THE LIGHT
BARRIER

THE LIGHT
BARRIER

THE LIGHT

BARRIER

THE LIGHT

THE LIGHT

BARRIER

BAR

THE L

THE LIGHT

LIGHT

BAR

THE L

BARRIER

ARRIER

THE LIGHT

BARRIER

TH

THE LIGHT

BARRIER

BA

THE LIGHT

BARRIER

THE LIGHT BARRIER

Understanding the Mystery
of Irlen Syndrome and
Light-Based Reading Difficulties

RHONDA STONE

FOREWORD BY ROBERT DOBRIN, M.D., F.A.A.P.

St. Martin's Griffin ☒ New York

www.stmartins.com

Design by Nancy Singer Olaguera

Library of Congress Cataloging-in-Publication Data

Stone, Rhonda.
    The light barrier : understanding the mystery of Irlen Syndrome and light-based reading difficulties / Rhonda Stone.—1st ed.
      p. cm.
    ISBN 0-312-30405-6 (hc)
    ISBN 0-312-32028-0 (pbk)
    1. Dyslexia. 2. Color vision. 3. Attention-deficit hyperactivity disorder. 4. Photosensitivity disorders. I. Title.
    RC394.W6 S765 2002
    618.92'8553—dc21

2002005137

First St. Martin's Griffin Edition: December 2003

10 9 8 7 6 5 4 3 2 1

For Katie and Jacob
and every child and adult interrupted by light

To help you
stay on top of the latest information
on light's effects on the brain,
look for "New Information" at
www.thelightbarrier.com

CONTENTS

CONTENTS CONTENTS

ACKNOWLEDGMENTS

ACKNOWLEDGMENTS
ACKNOWLEDGMENTS

Dozens of people in several parts of the world have made this project possible. First and foremost, our family's thanks to the experts who have worked diligently for years to document, understand, and address light-based reading difficulties: Helen Irlen, Arnold Wilkins, Bruce Evans, Greg Robinson, and Paul Whiting. Additionally, this project was made possible by every individual who allowed his or her personal story to be told. Our thanks to you for sharing parts of your lives with others. Our family is indebted to those who helped identify and address Katie and Jacob's challenges with aspects of light. To Jean Hawkins, Michelle Orton, and Kirstie Lewis, thank you. And to Kirill Federspiel, Mat Thompson, and Rich Villacres, special thanks for the graphic and photographic talents that helped us to understand how Katie and Jacob perceive the world and printed word. Special friends encouraged us when others were skeptical. On behalf of Katie and Jacob: Mrs. Davis, Mrs. Hiler, Mr. Adamson, Mrs. Van Beek, Mrs. Hamar, the Phillips family—you are the greatest. To each of our special Sunday-night friends, thank you for your support and encouragement. To those around the Northwest who sent prayers up for the completion of this book, may the peace you provided me be returned to you. Sue, Joanne, Jeanne, Anne, Linda, Mom, Jennifer Reeve, agent Jeff Kleinman, and editor Heather Jackson—my gratitude goes beyond words. Finally, to the love of my life, Paul: thank you for your support and encouragement.

FOREWORD
FOREWORD FOREWORD

One of the challenges in the practice of child psychiatry is obtaining an "authentic diagnosis." Each child is unique. Every child has individual complexities related to growth, development, neurobiology, personality, and genes. As a medical sleuth, putting the pieces of the puzzle together, describing the initial conclusions to the parent and the patient, and then watching for the reaction that reflects "that's it!" is a very satisfying feeling.

The Light Barrier, written by Rhonda Stone, is a search for authenticity. The book portrays a dramatic example of the frustrating and lengthy journey of a family in search of an underlying reason and a diagnosis for the complex reading difficulties of their children.

In my own practice, I became intrigued with childhood sensory problems when many of my young patients referred for symptoms of attention deficit/hyperactivity disorder were described by their parents as "sensitive." Some had unexplained anxiety when they were exposed to bright light. Many of these children disliked loud noises, had rigid opinions about the clothing they wore, and were diagnosed as having problems with reading. Their symptoms were often mistaken for obsessive-compulsive traits.

Patterns and associations began to emerge. Uncovering what is really going on is the goal for an authentic diagnosis. I asked myself, what is the cause of their reading difficulties and what triggers their anxiety? Then I questioned the children and the adolescents with an open mind and interviewed their parents. I also had teachers and parents fill out behavioral rating scales. I was looking for a diagnosis that fit the patient's difficulties at home and at school.

Then "S," a nine-year-old boy with a fifteen-year-old swagger, walked into my office. He had a history of poor attention in school, anger at home, and reading difficulties. He brought with him a pair of colored lenses that he insisted helped him read in class and do his homework. During the next thirty minutes, "S" and his mother talked of scotopic sensitivity syndrome, also called Irlen syndrome. I had heard of it previously, but had not spent time reviewing the subject.

As we talked, interesting similarities to complaints I had heard from patients who had trouble with reading and who were sensitive to light began to make sense. *Reading by the Colors*, a book by Helen Irlen, helped me organize an approach to the patients I saw who had reading problems and/or were light-sensitive.

I wanted to learn more about the subject. I found that many people, unless asked how they felt about light, did not know they had sensitivity that interfered with their reading. They assumed the patterns of white spaces (rivers) they saw within the dense text were normal. A graduate student I spoke with told me that she always thought it was common to see patterns on the page. A slow reader who regularly experienced eyestrain, she had worked very hard for her grades. Her reaction with her specifically chosen colored lenses: "I feel incredible and much calmer now; and I read much faster!"

It became clear to me that there was a common thread within these stories. Accompanying the difficulties with reading and, in many cases, depth perception was a feeling of stress, tension, and anxiety. Colored overlays and/or colored lenses could provide a feeling of calmness. For such people certain aspects of light were the problem.

Many teachers, parents, specialists in eye care, psychologists, and physicians are unaware of Irlen syndrome. But, more important, they are unconvinced that colored lenses have the potential to provide effective treatment for sensitivity to light.

Irlen syndrome is a perceptual disorder that may coexist with migraine headaches, ADHD, various developmental delays, learning disabilities, head injury, bipolar disorder, and a spectrum of anxiety disorders.

Is it rare? During a fifteen-month period, I evaluated 460 patients, including both adults and children, at a brain-imaging center. Using questions that would uncover problems related to light sensitivity and reading difficulties, I found 122 patients who met the criteria for further testing at an Irlen center. Fifteen patients had family members who also experienced sensitivity to light while reading. Forty of the 122 were treated with tinted lenses and either completed subjective rating scales or were interviewed before and after they used overlays and/or tinted lenses. All subjects were enthusiastic about their improvement. For these patients, Irlen syndrome is an authentic diagnosis.

The Light Barrier by Rhonda Stone should be read. It describes one parent's quest to uncover the reasons for her children's struggles with reading and, ultimately, how this important life skill impacts a child's sense of self. This book provides a road map for understanding the relationship of light to our perception of written language.

We need not hesitate to intervene because we do not have a conclusive answer as to why colored lenses or colored overlays help some of us who have perceptual distortions and physical discomfort when exposed to certain components of the light spectrum. Instead, we as parents, educators, health professionals, and scientists should continue to investigate this unfolding mystery of light.

—*Robert Dobrin, M.D., F.A.A.P.*

Dr. Robert Dobrin's professional background began in pediatrics as a clinician/researcher in pediatric nephrology/transplantation, immunology, and critical care. Since 1991, after additional training, Dr. Dobrin has practiced behavioral pediatrics and child/adolescent, adult psychiatry. His research interests have included subgrouping ADHD, childhood bipolar disorder, and sensory dysfunction in both children and adults. He has subspecialty training in addictionology and eating disorders.

In 2000, Dr. Dobrin began to work with the Amen Clinic, a brain imaging center in Newport Beach, California, that uses single photon computerized tomography (SPECT scans). Brain imaging provides a new technology for refining the diagnostic process and improving treatment strategies by correlating patterns of brain blood flow with neurological and psychiatric symptoms.

BEFORE YOU READ . . .

BEFORE YOU READ . . .

Some books are easy to drop into and out of, allowing for quick reference and learning. This is not one of those. *The Light Barrier* introduces a paradigm shift in how we see and visually perceive, a new proposition of science that is both controversial and dynamic, and with plenty of room for misinterpretation and misunderstanding.

The Light Barrier needs to be read cover to cover if it is to be useful to parents and other adults seeking solutions for children's learning needs. My family wants you to benefit from all that we learned. Doing so takes an entire book, not a few pages or single chapter.

There are as many as 10 million children in the United States struggling every day to read and perform in school. There are diverse opinions about the cause or causes. Teachers aren't teaching; parents aren't parenting; children have become television and video game zombies and are no longer motivated to learn. Other factors proposed include physiological and psychological disorders, from auditory processing problems to neurons with missing links to attention problems and mood disorders.

What if there was a way to improve reading conditions for some children with a simple remedy? What if this remedy was being ignored largely because of preconceptions? Would that technique be worth exploring?

The Light Barrier tells the story of our family's quest to understand how a remedy labeled snake oil by a few professionals has worked for our children—and worked well. Our children, seven and eleven when our quest began, now enjoy reading. Should we have abandoned the remedy because it was controversial? We didn't, and we want you to know why.

The Light Barrier is from our family to yours. It does not guarantee every child will read "one full grade level better or more in just weeks." Instead, it introduces a potential barrier to reading and a solution that has worked for many. It asks questions and offers answers.

Millions of children are waiting for adults to come up with answers as to why it is hard for them to learn to read. Please join our family in seeing that the questions are both asked *and* answered.

Best wishes,
The Stone Family

part I
A HIDDEN
PROBLEM

A HIDDEN
PROBLEM A HIDDEN

PROBLEM

THE RISE AND FALL
OF A CHILD

Katie is fair and lovely. At age thirteen, she is tall and slender with the kind of cheekbones I always wanted when I was a girl. At that age I remember sucking the insides of my cheeks together and puckering like a fish in an attempt to produce the high, full cheekbones she produces with just a demure smile.

Katie is a normal American youth through and through—normal in every way but one. Just before her eleventh birthday, Katie was spiraling downward into a pattern of frustration, irritability, and school failure. She struggled to read, rarely smiled, and found it hard to keep friends at school.

It is hard to watch a child struggle. And puzzling to see a normally developing boy or girl hit a wall in the second or third grade. That is what happened to Katie. She hit a wall that no one could explain—until a chance encounter introduced our family to an invisible barrier to learning.

TENDER BEGINNINGS

Katie came into the world on a crisp November morning. She was beautiful, her eyes almond-shaped and her brown hair distinguished by a single shock of gold toward the back. From infancy, Katie was fascinated with the world. On a shopping trip at a week old, she nestled in my arms in a sun-yellow pram and studied the bright lights and black-and-white images around her. The pupils of her eyes were like mysterious little pools of oil that had not yet committed to brown or blue or green.

As a toddler, Katie loved bold colors. Her favorite book at age two was *Moo Moo, Peek-a-Boo*, a brightly colored picture book that had us oinking, neighing, and hooting through its pages. Books were not strangers in our home. Katie's room, from the day we brought her home from the hospital, was full of books.

In some settings, Katie was a little shy. Her first preschool class was at a local gymnastics center, where the windowless gym was filled with murky fluorescent light. Initially, Katie preferred my knee to the noisy bustle of her classes. After a few weeks, though, she acclimated and joined in enthusiastically.

Katie's second year of preschool was spent at a Catholic school. The lighting in the old house where preschool classes were held was more like home—incandescent bulbs and plenty of large, unobstructed windows. She was very comfortable in that setting and adapted quickly. She no longer clung to my knee. There, Katie's teachers were loving and down-to-business. One afternoon, as the children played on the school's outdoor gym equipment, Katie's teacher predicted she would have an interest in science when she grew up. I asked her why. She pointed to Katie sprawled on the sidewalk, studying a column of marching ants. Katie, she said, loved to study and observe.

Katie's progress continued to be consistent with that of the other four- and five-year-olds in her preschool class. In fact, quite to our surprise, our non-Catholic daughter recited her Hail Marys so well that she was chosen to recite at the spring all-school program at the end of the year.

Our daughter did not lack for opportunities to learn and grow. Beginning at three and four, she took swimming and ballet lessons. In swimming, she started out a little fearful of the water, but quickly got over it. In ballet, she seemed a bit uncomfortable with the brightly lit classroom where she danced once a week. In the windowless room, Katie often stood timidly, knees pressed together, elbows bent and held tightly to her body. It was as though she were trying to make herself smaller. I thought it rather unusual, but never troubled her about it.

Just before the start of kindergarten, Katie knew her letters, shapes, and numbers and could pick out a few words in her picture books. In fact. the first word she could spell from memory was *book*.

Her kindergarten teacher inspired in her a love of preparing healthy foods. At age six, Katie appeared at our bedroom door for the first time, a black lacquer tray carefully balanced in her hands. She was treating us to the first of many breakfasts in bed. In a bowl, white liquid sloshed gently over the sides. Her creative masterpiece consisted of a bowl with seven small-sized shredded wheat biscuits in a mixture of half milk and half water. The concoction was sweetened with a sprinkling of sugar. I ate every bite with visible delight and lavished praise on Katie for the delicious meal.

Other than mild shyness and her unusual behavior in dance class, I cannot think of a single thing that might have suggested possible delays in Katie's academic development. Through first grade, she appeared to do fine in school. As long as the print was large and there were only a few words per page, her reading appeared to keep up with her classmates'.

One classroom reading activity, however, caught my attention. In this activity, the teacher worked with first graders all week to familiarize them with photocopied poems and short stories. On Friday, the text-rich pages came home in binders to be "read" by children to parents over the weekend. Nearly every Friday, Katie and I would snuggle together, usually on the sofa, and read. I would follow the words with my finger while Katie chanted the words. At first it appeared she was reading. Soon, however, it became apparent that Katie was using her memory skills to recite the verses. Her chanted phrases and the small print had little, if any, connection to one another. Even simple words she knew—*is, it, the*—were lost to her in the paragraphs of text. When I inquired about it, her teacher assured me this was normal and part of the program. The goal was not necessarily to develop reading skills per se, but to develop an understanding of the relationship between printed stories and spoken words. I accepted her explanation and thought little more about it.

Katie's classmates began to write letters, numbers, and short words in kindergarten. Inventive spelling was encouraged in the first grade. Katie was a master of inventive spelling and her teacher always seemed to be able to read and understand it. I was not as skilled. Katie's early print was erratic and difficult for me to read.

"MOMMY, I CAN'T SEE"

Shortly after the start of second grade, Katie complained she couldn't see to read. As soon as she shared this, I took her to a vision professional to have her vision checked.

Testing was typical of most vision exams. An assistant led Katie from the waiting room to a room in which she was seated in front of a boxlike device called a stereoscope. She was instructed to look through the dark box at illuminated images in order to measure her depth and color perception, as well as the ability of her eyes to work together. Katie passed all tests with flying colors. Then, in a dimly lit room, she was asked to identify large letters from a softly illuminated Snellen eye chart. She passed all her tests and her vision was pronounced to be fine—with a slight indication she might one day have trouble with distance vision. The optometrist recommended against glasses and asked to see her again in a year.

Soon after Katie's eye test, her teacher advised us that she was falling behind her peers in reading. Of greater concern to her teacher, however, was that Katie regularly engaged in daydreaming. Rather than pay attention during reading and instruction time, Katie would be off in her own world, looking out the window, at the ceiling, at the floor. When we asked our eight-year-old about it, she answered in her usual direct fashion: "Mom, Dad, school is boring." We gave her a gentle pep talk, put the issue on our ongoing radar screens, and marched her back to school.

My husband and I, for our parts, were sorely inexperienced in the area of child development as Katie progressed through school. I was the youngest of four children and my husband the second to the youngest of seven. Each of us had the academic achievements of older siblings to chase after as we progressed through school, and both of us found grade school remarkably easy. In retrospect, I realize now that neither of us had a clue as to what to expect our first child to accomplish in the early years of school. When she was a toddler and preschooler, we had a couple of paperback books to help track her progress—and she nailed every milestone. But the birth-to-age-six books ended just about the time Katie started school and, with her apparent normal development, it didn't seem necessary to track her milestones beyond what classroom teachers would tell us.

By the third grade, Katie appeared to have little interest in being an A or B student, although she did complain once again at the start of school that she had difficulty seeing in her classroom. This time, besides finding it hard to see the words in her textbooks, she specifically complained that she couldn't read the words on her classroom's white board. We took her to the optometrist again, where Katie's vision was checked once more. Her vision was again pronounced to be near 20/20, with the same caution that she might have a problem with distance vision in the future.

With her vision declared to be fine, we expected good school performance from her, and at first, she appeared to meet the challenge. But month after month, she slowly and steadily fell further behind. Occasional reports would come from her teacher that Katie struggled to keep her attention on the books and paperwork in front of her. She looked out the window too much or fidgeted in her seat—anything to avoid doing her work. The red flag we all ignored was Katie's handwriting. In the third grade, it continued to be the large, erratically spaced, and sloping print she began with in the first grade. She hated cursive with a passion and, whenever possible, avoided using it. Her loops and curls were just as erratic in size and configuration and the resulting words were difficult to read. When I asked her third grade teacher about Katie's difficulties in printing and handwriting, she shrugged it off: "We see this all the time. She'll catch up."

Another source of concern was Katie's spelling. After nearly three years of inventive spelling as the accepted standard, I began to wonder when she would understand that just any old set of letters scrawled on a page would not necessarily communicate meaning to the rest of the world. Adding to the confusion was the fact that Katie did fairly well on spelling tests, but couldn't spell even simple words when asked to write paragraphs. When I tried to encourage her to spell better, she became extremely defensive. "This is how we do it in class, Mom. This is how it is supposed to look."

Propped up with plenty of assistance at home, Katie passed from grade to grade with good to average marks. By now, her single lock of blond was long lost to a thick mane of shoulder-length chestnut hair. Occasionally teachers remarked that she needed to concentrate or focus more. These comments never came in the form of intervention, complete with cooperative problem solving. Her handwriting continued to be poor and her spelling inaccurate and inventive. I encouraged her to work a little harder at both. We began to have Katie do her homework at the dinner table after school so that her father and I could monitor her work. She resented our watchful eyes and our involvement. As she put it, such attention made her feel dumb.

It is difficult to look back on those days now. They are the types of memories parents prefer to throw in a boneyard of family moments best forgotten. Katie would open her social studies book and stare. Her eyes would lurch from word to word. She would get to the bottom of a page and remember nothing about the text she had just read. She would read end-of-chapter questions and stumble through the two or three pages where the information was located, unable to find a single key word. It was almost as if she were blind. More than a time or two, frustration ebbed to the top of my throat and I harshly delivered a shameful question. "Are you blind, Katie? Can't you see it? It's right *there!*"

"No, Mom!" Katie would fight back. "I *can't* see it!"

Katie became acutely aware that post-school-day life for her revolved around the dining room table and homework. It was a house rule that homework must be completed before the kids could engage in other activities. Because of the length of time it took Katie to do her homework, however, we modified the rule for her, allowing her about forty-five minutes of non-school-related activity before she cracked open the books. She worked for about an hour and a half before taking a break for dinner. After the hour-long dinner break, she returned to her homework until bedtime. During soccer season, when Katie participated on a team, she skipped the after-school break and we squeezed dinner into twenty or thirty minutes. This modification provided the necessary two to three hours for homework.

Katie's fourth grade teacher told us our daughter should not need to spend more than twenty or thirty minutes on each homework assignment. *Ha! What is she thinking?* I thought to myself. This should have been another signal that something was amiss. Clearly, what Katie ought to be able to do did not match what she was capable of doing. We couldn't seem to get this point across to any of the professionals we assumed would be able to spot an academic problem in the making. Our daughter clearly was falling into an alpine-size academic crevasse.

Homework was not the only struggle. I had known for some time that Katie had trouble sleeping at night. I attributed it to stress. Routinely she came home from school red-eyed and exhausted, the fatigue causing her to be irritable in class and on the playground. Her extreme moodiness at home by day's end explained to me why she might be struggling to keep friends. At some point during her third grade year, I spoke to Katie's pediatrician about how quickly her eyes would become red when she played outdoors. He assured me she was probably just more sensitive to light than most children and recommended sunglasses. It never occurred to me to press him about the red eyes and fatigue she experienced at the end of each school day—including bad weather days when children weren't allowed to go outside. I simply had not yet put together all the relevant pieces of our daughter's physical issues.

At the end of the summer just before the start of fourth grade, Katie complained again that she had difficulty seeing the words in her books. I asked her whether she would be willing to try glasses and she was enthusiastic. We returned to the optometrist, and after she had a thorough screening that yielded the same results as appointments past, I insisted she be fitted with a prescription for her slight nearsightedness. Katie's optometrist agreed, in light of the difficult time she was having in school. Katie chose a fashionable gold frame, and because she continued to come home every day with bright red eyes, I talked her into photo-gray lenses that would automatically darken in bright light. This, I figured, would address the problem with light sensitivity that Katie's pediatrician thought was caused by sunlight.

RISING TO THE CHALLENGE

Katie started fourth grade with her new glasses. Still, she read slower than other students and routinely stumbled over words. She qualified (sort of) for the school's challengers group for B students; I did a little begging to get her into the class. It was my position that she was bright and needed more hands-on activity, such as that offered through the challengers program.

Getting her into the class was worth the effort; no program inspired her more. She soared, scoring a perfect one hundred percent for the quarter, compared to a class average six or seven points below. Part of the program included an Invention Convention, where Katie's design for a self-cleaning pet cage, complete with indoor plumbing, took top honors in her category.

Katie loves animals the way chocoholics love chocolate. She came up with her mesh cage design as a method of improving sanitary conditions for animals in pet shelters. The cage's floor had two layers. Animals sat, stood, or laid on the top mesh layer, urine dropping through the mesh to a slanted tray three inches below. The tray operated like a drawer and could be slid out when pet attendants needed to sweep animal stools into the tray. The tray was also plumbed with a movable water hose and flexible drain for periodic flushing.

At the Invention Convention, held in a large room with high ceilings and row upon row of cafeteria tables and student projects, I listened as my daughter answered the judges' questions intelligently and thoroughly. The local superintendent of schools, a member of the school board, and the sheriff of our county were among the dignitaries. Minutes later, Katie was cool and smooth through photo and video sessions with the school district photographer and a local television reporter.

This, I came to understand, was what Katie was capable of accomplishing with her inventive mind and oral communication skills. Aside from the hands-on challengers program, however, Katie was not doing well in school. Her grades continued on a slow and steady downhill slide. Her papers were messy and her oral reading slow and choppy. Reading aloud, she lost her place routinely and continued to misread simple words such as *the, was,* and even *is*—as though she'd never seen them before. It was so odd. At times she couldn't read these simple words, and yet out of the blue, she would read a word like *misjudged* or *serendipity* as though she'd read and understood these words for years.

KATIE'S "GHOSTS"

By the end of the first quarter, Katie's grades had slipped to the point that she was no longer eligible for the challengers class. She had fallen even further behind her peers in reading. In spite of her photo-gray glasses, she was coming home exhausted, with bloodshot eyes and headaches. By the end of the year, her reading level was a full grade level or more behind. Over just a few months, our daughter plunged from stellar inventor to the brink of academic failure.

As I watched Katie's classmates begin to develop neat and even cursive writing, it was clear to me that something was not as it should be where my daughter was concerned. Yet teachers assured me some children developed eye-hand coordination more slowly than others. It didn't explain, however, how my daughter could score 80 to 90 percent in spelling one minute, and in the next, fail to spell basic words in the context of class compositions or to read and comprehend basic fourth grade books. It also didn't explain why, at the end of every school day, my daughter came home physically ill and with a fuse so short a bullfrog couldn't jump fast enough to get out of her way.

Something was *wrong*. The most frightening red flag ran up near the end of fourth grade. On a Saturday afternoon, our daughter, by now with blue-gray eyes the color of blueberries, came to me, tears brimming. Standing in our family room, towering over me as I sat in an old rocking chair, she tearfully pleaded to know whether ghosts were real. I knitted my eyebrows: "Of course ghosts aren't real, honey. Why do you ask?"

"Because," she answered, "I see ghosts everywhere, Mom, and they scare me."

The interchange frightened me. My first instinct was to scoop her in my arms and run full-speed to her pediatrician's office. With all the other difficulties she had experienced during the year, a dreadful thought flashed across my mind: *What if my daughter is bipolar or schizophrenic?* I calmed myself down quickly and assured her that her imagination had probably just run away with her.

"But, Mom, I see them every day," she said, tears beginning to spill down her cheeks.

I encouraged her not to worry or even think about it—*ever*. Then and there I should have taken her to see her pediatrician, but I didn't. We had already been for so many other issues—allergies, asthma, headaches, nausea, fatigue. Katie's file was over an inch thick and most of the time, her complaints were dismissed as nothing unusual, nothing more than an overanxious and paranoid mother. Fear stopped me from taking her then—fear, confusion, and self-doubt.

At the end of the school year, Katie received some comfort from her fourth grade teacher, who encouraged her to spend her summer reading. Her teacher assured her that improving her reading skills would make school easier and more enjoyable the following year. Katie pledged to do so and throughout the summer devoted her energies to reading. At first her chosen reading method threw me: bedroom lights off in mid- to late afternoon, the only source of light the sun filtering through her north window's partially closed mini-blinds. On the lower bunk of her bunk bed, Katie would curl up comfortably in the shadows near her bedroom wall. Light bounced off the ceiling and walls and softly cloaked the room. Katie remained in the room's darkest shadows. It was about half the light I felt she needed for reading, but she was reading, and doing so frequently and rather well. Occasionally I asked her to read aloud so that I could check her speed and fluency. When she was in the shadows, her problems with skipped words, skipped lines, and the struggle to read simple words like *is* and *the* disappeared. In very little light, she read smoothly and efficiently without fatigue or sore eyes. I, on the other hand, strained to see the words in her books. Even though I felt she needed more light, I found no reason to intervene.

When school began in the fall, Katie's reading level had taken a remarkable turn upward. The recreational books she was reading were at a fifth grade level. As we soon discovered, however, her classroom comprehension continued to be poor. The information was confusing. How could she be reading so well at home and still struggling in school? Why did school continue to be so difficult for her? The answer lay in a chance encounter just around the corner.

2

A CHANCE ENCOUNTER
AND A CHILD'S LIFE

Spiritual people believe God has the power to intervene in their lives. Non-spiritual people generally think of the twists and turns of life as luck or fate. Make no mistake, beginning the day my daughter took me into her confidence about her ghosts, I started to pray to God that we would find the source of her problems and a solution.

By the end of fourth grade, the issues were many. Except for the one hundred percent in her challengers class, her grades slipped to mostly Cs and Ds. Throughout that year, her father and I had taken up a tag-team vigil at the dining room table. I helped with language or social studies. Paul helped with math or science. Yet there never seemed to be enough hours in the evening. Poor Katie, just ten years old, poured heart and soul into her homework, routinely working at least three hours a night. Because of the length of time it took her to complete assignments, Paul and I propped her up with assistance in just two or three subjects at a time and let the other subjects go. To this day, I can track this activity on her report cards. When she received intensive help from her father and me, she scored a few Bs, but mostly Cs. Where she had little to no help, she got Ds.

By the beginning of fifth grade, after a summer of reading in a dark-ened room, Katie's recreational reading skills were much improved. At her request, we allowed her to start the school year without the conventional glasses she'd been prescribed the year before. They hadn't seemed to help and Katie had raised her reading level without them. Yet her increased reading level didn't seem to help her in class. October 1999 arrived, and with it came her first midterm F. It was during this month, shortly after I'd turned my prayers up a notch or two, that I had a chance conversation with a former colleague from my days working in public education.

Jean Hawkins and I had once worked in adjacent offices. Back then, she was a certified teacher working in our school district's evaluation office and I was a former newspaper reporter disseminating school district information to teachers, parents, and taxpayers. When we caught up with each other six or so years later, Jean was a principal for a neighboring school district and I was the grants coordinator for a regional hospital and foundation. I was contacting a number of elementary school principals in regard to a classroom health and safety education program when Jean's name turned up on the list.

I placed a call to Jean and we completed our business quickly. The conversation turned to family. Jean inquired about my children and I briefly expressed my deep concern for Katie's academic struggles. Jean, who hadn't seen my daughter since she was two or three, listened intently to every word, showing genuine interest and responding with an affirming uh-huh every time she recognized a specific behavior. For my part, it was a relief to finally find an educator who understood why I was so concerned.

Jean followed my description with one question: "Rhonda, have you ever heard of scotopic sensitivity?"

"No," I said, "what's that?"

"Well," she continued, "you might want to have Katie tested for it."

IRLEN SYNDROME

Jean was the first to introduce me to scotopic sensitivity, the term once used for a condition now referred to as Irlen syndrome. The condition is best described as sensitivity to aspects of light involving brightness, wavelengths we interpret as color, and dark/bright contrast. Symptoms typically include one or more of the following: light-based reading difficulty, fatigue, physical strain, burning or watery eyes, headaches, migraines, nausea, irritability, difficulty focusing on visual work (reading and computer terminals), and inattentiveness.

Some brains, Jean explained, appear to react to light and high contrast images with physical stress and/or an unpredictable pattern of mild to severe visual distortions. In these individuals, the problem worsens when print becomes smaller and denser and as brains become more fatigued. Children may have few problems reading in first grade because the print is large and well spaced, and only a few words appear on each page. These same children, however, begin to struggle with reading as soon as print becomes small, plentiful, and compressed—often in the second or third grade.

Distortions associated with sensitivity to aspects of light vary widely. They can be slight or difficult to imagine: flashing lights and blots of color, words that appear to float up or slide off the page, words that crowd together or altogether disappear. Some people see rivers and waterfalls cascading down pages, as white spaces group together and mysteriously dominate the brain's attention and focus.

Jean's school had just started training staff members to identify children who might have Irlen syndrome. She gave me the name of the certified screener who arranged the training and recommended I give her a call.

Within a week, Katie and I met Michelle Orton, a certified teacher and reading specialist. Because Michelle works full-time, she asked us to meet her on a Sunday afternoon in her home. It was a pleasant five-minute country drive from our home to hers.

Michelle greeted us with a warm smile and invited us to a back bedroom converted to an office. In one corner of the room was a desk, a computer, and an office chair. In the center of the room, a few feet from the desk and right beneath the room's only window, was a long worktable with two chairs. Above the table, a fluorescent light fixture hung, completely separate and independent from the room's incandescent ceiling light. Katie and I took seats at the table, side by side.

If asked to select one word to describe my observations during testing, I would not be able to choose. Shock, wonder, amazement, frustration, irritation, anger—all come to mind. As I sat there, observing the logical and methodical way in which Katie was asked how she felt physically while reading and what she saw on the pages before her, I couldn't help but wonder why she had never been asked these questions before. I wondered this because Katie's answers were no less than amazing.

"Do you accidentally skip lines or sentences?" Michelle asked.

Katie's answer: "Never."

My unspoken answer: "Often."

"Do you accidentally skip words?"

Katie: "Never."

My verbal interruption: "Umm, I would say often. I'm sorry, perhaps I shouldn't butt in."

Michelle: "It's okay. You can share what you observe. Okay, Katie?"

Katie: "Okay."

"Do you find that reading gets harder the longer you do it?"

Katie: "Sometimes."

Me: "Katie knows best."

"Do your eyes bother you?"

Katie: "Often."

Me: "Yes, but her doctor and optometrist don't seem to feel it's a problem."

Michelle flashed me a wry, knowing smile. "Do you rub your eyes a lot while reading?"

Katie: "Often."

Me: "There's a pattern here, isn't there?"

Michelle's wry smile returned.

Michelle asked thirty-four questions in all. She completed the questions, turned on the fluorescent light, and produced a few semi-glossy sheets of stiff paper. On the first card was a large three-dimensional cube, divided by lines into smaller cubes. Katie was asked to choose one of the lines of cubes and to follow this line across the top and down the side of the larger cube. She was to count the small cubes as her eyes followed the selected line. Katie struggled to keep her eyes focused and had great difficulty completing the task. When she was done, Michelle asked her whether the lines did anything as her eyes moved along them. Did they remain still on the page or did anything happen? Some of the cubes, Katie said, floated off the page. She was having difficulty following the line of cubes because things kept moving. Also, she saw a muddle of funny spots and colors and flashing lights. She saw these things even though the only image on the white card was the cube and its thin black lines.

Next, Michelle pulled out a card with a series of small Xs. The Xs were positioned to form the image of a jack-o'-lantern. Michelle asked Katie to focus on a continuous set of Xs across the center of the jack-o'-lantern's face. She was then asked to count these Xs out loud. Again, Katie struggled to complete the task, and once again, Michelle asked Katie what she saw. This time, Katie explained, the pumpkin's eyes and mouth grew larger each time she tried to focus on the center line of Xs. In fact, they grew so large they eventually swallowed up the rest of the Xs on the page. This made it nearly impossible for Katie to keep her focus on the Xs she was attempting to count.

We were only a few minutes into the test and Katie's eyes were already red. For the first time, I made a connection between her red eyes and her schoolwork. She began to rub them and squirmed to find a comfortable position. Michelle produced the next card. Except for a half-inch margin, the sheet of paper was covered, top to bottom, with indistinguishable groupings of letters simulating words. Rather than read the page, Katie was asked to chose one line of text near the center and read aloud the name of each letter on the line. Katie complied, getting no farther than four or five letters before she began to skip letters, jump over whole groupings of letters simulating words, and drift to the letters and "words" above and below. Katie struggled to keep her place. Once again, Michelle asked her what she saw. Some of the letters, she said, would rise up and fall down. She was trying hard to keep up with the movement. When she got to the center of the page, it seemed to her as if the whole page of text were swirling around a few letters.

Do words do that at home and school? Michelle asked.

Sometimes, Katie said.

I searched for something to explain what was happening. For a few minutes I thought Katie was making it all up. It was too remarkable. Not one of Katie's teachers had ever suggested she might have a problem with what she saw on the printed page. On top of that, her optometrist had said her vision was fine—not once, but three times. I knew that her read-aloud skills were poor. She found it hard to read more than two or three words at a time without interruption. But teachers had identified too little practice as the cause. Rather than weigh those remarks against how hard my daughter worked, I blamed myself for not having her read even more. Katie was, after all, my first and oldest child. I didn't have the experience of another child for comparison. None of it made sense.

Before Michelle tested Katie for Irlen syndrome, no one had ever asked my daughter what she saw on the printed page. What we learned on that October afternoon was that under the worst conditions, Katie could accurately perceive only a few syllables at a time. Depending upon the light source and Katie's fatigue level at any given moment, everything else might swirl in a circle around a few syllables or appear to rise up, fall down, or slide off the page. More revelations came. Under a certain type of fluorescent light, the white board in Katie's classroom appeared sickeningly lime green and the black letters mud brown. Overhead projectors in a dark classroom were a blast of light to my daughter's brain; projected words were blurry and difficult to read.

Physical evidence helped support what my daughter shared. During testing, long before light was suggested to my daughter as a potential problem, I watched Katie squint, squirm and shade her eyes in an effort to block out light and settle distortions. She gained relief only when Michelle turned off all the lights and partially closed the room's window blinds. Then, in a dimly lit room too dark for me to read without strain, Katie read to Michelle and me at the fifth grade level she had worked so hard to achieve.

Of course Katie struggled to read in class! Of all things, *light* was the cause!

A FAMILY PROBLEM

On October 17, 1999, using the seventeen-point Irlen Reading Perceptual Scale, Michelle Orton determined that Katie is severely impacted by aspects of light. By the end of the two-hour session, during which Katie was later tested with dense text for her reactions to incandescent, fluorescent, and natural light, the whites of my daughter's eyes had turned cherry red and she had a monster headache and an upset stomach. To my surprise, so did I—and it wasn't a reaction to the day's stress. Three minutes after the exam room's fluorescent light was turned on, my eyes began to sting and water. Irlen syndrome, Michelle said, commonly runs in families. For as along as I can remember, I have dreaded being in the presence of most sources of fluorescent light. It causes me to fidget and, depending upon the quality of the fluorescent light, my eyes to burn. Under other lighting conditions, I am prone to migraine and cluster headaches. Fortunately for me, thirty-five years ago, when I learned to read, schools were

SWIRL

From "Reading By the Colors," Helen Irlen, Penguin Putnam/Perigee Div. Publishing, New York, USA.

modestly lit by incandescent and natural light. Today, most classrooms are brightly lit by fluorescent light—the light source that caused Katie to see the greatest number of visual distortions.

When she had finished testing Katie, Michelle told me more about Irlen syndrome. Studies indicate that 12 percent of the entire population may have some form of sensitivity to aspects of light—from the more common mild fatigue and eyestrain to the rare individual who perceives *everything* as distorted. Few educators know about this type of perceptual problem, and even fewer pediatricians and family practice physicians know about the research that has been done by a handful of educators and psychologists to validate its existence. Ironically, optometrists and ophthalmologists, the medical doctors who treat issues related to the eye, routinely turn off or dim exam room lights to screen for issues related to vision.

As a parent, I wanted to kick myself. Why hadn't I recognized there might be a physiological reason for Katie's struggles? Was I not paying attention? This wonderful little girl—who loves to cook and serve her parents breakfast in bed, who can dream up detailed plans for indoor plumbing in pet shelters—was trying hard, but nothing had helped. Extra time on homework at the dining room table in truth was extra time seeing through eyes that saw words rising, falling, sliding, and moving. It was extra time that caused her nothing but discomfort and misery. Why hadn't I seen it?

After I had tortured myself for a few minutes, reason finally took hold: if vision professionals dim the lights, if pediatricians and family practice physicians don't know the problem exists, if teachers don't know about or understand it, what on earth is a parent to do? How are children—who spend over a thousand hours a year in classrooms and hundreds of hours doing homework—supposed to cope?

The implications flooded my mind. The visual distortions Katie described to us were not the fault of eyes that did not work properly. Her optometrist already had determined that she did not have a problem with visual acuity or with what her eyes saw. The problem involved how light interacted with Katie's visual system. A faulty reaction occurred, impacting the ability of Katie's brain to properly perceive images. Thus, she "saw" distortions that weren't actually there.

My mother's mind churned. I'd found Michelle only because of a chance encounter with an old friend. I wondered aloud: "If problems with visual perception are real, who's diagnosing it in children?"

"That's a good question," answered Michelle. As a reading specialist, she works with dozens of children each year who experience physical stress and visual distortions. By the time they reach her, most have passed one or more conventional vision exams and many have been labeled inattentive, lazy, underachieving, and even dyslexic.

COLORED OVERLAYS

Michelle produced a folder from her desk and introduced Katie and me to the best intervention she has found for individuals experiencing light-related strain and visual distortions. Inside the folder were nine transparent sheets, each of a different hue. The intervention: color.

What ensued was a thorough process of identifying the right color of overlays to calm Katie's visual system and settle her perceived distortions. By the time the process was complete, Michelle had prescribed three overlays for Katie to use together: two purple and a turquoise. The darkness of the combination reminded me of the subdued lighting in the room where Katie best liked to read. It was amazing.

Michelle tested this combination with text. She produced several sheets, each labeled by grade level. She chose a fifth grade passage and asked Katie to read the passage without color filtration. As she usually did, Katie read the first line aloud rather well and began to struggle as she continued down the lines of text. By the middle of the first paragraph, she was skipping words and whole lines. She completed the paragraph with great difficulty. Michelle pulled out Katie's combination of overlays. She laid them over the text and directed Katie to read the next paragraph on the sheet. Katie began to read. Her eyes followed easily from word to word, line to line. She completed the paragraph with just a few hesitations. The improvement was remarkable.

Michelle determined that Katie has severe sensitivity to aspects of light, or Irlen syndrome. She gave us the colored overlays and a few extra tips: position the overlays so that glare does not reflect off them; do homework on blue paper instead of white; and allow Katie to wear a visor in class to keep overhead fluorescent light from bothering her eyes.

Katie and I thanked Michelle and began the five-minute drive home.

We spoke only once. As we made our way down the road, past an October vineyard covered in yellow-green leaves, I asked Katie how her stomach and head felt.

"I have a terrible headache. I feel like I could throw up," she said.

"Me, too," I said, rubbing my own pounding head. "Wow, Katie. You really see all those things?"

"I told you I had trouble seeing," Katie answered. "Nobody believed me."

"Yes, you did tell me, honey," I said. "Yes, you did."

3

JACOB'S DILEMMA

Soon after Katie and I reported the results of her testing to her father, Jacob began complaining that his classroom lights were also "too bright." Jacob is not one to copy his sister. In fact, these competitive siblings are more likely to go in opposite directions. To Paul's and my dismay, Katie and Jacob rarely agree on anything.

One of the wonders of parenting is the reality that no two children—especially those born in the same household—are exactly alike. Paul and I know this well. Katie is gifted with a nurturing spirit. She is happiest in the presence of animals and young children, innately sensing their need for shepherding and attention. Jacob, on the other hand, constantly needs shepherding and attention. His joy often gets the best of him, carrying him to places and situations that are not always in his best interest.

Two examples of his effervescence come immediately to mind. During his first few years Jacob became acquainted with the freedom and power of his legs. At Jacob's first birthday party, nearly every grandma, grandpa, aunt, uncle, and cousin within fifty miles was present for the hallowed event. Sensing that this would be a great place to grab a lot of attention, Jacob, who had never taken a step alone, stood up in the middle of the room completely unaided and began to walk. He never crawled again. It was the most entertaining moment of the day and Jacob relished every minute of the attention he received.

TWO VERY DIFFERENT CHILDREN

Not long before Jacob's third birthday, his legs nearly got him into a whole lot of trouble. Occasionally, parents are wooed into a false sense of security by the behavior of older siblings. As a toddler, Katie had always been extraordinarily compliant. If I gave her instructions, she followed them. Jacob, however, was not his sister, and I occasionally forgot that. On this particular afternoon, Katie, Jacob, and I were at the grocery store picking up supplies. We were in the salad dressing aisle and I was stumped trying to find something other than the same old Italian or Ranch. Katie and Jacob were standing near me, out of the cart. I believed it was good for children to learn to obey instructions—and the grocery store seemed like a good place to practice.

I was lost in thought somewhere between Caesar and bleu cheese when Jacob drifted away. He was about twelve feet from me when I saw him grin and bolt to my left, between two short aisles of specialty foods. I figured he couldn't get far and sauntered casually after him. By the time I got to the short aisle, he'd cleared it, turned a corner, and was out of sight. My heart sank. Still, I figured he couldn't go far. I had a fairly open view of the front of the store, obstructed by only a few produce tables. With no sign of him there, we headed toward the back of the store. Again, no sign of my not-quite-three-year-old. By this time, I was pushing my grocery cart at a frantic clip, face frozen in an open-mouthed-stare. My face relaxed but my stomach knotted when I spotted someone at the front of the building walking *into* the store carrying my child. I can't remember if a woman or a man brought Jacob back to safety. I was fixated on my son and the stress of the moment. I remember only what the person holding him told me. Jacob, still beaming from ear to ear, had bolted straight out of the store onto the sidewalk and was about to step off the curb and into the path of an oncoming car.

I trembled with relief when the stranger placed Jacob back in my arms. A woman who had watched the entire scene promptly marched my way and scolded me for not paying closer attention to my son. Her rebuke was so thorough I think it was then that Katie decided that young children, like pets, need shepherding. And parents, stressed by the experience of raising children, occasionally need breakfast in bed.

To this day, Katie and Jacob are very different people. In a crowd, Katie is introspective and quiet and Jacob is outgoing and ready to go. From the time he could talk, Jacob has marched up to strangers and struck up conversations. He was only three or four when we walked into an old-fashioned ice cream parlor and he skipped (he rarely walked back then) straight for a stool between two somber-faced men. He started a conversation with both and had them smiling within seconds.

Paul, Katie, and I took seats at a table right behind the trio. Eventually one of the men turned to me and asked whether it concerned me that my son talked to strangers. "Only if I'm not watching" was my reply. I respect the fact that we have two very different children. They have been raised the same—both were given the same rules and cautions about life. But one is reserved, the other outgoing. One I can trust to obey basic safety rules, and the other I have to watch like a hawk.

Like his sister, Jacob demonstrated no early signs of difficulty in learning. He was hitting baseballs with a bat by age two and, at age three, could jump more than three feet from a standing position. He was and is remarkably strong for such a little guy. He knew his alphabet, numbers, shapes, and colors by the time he entered kindergarten. He was one of the first kids in his class to count to 100.

Jacob had just entered first grade when he, too, complained that he had difficulty seeing at school. When Katie had her vision checked by an optometrist before the start of fourth grade, Jacob joined us.

Like his sister, Jacob passed with flying colors—with one minor variation. His optometrist noted a minor differentiation in color discrimination. Jacob had difficulty distinguishing pinks from reds. Other than that, his vision was perfect.

"Okay," I said, "but Jacob is complaining that it's hard for him to see in class."

"Ahh!" his optometrist said lightheartedly. "We hear that all the time at this age. Some kids see others getting glasses and they want glasses, too. That's all."

"Oh," I said, thinking that Jacob was more of a leader than a follower. I left it at that.

In the summer just before the start of second grade, Jacob developed a weird attachment to an old pair of deep-orange ski goggles. He put them on for play one day and decided they were the coolest things on the face of the planet. He tried to wear them everywhere. As school started, the resulting tug-of-war to dissuade him from wearing them to school or the store was beginning to get on my nerves.

"What's the deal with the goggles, Jake?" I eventually asked.

"I don't know, Mom," he said. "Everything looks better when I wear them."

It took me two or three weeks to get him to give them up.

JACOB'S "MONSTERS"

Jacob started second grade enthusiastic about school and his new teacher. His new classroom was considerably different from that of the year before. The outer wall of his first grade classroom included several evenly spaced, unobstructed windows and pleasant white fluorescent light bounced off the room's warm cream walls. The second grade classroom's walls were a dull blue-gray and the room's outer wall had only two narrow windows, one on each end of the room. The fluorescent tubes cast a murky grayness throughout the room.

About six weeks into the year, I received a call from Jacob's principal. My son had been sent to the office for refusing to do his work. Jacob's teacher had taken the extreme measure due to his resistance to journaling, a weekly activity in which the children were instructed to write something—anything—about their weekend. In a half hour, his teacher could rarely get him to write more than a sentence or two. On this particular day, like several others, Jacob hadn't written a thing.

It was time for a parent-to-child pep talk. At home that evening, we asked Jacob what was wrong. He said he couldn't think of anything to write. We encouraged him to write *something*. The encouragement produced a heavy sigh and a sad face from our usually joyous son.

"Okay," he conceded.

A couple of weeks later, days after Michelle Orton had determined that Katie was severely sensitive to certain aspects of light, I met with Jacob's teacher for a regularly scheduled school conference. She shared with me how well Jacob was doing in all but two subjects: journaling and reading.

"It's the strangest thing," she said. When a word was isolated—presented to Jacob free of text—he could easily read it. When the same word appeared in the middle of a page of text, Jacob couldn't even find it.

As she said this, information Michelle had shared with me came flooding back. Irlen syndrome runs in families, and kids pass conventional eye exams because the problem is related to dense text. Kids begin to have difficulty in the second or third grade because the print in their books becomes smaller and denser.

There were other things I knew about Jacob, but didn't share with his teacher. Jacob didn't like to draw. He never had. I suspected his aversion to paper and pencil had something to do with why he didn't like to write. And although at age two Jacob could hit a pitched ball, at age seven he struggled to track a soccer ball amid the chaos of flinging arms and legs. Finally, since the beginning of second grade, I'd noticed that Jacob was no longer his usual outgoing self. He had become increasingly fearful of his own classmates.

Within days, I called and scheduled an appointment for Jacob with Michelle Orton. During screening, we learned that Jacob also reacts severely to light. He too has problems with rising, falling, sliding, and swirling words—terms that I had intentionally not introduced to him when his sister was diagnosed. I didn't want to put any ideas into his young head. Intriguingly, we discovered Jacob had one other problem that his sister did not: Jacob did not describe seeing ghosts; instead, out of the blue, he explained that his classmates looked like monsters under his classroom's fluorescent lights. Their outlines blended together with the outlines of their desks and chairs, the images joining in one difficult to distinguish blob. He said this scared him, and because of it, he didn't like to talk to his peers.

Ghosts and monsters. The information was overwhelming. It made sense, though, in so many ways. Despite the hours I'd spent reading to and with my children, Katie and Jacob were struggling to learn to read. At the time of Jacob's second grade school conference, his reading level was several months behind those of his peers. Katie's red eyes and headaches hadn't started until the mid- to late second grade. And in fourth grade, she was struggling to move beyond third grade readers.

I was feeling as though I'd already failed my daughter and I didn't want to fail my son. For both of my children, I was willing to give the theory of sensitivity to aspects of light and color filtration a try. Two weeks after Katie's appointment, Jacob came home with two purple overlays.

I had a lot to think about. How could reading through such dark colors help my children? Most of us grow up being told that dim light is bad for the eyes. Wouldn't reading through dark overlays ultimately hurt Katie and Jacob's eyes?

For two years, Katie regularly came home from school with bright red eyes and headaches. During the summer just passed, she raised her reading to a fifth grade recreational level by reading in very dim light. And, for the first time in her life, Katie had been asked what she saw on a dense page and her answers were too remarkable to ignore.

Katie immediately began using her overlays at home and school. Aided by the overlays, her oral reading was somewhat smoother and more efficient. Katie often complained, however, that light overhead bounced off the plastic sheets and caused problems with glare. The stack of colored transparencies also was not helpful with another of Katie's other complaints—the strange variation in color she saw under fluorescent light, such as lime-green white boards.

Jacob started using his overlays too. But Michelle had told us about another method for addressing problems with aspects of light: specially tinted colored lenses worn as glasses or contact lenses. Such testing was much more expensive than the $80 for the two-hour screening session with Michelle, but Katie and I had both arrived at the conclusion that tinted lenses would circumvent her problems with glare and her classroom's white board. After just a few days of using the overlays, Katie asked if she could have a pair of tinted lenses. I told her I would talk to her dad.

4 FAMILY REVELATIONS

There are more pairs of sunglasses lying around our house than there are drinking glasses or coffee cups. Rifle through our large, family pencil box and—voilà!—a pair of sunglasses. Dig into our car or truck's glove compartment and—wow!—a pair of sunglasses. Atop windowsills, in bathroom drawers, on countertops—sunglasses.

Yikes! I just reached for the *Oxford Concise English Dictionary* sitting on the credenza shelf of my computer station and what do you think was lying in front of it? A pair of sunglasses! No kidding. In our house, sunglasses seem to multiply like Star Trek tribbles.

For the most part, the sunglasses belong to the same owner: my husband. He rarely goes out on a sunny day without them. They are almost always the same color—very dark gray. If he forgets his sunglasses when we leave the house for a short day trip, you'll find us at the nearest convenience store hunting for a pair. He doesn't think this is unusual. I think it's odd. I don't like sunglasses; I find them annoying. On my face, they routinely last about two minutes before I yank them off and stuff them where they can be quickly forgotten. The blue-grays and grays are worst. The ambers and browns are almost tolerable, but not quite.

A few months before our family was introduced to Irlen syndrome, an interesting thing happened. We were preparing to leave for a summer vacation the following week. My husband suggested I get a pair of sunglasses for the trip. Summers in central and eastern Washington state are very hot, a few days commonly pushing 100 degrees, and we were headed to the Canadian Rockies, where it can also be very bright. I resolved to find a pair and headed to town. Two stores later, I found a pair of clip-on shades for my prescription lenses that changed my opinion of sunglasses forever. The clip-ons were a shade of amber I had never seen before—more peach than yellow, more warm and natural than the usual dull ocher or bronze shades.

I loved those clip-ons. On sunny days, the sky looked slightly blue-gray and the clouds faintly orange, but the golden hills around our home appeared sharper and more distinct than my naked eyes had known them. The color was strangely soothing. A couple of times I even wore them while I worked in my office. It was with great satisfaction that I put them on my face for the nine-hour drive to Fairmont Hot Springs, Canada. And it was a crushing blow when four hours into the trip, fifteen to twenty miles from where we stopped for lunch, I realized I had left them in the restaurant. Because we were part of a four-car caravan, there was no turning back. Five days later on the return trip we went straight to that restaurant. My clip-ons were nowhere to be found. Within days I returned to the department store where I had purchased them with no luck. They were sold out. For weeks afterward I tried to find the exact shade at local department stores and quick stops, to no avail. I never found that warm, soothing peachy-amber hue again.

CERTAINTY AND SKEPTICISM

All of this was far from my mind the following October when Katie and I arrived at Michelle Orton's home for the first time. I entered that appointment certain about only a few things: My daughter was struggling in school. Her daily life was ruled by red eyes, headaches, and fatigue. And each year she asked—no, begged—me to take her to have her vision checked.

I remembered the summer clip-ons as Michelle explained the importance of precisely chosen colored overlays. For many with Irlen syndrome, she said, some colors are downright offensive. Only a narrow range of hues provide maximum benefit. It was then that I recalled my experience with the summer clip-ons. In that brief moment, my mind opened and became receptive to Irlen syndrome. My experience with the peachy-amber color led me to believe there was something to this connection between light and color filtration. During the first appointment, as Michelle worked with the overlays, laying a rose overlay beside a peach and a peach overlay beside a goldenrod, that I found myself once again drawn to the soothing peach hue. I liked it. The puzzle pieces began to fit together.

It did not make sense, however, to my pragmatic and cautious husband. He had never heard of the condition before and he couldn't understand why Katie's optometrist or pediatrician had never suggested it. Surely, if it were legitimate, one of them would have. He agreed to have Katie tested for Irlen syndrome because she was struggling in school. Also, the recommendation had come from a friend of mine, who also happened to be a school principal. When we came home from the screening with the stack of colored overlays that made book pages look as dark as grape juice, Paul was skeptical. Katie's difficulties, however, overrode his reservations. It was worth a try.

We were just a week into colored overlays for Katie when Jacob's school conference took place. I delivered the information to Jacob's dad and watched as his eyebrows furrowed.

"Jacob isn't having a hard time in school," he countered. "He's a little slow in reading, but he'll catch up."

"Maybe," I said. "But he has complained that he can't see in class and Michelle says it runs in families. It might be worth having him tested—just to make sure." Paul can tell by my tone of voice when my mind is made up. Suffice it to say, he conceded.

Given the opportunity to go back and do Jacob's initial testing again, I would change one thing: Jacob's dad would have come with us. It is difficult to communicate in person or print what happens when people go through testing. Supposedly only 7 percent of communication between human beings depends upon the words they use. Screening helped me to understand this notion. I watched both of my children struggle to keep their attention focused on busy black images on bright white paper—they squirmed, averted their gazes, looked out the window—and I listened as both of them described movement on the page that I struggled to imagine. Both times, I wondered whether my children were making up the visual distortions they claimed to see, and each time Michelle assured me that what they communicated was not unusual. At the end of each session, she pulled eight to ten sheets from the testing manual, each recreations of the distortions Katie or Jacob described. Paul needed to see it all. It would have prevented the tension in our house after Jacob too was identified as severely sensitive to aspects of light.

From Michelle, Jacob learned that two purple overlays could help reduce the visual distortions he saw on the printed page. The overlays would not, however, get rid of Jacob's monsters. Only tinted lenses could do that. We brought home the overlays, but Jacob was not satisfied. He wanted tinted lenses to rid him of the scary blobs he saw when his class-mates' shapes became one with their desks and chairs. After several days of pestering, he convinced me to try an experiment, even though Michelle had indirectly cautioned against it. Michelle's caution was that the purple identified for Jacob's overlays would not match the color of tinted lenses he needed to most effectively remove all his discomfort and distortions. Yet, at Jacob's request, I decided to let him try a pair of purple dime-store sun-glasses. When you are in the second grade, seeing your classmates as mon-sters is not a pleasant experience.

I took Jacob to the nearest department store and let him try on over-the-counter purple sunglasses. He tried on several pairs and one particular hue caused an instant reaction. "Mom, these are great! Everything looks clearer!" We bought one pair and returned some time during the first month to buy three more on clearance. Jacob had already broken the first.

What worked for Jacob, however, did not work for his sister. She tried on her brother's brand-new purple glasses and reacted immediately. They made the page even brighter, she said. She didn't like them. Her brother, on the other hand, would have rather given up pizza for life than go another day without colored glasses. A boy in *purple* glasses, no less. From the day we bought them, they became the first thing he reached for when he got up in the morning and the last thing he took off his face at night.

Through the years, I have known a number of children prescribed conventional spectacles for near- or farsightedness who struggled to adapt to their glasses. Not Jacob. He would go to bed with his purple glasses still on, waiting until the last possible moment to take them off. To this day, when we tuck Jake into bed at night, we occasionally find him with his glasses on. They are as much a part of him as the hair on his head.

Considering Jacob's behavior, we found it hard to deny Katie the opportunity to have her own tinted lenses. She was, after all, having the greatest difficulty in school. It took about two weeks to convince Paul to risk $275 plus the cost of frames and lenses on a little-understood theory. Frankly, that's how desperate I was. Desperate to do something for a daughter who, although reading better at home with overlays, continued on a downward slide in school.

By the end of October, Katie had an appointment with Kirstie Lewis, Ph.D., at the time the only diagnostician in the Pacific Northwest trained and certified in the Irlen method to help children and adults find the right color of tinted lenses. Dr. Lewis was based in the Seattle area and traveled to Yakima several times a year to screen Michelle's clients. It just happened that her next trip to Yakima was coming within weeks of Katie's initial screening.

TESTING FOR TINTED LENSES

Once again, Katie and I made our way to Michelle Orton's home, down the country lane, past the meandering rows of grapevine, now covered in copper leaves. Dr. Lewis led us back to Michelle's office and switched on the room's overhead fluorescent light. To confirm Michelle's original conclusion, Dr. Lewis repeated the list of questions and the initial Irlen screening procedures. She too determined that Katie was severely impacted by sensitivity to aspects of light. Once again, Katie's eyes and head began to ache halfway through the screening and I watched as streaks of red slowly took over the whites of her eyes. Dr. Lewis completed the screening and produced a briefcase. She popped opened its locks and revealed the contents. About eighty lenses rested neatly in foam slots—row upon row of colored lenses, each nearly three inches across and in varying shades.

Dr. Lewis began to work with the lenses, asking Katie to look through the various shades at a dense page of text to see which colors made any improvement. From the beginning, Katie clearly preferred lenses in the blue-green and purple range. Dr. Lewis focused on variations in these hues. Finally, she combined three lenses to create a rich shade of teal. Katie indicated a preference for a fourth lens, a purple, but she was uncertain.

Dr. Lewis began to modify the light in the room to determine whether light source affected Katie's color preference. Under incandescent light, or the standard home lightbulb, Katie preferred the teal combination. With the overhead fluorescent light on, she reported that her visual distortions worsened. Dr. Lewis added the extra purple and Katie reported improvement.

This part of the process completed, Dr. Lewis invited Katie to follow her outdoors. There, in natural light, Katie was asked to walk a dozen or so feet and describe her reactions. It was rather funny to watch. In each hand,

Katie held a set of the blue, green, and purple filters stacked together. She raised them to her eyes and began to walk, raising each foot high as though stepping over the curb, similar to how people respond to overcorrection in a conventional pair of glasses. Then Dr. Lewis helped Katie remove the purple lenses and asked her to try just the blue-green stack. This time Katie walked comfortably, her step normal, quick, and natural. I marveled at the difference.

"Is that common?" I asked.

"Not really," Dr. Lewis said. "Katie is a little harder to pinpoint. Usually I can find one tint that works for kids. She shows a strong reaction to different lighting conditions."

"Does that mean two pairs of glasses?" I asked.

Dr. Lewis led us back to the office. "Well," she said, "here's what I recommend. Clearly the blue-green tints work for Katie under normal room light and outdoors. Under fluorescent light, she needs something extra. If you can do it, I would consider a blue-green base pair of lenses with a purple clip-on. Then she has a little flexibility."

Dr. Lewis added one caution: "About twenty-five percent of the kids we see need to have their tints adjusted in the first year. It is something to watch for."

We thanked Dr. Lewis and made our way home. Once again, Katie had a whopping headache. During screening, though, I protected myself. When Katie was asked to look at busy images and dense text under fluorescent light, I looked away to avoid the physical discomfort that came with the first experience. It worked. I left with only a mild headache and a mind churning with questions.

We arrived home and I attempted to describe the experience to Paul. I didn't do a very good job. He was still smarting from the hole the bill would leave in the family checking account.

BEING DIFFERENT IS HARD

Katie received her first set of Irlen colored lenses in November 1999, just months after she started the fifth grade. When she used them, she came home rested and in good spirits. But fifth grade is a difficult age for any child to be singled out as different among her peers. It is the height of preadolescent social awareness. Katie resisted wearing her tints for the same reason many fifth graders struggle to wear conventional lenses. They made her different from the other kids. And, on top of achieving the distinction of having four eyes, Katie's lenses were as dark as a dusky sky. No other child in Katie's school of 500 wore lenses like that. It was like wearing a neon sign that said "kick me." What this meant to her didn't really sink in for me until I heard a classmate call her "devil woman."

The year came and went, and in spite of being able to read better aloud, Katie continued to struggle in school. I visited her teacher several times for progress reports and she repeatedly brought up Katie's difficulty with comprehension. I asked whether Katie was wearing her glasses every day in class because I was trying to gauge whether they made a difference. Katie's teacher claimed Katie was. I asked her to make sure of it—to call me, if need be. She never called.

In early April, I finally began to notice that Katie was once again coming home daily with bright red eyes. In retrospect, I realized it had been happening frequently, although not daily.

"Are you wearing your glasses?" I asked.

"Sometimes," Katie answered. "Well, not much."

"Why not?" I asked.

"Mom," she said, "I hate being different. The kids make fun of me."

"That has to be hard," I said. "But, honey, do the glasses help you? If they do, then you need to wear them. If they don't, then let's get rid of them."

That drew a reaction: "*No*, Mom. I don't want you to do that. They do help. I just don't like to be different."

The next day I spoke to Katie's teacher again and asked her to make sure Katie wore her glasses. For a couple of weeks, Katie came home with clear white eyes. At the end of the month, the telltale red showed up again. Not one or two days, but nearly a week of red. I approached her teacher. She acknowledged Katie hadn't been wearing her glasses. I'd had enough.

Just five weeks before the end of the school year, we moved Katie from her public school classroom of twenty-seven students to a private school class of fifteen. It was a hard decision to make. It meant pulling Katie from a routine and people she knew and dropping her smack-dab into an unfamiliar situation—and just a few weeks before summer vacation. On the one hand, it seemed extreme. On the other hand, I needed to know whether there was anything to this connection between light and color. Could tinted lenses help Katie in class? Her use of them had been so inconsistent, I couldn't tell.

At a cost for tuition of about $350 per month, we made the move.

Before we did, we made certain that Katie's new school would cooperate with our request to have Katie wear her glasses consistently. She immediately began coming home rested and with clear white eyes. She began to sleep better, too. But Katie had lost a lot of ground compared to her peers and her new teacher agreed that her learning had been delayed. She continued to struggle with cursive writing and her printing continued to be erratic and sloppy. A single homework assignment continued to take an hour and a half, while it took other children just thirty minutes. In the last week of school, Katie's new teacher recommended that she repeat the fifth grade.

We took the recommendation seriously and began to think through the last year. Katie had used her lenses sporadically, and when asked to read aloud at home, she did show improvement. She could read several paragraphs from a textbook aloud with relative smoothness—not perfectly, but better than without her glasses. Clearly, however, her comprehension was poor. She could read two or three paragraphs of text and have no recollection of what she'd just read. It was a puzzle begging to be solved.

A SECOND LOOK

I remembered what Dr. Lewis had said—25 percent of individuals with Irlen syndrome need to be retested in the first year. I decided to have Katie tested again, just in case. I asked Katie's fifth grade teacher and school principal if we could wait until August to decide what to do about placement. I wanted a little more time to sort through Katie's issues.

Buying time paid off. The second round of testing provided one more revelation in a year filled with them. What we learned from Katie was that the first attempt to improve what she saw on the printed page had lessened the distortions, but it had not resolved all of them. The first set of teal and purple lenses moved Katie from a mishmash of words that appeared to rise, fall, and slide down the page to words that did not move, but instead grouped together two and three at a time without spaces between. White space she did perceive occurred every third word or so and lined up vertically with white spaces above and below to create an optical illusion that looked like rivers or waterfalls flowing down the page.

Katie's ability to perceive the printed page had improved and she was experiencing less stress, but now she had to wade through rivers of white and decipher words grouped together. She was working so hard just to

Katie's River Pattern

What is known today in the United States as scotopic sensitivity/Irlen syndrome and in the United Kingdom as Meares-Irlen Syndrome is incredibly complex. When I first heard about it, I thought, "They've got to be kidding." When I sat beside my child, though, and she described for the first time how letters rose up and fell off a page, or slid like words on an invisible sled on a downhill slope, I was amazed. When she talked of seeing only two and three syllables in a book at a time and the words on the rest of the page swirling nauseously around them, of white spaces looking like waterfalls, or of classroom white board's appearing lime green, I thought, "How could this be?" The more I learned about how the brain interprets what the eyes see, however, the more what she told us made sense. What we see comes to the brain via wave lengths of light. If this is true, why couldn't those wave lengths be distorted by abnormal brain activity? Why couldn't the extreme contrast of black words on white pages overstimulate the brain to the point that visual distortions would occur? Just as some people taste salt more strongly than others, just as some hear frequencies of sound more accutely than others, just as some people are more bothered by smells than others, just as some people have allergic reactions to food or airborne particulates, why couldn't some brains overreact to light and high contrast?

The best proof I have that SS/IS is a real and appropriate diagnosis are my children. In the first and second grades, both of my children figuratively "hit a wall" when it came to reading. Both began to fall behind their peers. By the fourth grade, my daughter was a full year or more behind her peers. At second grade, my son already was a full year behind. My daughter figured out on her own that if she removed light from her environment, she could read comfortably and efficiently. Months before she was diagnosed with SS/IS, she began reading in remarkably dim conditions and, in three short months, brought her reading level up a full year. Reading in dim light, she had far less problem with bloodshot eyes and headaches. From the day she received her Irlen Filters and began wearing them in class, the red eyes she normally came home with at day's end disappeared. Immediately she stopped suffering from headaches, nausea, and fatigue. Within 15 months of receiving his colored lenses, my son's reading level increased from .9 (less than first grade) to 3.9 (just below fourth grade). Any classroom teacher will tell you that this is impressive progress. The first day he wore colored lenses to school, his fear of his classmates disappeared. The difference was physically noticable. He came home joyful and relaxed. As he explained, he could finally see his classmates clearly under fluorescent lights. Their shapes no longer blended together with their desks and chairs. In his words, they no longer looked like "monsters". stopped suffering from headaches, nausea, and fatigue.

separate the words that her brain was not free to take in the meaning of what she read. The distortions made it very difficult for her to find the answers to chapter questions in her books.

Why wasn't this caught before? The answer came from Katie herself. In all her life, she had never before been able to read a page of dense text without physical discomfort and distortions. Consequently, she assumed river patterns were what everyone saw. It was better than the shifting, sliding, pulsating words she saw without her filters. And it was a great improvement over the nauseating swirl of words she'd seen occasionally under fluorescent light, when her brain was too tired to hold the whirlpool in place.

Educators will tell you that the ability to scan a page is an important ingredient in reading and in the development of efficient study skills. Without this skill and the related ability to efficiently and quickly identify words, Katie remembered little of what she read. Most of her energy and brain power went into separating and deciphering the connected groupings of words.

At Katie's second appointment in mid-June, Dr. Lewis once again involved Katie in the painstaking process of determining the proper tints to settle her distortions. Through the process, she arrived at a rich combination of blues and greens—the same teal prescribed before—and the additional purple. This time, however, Dr. Lewis added a filter: a special type of gray that filters a different part of the light spectrum. The coating could easily be added to Katie's purple clip-on filter.

During this round of testing, I once again observed improvement in Katie's ability to read aloud. With text she had never seen before, she was fluid and efficient. The true test came a month later, in mid-July, when the newly coated clip-on arrived. I had borrowed a set of fifth grade textbooks from Katie's new school for the summer. The very day she received her glasses, I had Katie do a sample assignment. I chose the textbook she liked least and struggled with most in order to test the effect of the new lenses. The social studies text had highly reflective glossy pages and small print.

When Katie used the improved lenses, the difference was remarkable. The type of assignment that week after week had taken her an hour and a half to complete now took Katie only *twenty* minutes. The only difference between June, when she had last used the book, and mid-July had been the newly coated lenses.

Never count out a child who will teach herself to read in the dark. With her new tints, Katie invested one more summer of hard work in helping herself and had the last word in the question of being retained in the fifth grade or promoted to sixth. She voluntarily did a book report and social studies assignments, and she read. I watched as she completed assignments in one-third the time it had taken before. She invested about eighty hours during the summer in remedial activities and even more reading. The last of the barriers had been removed, leaving her to enjoy the process of learning.

By now, Katie was developing a dependence upon her glasses and becoming much more cooperative about using them. This fact became clear during an outing for a report on frogs. A friend whose country home has a small pond inhabited by tadpoles offered to let us harvest a few. Katie's plan was to raise the tadpoles and watch them mature into frogs. She would add her observations to the information she was gleaning from books and the Internet.

This particular sunny afternoon, Katie had her glasses on as she stood in the pond. Water lapping at her bare knees as she searched for tiny amphibians eventually splashed onto her lenses. She took them off and asked me to hold them. I put them in the breast pocket of my denim shirt. Later, without thinking, I leaned over to add water to our five-gallon bucket and the glasses slid out of my pocket into the water and disappeared.

Katie became hysterical. "*Mom!*" she screamed. "Those are my glasses! You can't lose them! You've got to find them! Mom, how *could* you!" She finished in tears.

What else could a mother do? Long pants and all, I plunged in after the glasses. Fortunately, silt on the bottom of the pond that I had stirred up cleared in a minute or two. I spotted the filters, pulled them out of the water, and calmed my daughter down. I knew then how Katie felt about her colored lenses.

My children's lives were changed by special colors. In the realm of human experience, it is unlikely that they are unique. In the eight months it took to find the right tints for Katie, my desire to know more about sensitivity to aspects of light and its mysterious connection with color only grew. I wouldn't be satisfied until I could understand this phenomenon and its implications, until I could finally look my husband in the eyes and know we agreed—for *or* against—on the question of color.

KATIE AND JACOB AND JACOB

5

KATIE AND JACOB
ARE NOT ALONE

Summer is my daughter's best season. She has demonstrated this twice: during the summer she taught herself to read in the shadows and during the subsequent summer, when she faced the possibility of being held back in the fifth grade. She was willing to pour her heart and soul into catching up.

One of my most vivid memories from the second summer was Katie's graduation from a babysitting class held at the hospital where I work. At the final session of the week-long series, each student gave a presentation on a relevant topic. I was a little nervous for Katie. The students read their material aloud in front of a large group of parents, grandparents, siblings, and other adults, and Katie decided to do it without her tinted lenses. She knew from experience that wearing dark glasses anywhere other than outdoors has the potential to cause a stir, and she didn't want to distract the audience.

Katie and her partner were the second to last to give their presentation. Katie read first and I held my breath. I expected the laborious, halting pace I'd come to know so well. I was wrong. Instead, Katie didn't falter over a single word. Her voice rose and fell for emphasis in all the right places. She held the laminated sheet, its purple back to the audience, lifted her gaze from the page frequently to engage the audience, and returned to her precise place on the page with no difficulty at all. It was the first time since the pet cage demonstration that I had seen such confidence in my daughter.

Katie's partner was the one who struggled. This young lady stumbled and jumped over words. She never lifted her eyes from the page. In fact, she brought the page closer to her face, fixated on the words.

A MOMENT OF DOUBT

I shook my head. Why had Katie read so well under the room's fluorescent lights? I had sudden doubts about everything that had transpired so far. Had I been duped into believing Katie had a problem with light and that color was the answer? If so, what was I going to tell Paul? I'd just convinced him to allow Jacob to be tested by Dr. Lewis for tinted lenses. It hadn't been easy; he remained skeptical. The dime-store purple lenses had taken care of Jacob's classroom monsters and his reading had improved a full grade level, but he was still a couple of months behind his peers. If Katie had indeed just read flawlessly from a sheet of white paper, there was plenty of room for doubt about color.

Also attending the graduation was a friend of mine who knew of Katie's tinted lenses and prior reading difficulty. At the end of the program, she made a beeline for me and asked the obvious question. "Hey, Rhonda. If Katie has trouble reading without her glasses, why did she do so well?"

"Good question," I said, forcing a smile. Katie was making her way through the crowd toward me. I greeted her with a hug. "Congratulations, hon! You were fantastic! Can I see the sheet you were reading from?" I didn't wait for a response. I reached into her new canvas bag, a gift for completing the class, and pulled out the laminated sheet from which she had read. From the audience, I saw only the sheet's deep purple back. It all became clear to me when I saw the sheet. The black print was muted by the color of the page, the same purple I had seen from my seat. The color was similar to Katie's overlays. The dark purple-blue sheet probably offered good reading conditions for Katie, but may have posed a problem for her partner.

I smirked as I pulled the sheet out of the bag. "*This* is why. The sheet isn't white—it's purple. Purple is one of Katie's best colors."

"Interesting," said my friend, with a hint of skepticism. It wasn't her fault. It was too complicated to explain in a crowd.

On the one hand, I felt great relief at not having been duped into accepting a diagnosis and treatment that weren't genuine. No one likes to be taken for a fool. On the other, I realized that my children truly do have a problem with how they perceive the printed page. I'd rather they didn't face this challenge, but they do.

About a week later, Jacob and I kept his appointment with Dr. Lewis, and, just as Michelle Orton had originally suggested, his prescribed tint did not match his overlays. The tint was darker than I had anticipated. It was a shade of deep blue-purple, similar to a twilight sky. We requested a rush on the lenses and they arrived just before the beginning of the school year.

Jacob started that year with a reading level of 1.8. By the following spring, he was a 4.3—an improvement of 2.5 years in nine months. He credits his new and improved tinted lenses. By his own description, Jacob's dime-store glasses for correcting distortions were an eighty on a scale of one to one hundred, and his carefully prescribed tinted lenses were a ninety-nine. I asked him why just ninety-nine. Eight-year-old Jacob paused, looked thoughtful, and answered: "I *would* say it's one hundred percent, but nothing's perfect."

It was a pivotal summer for us all. The more we explored color filtration, the more we learned, and the closer we came to understanding our children's difficulties with visual perception. Clearly none of this was as simple as it appeared. It required precision. Realizing that only made me want to know more.

OTHERS WITH IRLEN SYNDROME

During Jacob's testing, Dr. Lewis invited me to visit her Seattle office at a future date to see the sheer volume of cases in her files. I made the trip in October, nearly a year to the day from Katie's first testing. She motioned to a four-drawer filing cabinet packed with the stories of children and adults who have sought her help to understand why they struggle to read, or suffer physical discomfort while reading when they've been told their vision is fine.

Dr. Lewis walked from the filing cabinet to a counter and produced a looseleaf binder full of stories from a few of those she had tested. The stories were written to be shared with others trying to understand an aspect of visual perception that is overlooked. These stories were the first accounts I encountered from other people living with sensitivity to aspects of light. I was immediately struck by the similarity of these stories to those told by my own children.

Mirandy

Mirandy Archer lives in Washington state and was diagnosed at age fourteen.

Before I got my [lenses], it took me hours to do my homework. I would get frustrated easily. I didn't know what exactly was wrong. I had low self-esteem and got bruises all the time. But I didn't know why. . . . My new glasses helped my depth perception (why I ran into things and got bruises), light sensitivity, and slow reading. All of a sudden, I enjoyed school, school activities, and reading for hours on end. I started feeling good about myself. My grades went from 2.6 to 3.8 [GPA]. My parents couldn't be happier and I could finally enjoy my true passion: mystery novels. Whereas before, a page of print looked very bright, the letters moving around and all of the words "squishing" together, now they are still and evenly spaced.

Jocelyne

Jocelyne lives in British Columbia, Canada, and is an adult woman diagnosed in 1996.

I hated reading until I received my glasses. Because of the movement of the letters on the page, I was a slow reader, one word at a time. The letters and the lines were always moving. . . . This blurred vision affected lots of things. It slowed me down. In math, I had problems with columns. I had difficulty working out the numbers, as well as the sign. . . . For the most part, I hated school. Teachers thought I was lazy and should put more effort in my work. Kids laughed at me and called me names. Half of my teachers told me to give up; I didn't have a hope. Teachers and parents often compared me to my siblings. When I would pause to think, my father asked, "What are you? Stupid? Even your little brother knows that, and he is 10 years younger than you."

. . . I now have [tinted lenses]. They work great. I can read for hours; no problem. I can work on the computer for hours. I remember more of what I read and do less re-reading. . . . Now I believe the sky's the limit.

Gene

Gene (a pseudonym) lives in Oregon and was diagnosed in 1994.

I am a fifty-year-old man who has had immense trouble in school, as well as in activities and daily living. . . . I have had tremendous problems with light sensitivity, headaches, difficulty with reading and writing, and attention problems, especially now, as I return to school to learn another vocational skill. Over the last couple of years, I have been working on getting an associate's degree in nursing to become a registered nurse. I have always had an intense desire to be part of the academic world, as I was and continue to be a person who likes to know. However, the act of learning has always been an agonizing and painful experience for me. Reading proved to be a skill that I needed, but it was one that always caused dizziness, headaches, stomachaches, and tiredness due to the strain of dealing with the glare off the paper and preventing words from separating and jumping all over the page. Because of these difficulties, reading had to be done at a very slow pace with many rest periods. Therefore, I was always behind in my schoolwork and found learning from reading a dreadful experience. Since the use of [tinted] eyewear, what was always a nightmare has become an enjoyable and pleasurable time.

These three cases were my introduction to thousands of other people just like my children. In the year that followed, I read or heard about, met, and spoke with many others.

A VIETNAM VETERAN

A resident of South Dakota, Dan Horner is a decorated Vietnam veteran and member of a small rural hospital's board of trustees. For more than twenty years he has owned an office equipment and supply store. Dan also is a volunteer firefighter, and recently was doing something he never thought possible. He was on the verge of passing a highly technical forty-hour course to become an emergency medical system first responder.

"When I started school, if you were not succeeding, you were either dumb or lazy," he writes in a personal memoir. "By the time I reached the third grade I was falling behind. It was especially noticeable in my reading. I was attending a rural one-room school. My teacher called me to the front of the room, saying, 'Danny won't work hard enough to learn to read like a third grader, he reads like a first grader. He's going to show you how he reads.' With that she put a first grade reader into my hands. I struggled to read, 'Oh . . . look . . . look . . . and see.'" It hurt deeply when the first through eighth graders in the class laughed. "I was," he adds, "from that point, an outsider."

Dan struggled all through school and didn't realize he had a keen mind until he joined the military. There he excelled at working with his hands and on machines. After the service, he attended a vocational school and made a career of office machine repair. It wasn't until 1988, at the age of thirty-six, that he discovered there might be a reason that he struggled to learn the conventional way, through reading and writing. After seeing a news story on television about scotopic sensitivity syndrome, he drove 600 miles to Denver, Colorado, to see an Irlen specialist. Dan left that appointment with a new understanding of why he had struggled in school, renewed hope, and a prescription for four layers of color, resulting in a pair of blue-tinted lenses.

Within seven months, Dan saw tremendous improvement in his reading, handwriting, and spelling. His confidence surged. He began to see new possibilities for himself. Today he is a different person.

"I can now tell a scapula from a clavicle and a tibia from a fibula," he writes with precision. "I'm learning, and I'm enjoying it."

FROM A MOTHER AND SON IN AUSTRALIA

Beth (a pseudonym) is a mother in Sydney, Australia. She wants to know why she had to spend thousands of dollars for little to no help for her son, Ian (also a pseudonym), who struggled off and on with reading problems.

"I am mad that I spent a lot of time and money seeking help from people who should have known that such a disability exists and should have referred us to the appropriate clinic many years ago," says this mother, who has a Ph.D. in psychology. "What makes me even madder is that I suspect that many of them have heard of this problem, but because of the professional politics and their own financial interests, they have refused to acknowledge the existence of the disability. What makes me most mad, however, is that as a psychologist who works in Sydney's working-class western suburbs, I *know* that there are many children who probably have this problem, who will go undiagnosed and grow up illiterate because of professional biases."

The excerpt is from a letter Beth wrote to a Sydney news organization. She was attempting to stir interest in a story on sensitivity to aspects of light. Beth spent *four years* and thousands of dollars trying to pinpoint the source of her son's learning difficulty, and by the time she wrote the letter, she was far from calm.

Like my children, Ian performed well through his first few years of school. At age seven, however, he began misreading small words like *of, off, the*, and *a*. He also began changing the endings of words from *-ing* to *-ed* or *-s*, skipping whole lines, and jumping to sentences above or below the line being read.

"It was taxing listening to him read out loud because he made these mistakes frequently and often changed the meaning of the text," Beth recalls. "He complained that he did not like to read, and he rarely read spontaneously or for extended periods."

Ian also started complaining frequently about headaches. "Over the next four years," Beth writes, "I consulted an ophthalmologist, an optometrist, two different behavioral optometrists, and two different orthoptists." Her son spent about a year doing prescribed eye exercises. His reading and spelling improved minimally.

She consulted three other educational specialists to see if anything else could help his reading, paid for several months tuition through two commercial tutoring organizations and another $400 for assessment from another private educator. At a cost of $200 a month, the latter offered to provide additional instruction in phonics, which, she says, "I knew [my son] was already very good at. Nothing of these interventions made any difference to his reading."

In New South Wales in Australia, children take a selective school exam at grade six for placement in more challenging academic programs. Commercial coaching systems have been devised to help children prepare for such exams. Beth experienced a chance encounter of her own when she contacted one of these coaches to help her son. He immediately recognized Ian's difficulties with language, avoidance of reading for pleasure, and headaches, and asked Beth if she had ever heard of scotopic sensitivity syndrome. He referred Beth to an Irlen screening center.

Beth had Ian tested and discovered that under certain lighting conditions her son saw only a few letters at a time. He was coping daily with a blur of words and rivers flowing down the page. He is prone to headaches, especially under fluorescent light.

Beth explains what happened next: "When we left the clinic, Ian was given a colored, plastic filter to place over the page he is reading. The filter was nothing short of a miracle—he went home and, without any suggestions from me, read four books over the next two days, reading three or four hours at a time. When he—at his insistence—read out loud to me, he read without skipping words or lines and without mixing up little words or endings. He said he could now understand why people read for pleasure."

Ian's recovery from years of not being able to properly perceive the printed page began immediately. He scored well on the selective school exams and was offered a position in a selective class. Beth became certified to test children for the condition and is an ardent advocate for accessible testing for all children.

A TALENTED ARTIST

Abbie Mott is from the state of Washington. She was in her early twenties when we talked about what life was like growing up with an inexplicable barrier to learning. A gifted artist who loves to work with rich, deep colors, Abbie is tall, bright, and beautiful. As a child, she loved the pictures in her storybooks, but detested the words. Her mother, Anne Caffery, recalls the many times her preschool daughter took crayon in hand and blackened the printed words—as well as the eyes on picturebook characters. A devoted mom, Anne still has the books.

When Abbie didn't catch on to reading, her mother and grandparents began recording books on tape so the little girl would have access to good stories. Abbie would sit for hours with the tapes and the books and "read." In this way, Anne and her parents hoped Abbie would catch on. Abbie's verbal language grew, but her reading skills did not. In the meantime, Abbie loved the tapes and literally wore them to pieces.

Abbie's struggle with reading continued for years. By the fourth grade, she developed a sense she was different. She didn't read like the other kids. Instead, she stayed on top of classroom assignments by listening intently to every word her teacher spoke or read. After school, her parents and grandparents were ready and willing to help. Because fifth grade academic concepts were verbalized so well by her teacher in the classroom, she says, she didn't need to read textbooks. On the surface, it appeared Abbie was doing fine.

Everything changed in the sixth grade. It was the year Abbie hit the wall—and she knows why. It was the year teachers began assigning chapters for reading at home, no longer reading aloud in class. Abbie couldn't do the work because, when she opened a book, she struggled with moving, shifting text. Abbie began to fail and, as her grades sank, so did her self-confidence and self-esteem. By ninth grade, she lapsed into self-destructive behavior. She believed the only kids she deserved to have as friends were the kids who were like her—academic failures.

Amazingly, Abbie didn't realize that words were not supposed to rise up and fall down on the printed page. Words had always behaved that way, so she assumed it was the way everyone saw them. She never mentioned it. Abbie reasoned that she was simply "too dumb" to make sense of it—after all, everyone else could.

It wasn't until Abbie was an adult and she and her mother took a trip together that both realized something was not right about the way Abbie read. On a flight to a friend's wedding, Abbie brought a nutrition textbook from a college in which she had enrolled. Her mother was interested in the subject and asked to look at the book. Abbie sat with rapt attention as her mother quickly read page after page.

"How can you do that?" she finally asked. "How can you read that so fast? It takes me fifteen minutes just to read three paragraphs." She then demonstrated for her mother.

Watching her twenty-one-year-old daughter struggle to progress through the text, Anne realized something truly was amiss.

Abbie eventually was tested for Irlen syndrome and found to be in the severe range. For years she lived with an unrecognized obstacle to reading. Now she modifies the light in her environment and reads comfortably and efficiently.

A SIMPLE CONCEPT AND A COMMON PROBLEM

The concept does not have to be difficult to grasp. One ten-year veteran of tinted lenses cited one example to which everyone can relate: polarized lenses. Few fishermen would be without them. Outdoors most people experience the glare caused by bright sunlight. On the water, it can be particularly bad. For just about everyone, a polarized coating on lenses helps to reduce glare by causing the light to be filtered through microscopic layers of crystals.

People sensitive to aspects of light commonly struggle with glare—not only outdoors, but indoors, too. For them, color helps reduce the perceived brightness and indoor glare, preventing physical discomfort, fatigue, and visual distortions.

Are my children unique in their struggle? Far from it. Rather than asking "Is light really part of the problem?" perhaps we should be asking "How many suffer from its adverse affects?" How many children are labeled lazy or inattentive or are diagnosed as having a learning disorder or ADHD when they simply struggle because sensitivity to something within light interferes with their ability to read?

Lazy. Inattentive. ADHD. I know these labels well. At one time or another, they were used to describe Katie. I didn't wait for someone to pin them on Jacob. Dr. Lewis and other professionals trained to test for sensitivity to aspects of light have heard these same words countless times, frequently along with complaints about headaches, stomachaches, and fatigue. How can so many people of all ages describe similar symptoms and not get the help they need?

Gene, the fifty-year-old man who wrote to Dr. Lewis about his lifelong struggle with learning, articulates well the difference intervention for Irlen syndrome made in his life:

> After being tested . . . and the use of tinted glasses, my dizziness, headaches, stomachaches, tiredness, as well as attention problems, have diminished considerably. I now look forward to the time spent reading and find that I can perform this exercise for a much longer period of time. I can now read faster and comprehend a lot more information because my eyes are relaxed and the glare from the printed page is greatly diminished . . . School, as well as learning about life in general, has turned from an agonizing and painful experience into one of enjoyment and pleasure.

Should a person have to wait nearly fifty years to get the help they need to read comfortably? Is Irlen syndrome unique to Gene, Mirandy, Jocelyne, Dan, Ian, Abbie, Katie, and Jacob? In point of fact, it may be typical of five to twelve percent of people around the world.

Research conducted on three continents suggests that the number of people affected is in the millions. Most experience mild symptoms, such as fatigue and discomfort. But some, like my children, exhibit light-based reading difficulties.

As many as *one in twenty children* may be at risk of school failure because of problems associated with light. That amounts to at least one child in every classroom around the world. What if that child happens to be yours? How important is sensitivity to aspects of light then?

A THREAT TO
SCHOOL SUCCESS

6

A THREAT TO
SCHOOL SUCCESS

I grew up the daughter of a schoolteacher. From my mother I learned the importance of lifelong learning and developed an affinity for children and public education. My college degree is in journalism, but for a time I chose to work for a school system communicating school improvement goals and objectives for administrators, teachers, parents, and the community's general population of 64,000. The project's mission statement was simple: "All children *will* succeed." Countless hours and millions of federal grant dollars were poured into the project over four years.

Did every child succeed? It was a noble goal, but no, every child did not. Build a community where kids are immune to alcohol, drugs, crime, teen pregnancy, or negative self-perception and nearly every family in the industrialized world will fantasize about moving there.

I worked for the school district for two years before Katie was born and quickly learned that most new parents experience some level of anxiety about their children surviving adolescence intact. Working in education has likely made me more aware of the potential hazards.

Children and youth at risk of school failure frequently were the topic of discussion. As we worked through the details of the school improvement project, we invested a lot of time figuring out how to spot children struggling to learn and how to right their course. Mastery, meaning the ability to achieve a score of eighty percent or greater before advancing to a higher level skill, was the buzzword of the day. Teachers were encouraged to test children for mastery, teach the subject again when mastery was not achieved, retest, and repeat the cycle until students had mastered a skill. Teachers were encouraged to use a variety of visual, auditory, and hands-on methods to help children, including those who struggled. *All* children were supposed to learn according to their best learning style. In this way, success would be guaranteed.

Behind the scenes, however, an interesting dynamic took place. In hallway and lunchroom conversations, educators talked about their own children. I listened for a half-dozen years as these hard-working, well-educated mothers and fathers expressed heartbreak when their teenage children fell victim to truancy, alcohol, drugs, and teen parenthood. Without exception, these children had one thing in common: each had struggled in school as a young child.

"Terry" was one of those teens. His problems began in elementary school. Over the years, Terry was diagnosed with dyslexia and channeled into remedial programs. By high school, it was a struggle to keep Terry in school. Terry felt stupid and resented his inability to keep up with peers.

"Chris" had troubles, too. By the tenth grade Chris was in and out of rehabilitation for alcohol abuse. Unlike Terry, though, Chris was never diagnosed with a learning disability. The youth simply didn't excel in school. By the time high school graduation rolled around, Chris had parented a child.

Statistics indicate that children from low-income single-parent households are at greater risk of dropping out of school, substance abuse, and teen pregnancy than teens like Terry and Chris. But bright, well-educated parents struggle to keep their children in school and off drugs, too. You would think educators, with all their knowledge of what it takes to help children be successful, could figure out how to help their own children succeed, but many haven't. And it's not because these families don't try. Terry's mother and father and Chris's parents were responsible and conscientious. Yet they, too, were at a loss to know what to do for their children and why they struggled to succeed in school.

Why? Because how a child learns is not as simple as repeating instructions until he or she masters a skill. Far more is involved. And children with hidden learning issues face even greater challenges.

THE WAY WE LEARN

Individuals learn in different ways and through different strengths. Some learn best through visual tasks such as reading textbooks and completing worksheets. Others hear a lesson and can instantly understand and apply everything they've just heard. Others work and learn best using their hands. Yet in most schools, reading, writing, and lecturing are the predominant ways to teach, favoring individuals with better visual and auditory skills.

What happens to a child in a visually oriented classroom if words on the printed page appear to move, shift, or blur? If there is little spoken or hands-on support, would it be easy or difficult for that child to learn?

Optometrists and ophthalmologists know what would happen. They see children regularly whose ability to function in school is hindered by nearsightedness, farsightedness, or poor eye-muscle control. Eye-care professionals urge parents to have children tested early for problems associated with vision for a good reason—because they are well acquainted with the damage that can result when vision problems go undiagnosed for years. Children with such problems often experience failure at school and commonly lack self-confidence.

Willard B. Bleything, an optometrist with Pacific University's well respected College of Optometry, proposes a direct link between undiagnosed vision problems and juvenile delinquency, including substance abuse and crime. In a study unrelated to light-based reading problems, Bleything screened 477 teens entering the Stanislaus County Juvenile Hall in California. Sixty-two percent failed the visual screening battery. Complaints noted most frequently were headaches, watering eyes, blurred vision, and difficulty staying in place on the printed page. Bleything concludes:

So we find the visual profile of the juvenile delinquent to be similar to that of the learning-disabled, the key point being the preponderance of dysfunctions impacting reading activities. We know there is a strong literature base on the association between juvenile delinquency and learning disabilities. This suggests, then, that the juvenile delinquent may be a subgroup in the visually-related learning-disabled population.

HOW SCHOOL SUCCESS SHAPES A CHILD

Many organizations stress the importance of early school success. In October 1995, for example, the Carnegie Corporation of New York released *Great Transitions: Preparing Adolescents for a New Century*. The report is considered an excellent summary of the factors contributing to adolescent success and failure. The Carnegie Council on Adolescent Development concluded that obstacles in the path of developing youths "can impair their physical and emotional health, destroy their motivation and ability to succeed in school and jobs, and damage their personal relationships. Many reach adulthood ill-equipped to participate responsibly in our democratic society."

The report goes on to note that for the most part, adolescent interventions target substance abuse and teen pregnancy. Seldom, however, is this where problems begin. The report cautions that such programs overlook two important findings from research:

(1) serious problem behaviors tend to cluster in the same individual and reinforce one another; and

(2) such behaviors often have common antecedents (preceding circumstances) in childhood experience and educational failure.

Additionally, a child who struggles early in school is at greater risk of not developing many of the fundamental requirements the Carnegie Council found to positively influence adolescent development. Children struggling to learn often have a hard time earning the respect of their teachers and peers and as a result, frequently have difficulty developing a sense of belonging. Also, children struggling to learn may develop an invisible wedge between themselves and the most important adults in their lives—their mothers and fathers. Such wedges can hinder development of the close relationships necessary for youth to feel supported during the turbulence of the teen years.

What happens to kids who cannot find a safe harbor in the framework of home or school? Mental health professionals have long been aware that some teens turn to substance abuse as a way to dull the pain of failure and disconnection. A fact sheet entitled *Getting the Facts About Adolescent Substance Abuse*, available through the National Clearinghouse for Alcohol and Drug Information, states: "In these teens substance abuse may disguise, exacerbate, or be used to 'self medicate' psychiatric symptoms." The fact sheet notes that adolescents with substance abuse issues are more likely than their abstinent peers to have other mental health problems—anxiety disorders, attention deficit-hyperactivity disorder, and depression.

The National Center on Addiction and Substance Abuse at Columbia University (CASA) is one of several organizations monitoring youth attitudes about substance abuse (Web site: **www.casacolumbia.org**). CASA's work began in the mid-1990s. The earliest findings revealed that forty-one percent of all youth—two out of five—are in peril of using drugs. The most vulnerable age appears to be fifteen, years *after* a child's ability or inability to succeed in school becomes apparent.

I was aware of much of this as I watched Katie slide into school failure. I knew it well the day she came to me with tears in her eyes, desperate to know whether ghosts were real. When she spoke those words, I did not overreact, but I knew that all was not well. In the back of my mind was awareness that certain factors place children at greater risk for later drug use. "She'll catch up" and "she just needs to work harder" were no longer sufficient answers for what was happening to my child.

GENE'S STORY

The story of Gene, the man who waited nearly fifty years to discover that words on a printed page were not supposed to move, shift, or blur, provides an example of what can happen when problems remain undiagnosed. From the time he was young, reading from books made Gene tired, dizzy, and nauseous. What took other students an hour to do took him three. He recalls telling an eye doctor once when he was a child that he was seeing double, but the doctor turned down the exam room's lights, conducted his tests, and told Gene's parents the boy was just playing games.

"I learned to just shut up about it," he says. And when the same doctor shone a bright light into his eyes during a routine examination, Gene told the doctor it felt like an ice pick being jabbed through his eye and into his skull. That, too, was discounted. Bright lights, strobe lights, and even a few seconds of rapidly flickering high-contrast images on TV would put Gene "to the floor," the result of a reaction deep within his brain.

Gene's situation grew more difficult every year. His Ivy League parents weren't without resources. Gene says he felt loved, but lived with a constant sense of being a disappointment. It wasn't anything his mother or father said or did; he describes it as an internal sense that he was less than he ought to be. "My dad used to say 'a good mechanic is worth his weight in gold,'" he recalls. "There was no pressure from him in that sense, but there was internal pressure."

Throughout his school years, Gene struggled to read, was poor in spelling, and regularly switched numbers in math—traits that would challenge any individual to succeed academically. Gene compensated by developing into a gifted athlete. Through sports, he earned his peers' respect and developed a group of friends and a sense of belonging.

A wedge grew between Gene and his parents. He is hesitant to pinpoint its cause, but he acknowledges that he could never shake his nagging sense of inadequacy. In his heart, he felt he could never measure up.

In high school, Gene severely injured a knee and his hopes for a career in sports ended. His academic abilities were so poor he felt he had no hope of making it through college. It was the era of the Vietnam War, so he decided to enlist and attend officers' candidate school. But that hope evaporated as well when additional health problems related to allergies and asthma emerged. He was bounced out of officers' candidate school and ended up as an enlistee in a desk job.

"I quit making goals. Nothing ever seemed to work out," he says. "By that time, I was pretty messed up. I ended up in the drug world and that started making all the decisions for me."

He was assigned a job in a city where drugs were plentiful. A social interest in alcohol and drugs grew into a lifestyle. Gene says he graduated in just a week from marijuana to heroin, which he describes as a big "pain reliever." This lifestyle would last for nearly thirty long years.

Gene began to turn his life around in the early 1990s. He enrolled in a college program in 1994. He decided he needed to do something with his life and to give college a try. A chance encounter at the college where he was enrolled led to his introduction to Irlen syndrome and colored overlays. The overlays provided some relief, but not much. In 1996, he scratched together enough money to be tested for tinted lenses. With lenses, he received immediate relief from the distortions. "The glasses quadrupled overnight my reading ability. I could read for much longer periods and do my work faster," he says. The fatigue that characterized most of his school years diminished. School became much easier, even enjoyable.

Like so many others diagnosed with sensitivity to aspects of light as adults, Gene wonders what life for him might have been like if as a child, he'd had the yellow-gray lenses he now uses to read. Might academic success have made his parents proud and kept him from feeling inadequate? He'll never know. What he does know is that drug and alcohol abuse cost him a great deal—nearly thirty years of his life and every link he had to his parents. In the 1970s and 80s, Gene's parents were offended by his chosen lifestyle and communication broke down.

Gene's story and my daughter's struggles in school are mindful of kids many of us knew growing up. "Hugh" was a classmate of mine through grade school. Towheaded, with a knack for mischief, Hugh hated school. He struggled to perform basic tasks. He was a poor reader and rarely followed discussions in class. Over time, he became disruptive and downright combative. One of the low points of elementary school for me was watching Hugh wrestle our fifth grade teacher, nearly twice his size, to the floor. Sadder than Hugh's difficult school years was the waste of his young life. When he was fourteen or fifteen, he drowned in a community swimming hole, while under the influence of alcohol.

Then there was "Lynn." She and I were in the same class in first or second grade. She was a tall, pretty girl with long brown hair. We were very different: I loved school and had a sponge for a brain, soaking up every word my teacher produced; Lynn struggled. Aside from the difficulty she had with schoolwork, she didn't seem different from me. Both of us were quiet, neither of us came from affluent families, and both of us wore hand-me-downs. I suspect life may have been a little turbulent in both of our homes. But Lynn grew up to become one of the first unwed mothers in our class. A few years later, she drowned in a boating accident.

READING AND VISUAL PERCEPTION

I don't know why school was hard for Hugh and Lynn, but I do know they were not alone and that issues related to visual perception may have been part of the problem. Studies conducted by the National Institutes of Health in the mid-1990s found that as many as twenty percent of all school-aged children struggle to read. Reasons vary widely—for example, insufficient exposure to language, poor teaching, lack of support at home—but one issue is not yet taken seriously by medical science: visual perception.

In the summer of 1999, one of America's largest parent advocacy organizations, the National Parent-Teacher Association, passed a resolution calling for improvements in vision assessment. The primary author of the resolution, Maryland mother Nora Putt, pulled together the following pieces of information for the resolution:

- Eighty percent of what a child learns in the classroom depends on the efficiency of the visual system.

- Visual skill deficiencies may contribute to poor academic performance.

- Typical vision evaluations test for only a few learning-related visual skills (distance acuity—20/20 eyesight—stereo vision, and muscle balance), leaving most visual skill deficiencies undiagnosed.

- Ten million or more children ages 0 to 19 may suffer from undetected vision problems due to a lack of appropriate evaluation.

- Many states require vision screening and leave it up to individual schools to decide what type of tests will be done.

- The connection between poorly developed visual skills and poor academic performance is not widely known by students, parents, teachers, administrators, and public health officials.

The resolution was passed by the Maryland PTA in 1998 and brought to the convention floor of the National PTA in July 1999. According to those attending that session, something interesting happened when the resolution was read. Time provided for spontaneous testimony was filled with an unanticipated outpouring of support as parents and educators took the microphone to share stories of children who struggled to read because of mysterious problems associated with vision. The response was not staged; it simply happened.

The National PTA resolution had nothing to do with sensitivity to aspects of light or Irlen syndrome. Instead, it dealt with aspects of vision being treated via vision therapy (specially designed eye exercises) by specialists in the field of behavioral or developmental optometry.

Enter the great paradox in the quest to understand overlooked aspects of vision and visual perception, and their role in the ability of some children to succeed in the classroom. The splits and shifts and disagreements run rampant—and they can be difficult to follow.

In the United States, behavioral optometrists in general don't believe children and adults experience problems related to sensitivity to aspects of light. They believe problems related to visual perception can be corrected with vision therapy, a system of eye exercises, thereby retraining the eyes and the visual system to work together.

But the nation's leading ophthalmologists, medical doctors specializing in disorders of the eye, have called vision therapy costly and ineffective. Optometrists *and* ophthalmologists in the United States have both gone on record against what they call the non-diagnosis of scotopic sensitivity syndrome, the old term for sensitivity to aspects of light or Irlen syndrome, and intervention through color filtration. They criticize research done to date as inadequate. Ophthalmologists, for their part, have chosen not to develop any diagnostic methods to help families identify children who experience visual distortions, instead leaving it to public education to identify and remediate children.

Educators, however, do not routinely screen children for problems with reading-related visual perception. A few schools have developed active screening programs for sensitivity to aspects of light, but most school systems do not support it because ophthalmology and optometry do not support it. For reading problems in general, only a small percentage of children are tested. A thorough evaluation takes several hours, for which schools receive little to no compensation. Keep in mind that schools are overwhelmed with millions of children struggling to learn to read in classrooms.

In a nutshell, millions of kids struggle to read, experts in vision disagree on what can be done, and education is too overwhelmed to do much about it. So what are parents to do? Put children's futures on hold and wait for the experts to sort it out? Whenever my kids propose a risky activity, I have just four words for them: "I don't think so!"

Parents can take matters into their own hands. It may be another decade or two before vision experts sort out problems related to visual perception, but parents can't wait. Children who are unsuccessful in school are at greater risk of alcohol abuse, drug use, and teen pregnancy. When someone offered us a possible explanation for Katie's difficulties with learning, I jumped at the chance to explore it. The diagnosis she received explained a long list of concerns accumulated over many years—bright red eyes, headaches, fatigue, an aversion to classroom work, and an inability to follow and comprehend large volumes of text. The pieces of the puzzle fit together.

What we found was that color and managing light worked for Katie and Jacob *in spite of* medical opinion. My husband and I were torn between believing our children and trusting vision experts. It left us doubting our children, and that wasn't good for their confidence or ours.

So we decided to investigate Irlen syndrome, light-based reading problems, and the color solution ourselves. We were amazed by what we found. It is information every adult with the power to influence the life of a struggling child needs to know.

part II

THE PROBLEM REVEALED— SENSITIVITY TO ASPECTS OF LIGHT

THE PROBLEM REVEALED— THE PROBLEM REVEALED—

7
LIFE-CHANGING
DISCOVERIES

Our family's journey to understand sensitivity to aspects of light was not an easy one. When it was first suggested that our daughter could benefit from colored overlays or tinted lenses, my husband and I reacted in different ways. I wasn't entirely convinced, but I was willing to give it a try. Katie's difficulties with school had reached a point that I decided to do it first and ask questions later. Paul was more conservative. He feared that both testing and intervention would be a waste of time and money.

What ensued was a two-year journey to understand the invisible barrier preventing both of our children from being successful in the classroom. Along the way, we found ourselves knee-deep in research and other paper. As logical and strong a case as all the paper made, it was not the most convincing factor. That distinction belonged to our children.

The paper came to us via books, articles, journals, a hospital library, and select sources from the Internet. It was a process of "hunt and gather." Seek all you can find and search for more. Ultimately, the fact-finding mission connected our family with experts and resources in Australia and England and with individuals in places throughout the United States. Several times, from exhaustion, I resolved to quit the moment I found one document definitively proving wrong the theory of light as a source of physical discomfort and visual distortions and color as an effective intervention. I never located that document. Instead, I found studies supporting color as an appropriate intervention and others claiming no effect that ignored the very culprit in light-based reading difficulties—the type, quantity, and quality of light. While all this was going on, Katie and Jacob were wearing tinted lenses and their reading was improving by leaps and bounds.

THE PAPER TRAIL

The paper trail begins in 1980, the year a New Zealand schoolteacher named Olive Meares described visual problems encountered by some of her students. She was the first to suggest that reduction of contrast between a bright white page and black print assists some children with the process of reading.

In the early 1980s, the director of a learning disability program at California State University–Long Beach undertook a multiyear government-funded research project to identify barriers to learning. The researcher, Helen Irlen, focused her study on a group of adults who had always struggled to learn and a control group of graduate students with no difficulties reading or learning.

Irlen worked over five years with hundreds of learning-disabled students to document discomfort and a collection of perceived visual distortions associated with reading. Most of these students had come to believe that visual distortions and/or physical discomfort were just a normal part of the reading experience.

The distortions they reported were vastly different from the stereotypical letter reversals sometimes associated with dyslexia—such as *b* appearing as *d*. Their distortions ranged from white space between words dominating a page and causing words to disappear, to print that would "dance, vibrate, pulsate, jiggle, shift, shimmer, move" and more. Other distortions they reported: lines of text that appeared to slide sideways across or down a page, words washed out through the center, words with halos, and words crowded together with little or no space between.

In an era rich with information and technology, how could such a vast array of visual distortions be missed? Easily. First, screening practices used by vision professionals have evolved to remove conditions that typically produce visual distortions—bright light and dense text typical of the reading experience. Additionally, during the 1970s theories about why children struggle to read implicated the auditory processing system of the brain as the source of reading difficulties, not the visual system. Consequently, before Irlen's study, no standard procedures existed to identify physical discomfort and visual distortions associated with reading. *Nobody asked.*

Descriptions provided by Irlen's students provided a common language she used to move forward with her work. In the next part of her study, a sample group of thirty-seven subjects with learning disabilities were examined and treated by a host of experts, including optometrists, ophthalmologists, developmental optometrists, neurologists, psychologists, and reading specialists. Over nine months, Irlen says, not one of the conventional or innovative treatments the specialists recommended successfully addressed issues identified by her learning-disabled students.

Irlen looked for a new approach. She scrutinized methods of testing and therapies used through the years to treat learning disabilities. She was examining treatments developed within optometry—in particular, red overlays and red-green glasses used to help individuals develop a dominant eye—when one of her students put a red overlay over a page of text and shrieked. Before the young woman encountered the overlay, print on a page had always swayed back and forth. With the overlay, the words stopped moving and appeared steady and stable. The reading-disabled student went on to read the page of text aloud smoothly. When Irlen tried the red overlay with other reading-disabled students, however, they said it did nothing to improve their discomfort or visual distortions.

Curious, Irlen returned to class one day with a variety of other transparent colored sheets. Over many weeks, she encouraged students to take turns placing different colors over text. Eventually, thirty-one out of thirty-seven of the learning-disabled students reported relief from visual distortions using carefully chosen colors—different colors for different students. Study participants were asked to use their chosen color of transparency for one month and keep a journal of changes in their reading rate, comprehension, and comfort. At the end of the month, 78 percent of the students noted a reduction in visual distortions, improved attention and comprehension, and decreased strain and fatigue. Additionally, their grades improved.

As work continued with the experimental group, Irlen began to work with a control group of graduate students—individuals quite different from the study group in that they had demonstrated no difficulty in reading or learning. Each of these students was also encouraged to experiment with color transparencies and to choose a color that would make reading more comfortable. Intriguingly, this group didn't like the colored sheets.

They didn't want them and wouldn't use them. In the early 1980s, Irlen was invited to report her findings at a conference of the American Psychological Association.

Irlen thus discovered that specifically chosen colors could calm physical discomfort and visual distortions in individuals experiencing invisible barriers to reading. Her findings resulted in the Irlen Method for assessing individuals sensitive to aspects of light and the development of Irlen tinted lenses worn as glasses as an alternative to colored overlays.

Since the mid-1980s, several Australian researchers in the field of education have been captivated by Irlen's work. Paul R. Whiting, Ph.D., retired from the University of Sydney, and G. L. Robinson, Ph.D., University of Newcastle, studied the long-term benefits of Irlen tinted lenses for 267 individuals first diagnosed in 1988 with sensitivity to aspects of light. Six years later, researchers located 114 subjects willing to participate in follow-up surveys. Of the 114, 94 percent said Irlen tints were of "some" or "large" help with visual discomfort and/or visual distortions, with 58 percent indicating a "large" degree of benefit and 36 percent indicating "some" benefit. Only 6 percent indicated that they received no help from their Irlen lenses.

Studies by Dr. Robinson confirmed one other conclusion Irlen had drawn: the number of individuals affected by sensitivity to aspects of light is as high as 12 percent of the general population. Dr. Robinson also has found evidence that such sensitivity runs in families. Examining family histories, he found 84 percent of sufferers have relatives who complain of problems associated with photosensitivity, a general term for sensitivity to aspects of light. One of the most common threads he and other researchers have found is a family history of migraine headache.

In another part of the world in the 1980s, Arnold Wilkins, Ph.D., a psychologist formerly with the British Medical Research Council, was studying photosensitive epilepsy, in which seizures are induced by pulsating bright lights or busy, high-contrasting patterns. He became intrigued with Irlen's work and methods and began to work with color filtration. He began his own independent research and as a result developed testing and color methodologies to identify and lessen what he calls visual stress. In 1994, he conducted a double-blind placebo-controlled study with, among others, Bruce Evans, Ph.D., an optometrist and research director of London's Institute of Optometry, and found that 1 in 5 randomly selected children *preferred* viewing text through a specifically chosen color. More important, he found that 1 out of 20 randomly selected children demonstrated a 25 percent or greater improvement in reading fluency when aided by colored overlays or tinted lenses.

In the late 1990s, Dr. Evans led another study in an optometric clinic specializing in specific learning disabilities. Half of 323 patients there were prescribed colored overlays or tinted lenses to address issues related to visual perception, eyestrain, or headache. More than a year later, half of those given tinted lenses were contacted by phone and asked whether they were still using them. The response: more than 80 percent still wore their tints *daily*.

In 1998, the year before our daughter's reading and learning issues came to a head, Harold Solan, an optometrist and researcher from the State University of New York, State College of Optometry, also encountered positive evidence that color filtration could help some children who struggle to read. In a study, he found that 75 percent of children with reading disabilities could be helped to some degree with *blue* tinted lenses, a concept first suggested by Mary Williams, Ph.D., of the University of New Orleans.

According to Irlen, as of 2002, about 100,000 children and adults in the United States, Canada, Australia, the United Kingdom, and many other parts of the world had been tested for and aided with tinted lenses via the Irlen Method. According to Dr. Wilkins, another 20,000 had been treated through his testing methods. Thousands more children have been tested by school-based screeners and are using colored overlays in classrooms.

America's leading optometry and ophthalmology associations have not supported the use of specific therapeutic color to ease physical discomfort and distortions. The reasons are complex.

One of the first issues is the name. According to Irlen, the old term, scotopic sensitivity syndrome, refers to a connection she drew between scotopic aspects of light—or those parts of the light spectrum that activate the rods of the retina—and problems with visual perception. The theory has been criticized, however, because rods in individuals who experience discomfort and distortions do not appear to differ from the rods of those who experience no problems.

Irlen, however, points out that the makeup or quantity of rods may not be the problem. The problem may be how both the rods and/or cones *react* to light and the type of reaction they trigger for the rest of the visual system and brain. New research opens the door to the possibility that light-receiving cells in the retina are involved. Today, among Irlen-trained practitioners in thirty countries, sensitivity to aspects of light that responds to color filtration is referred to as Irlen syndrome. Among optometrists in eighteen countries using the Wilkins method, the condition is called Meares-Irlen syndrome.

Second, standard vision assessment for the most part continues to be limited to visual acuity, and the ability of the eyes to focus and work together, and does not take into account how the visual system may react to aspects of light. I once asked an optometrist screening my children why the lighting is dimmed during testing. He said it was in order to avoid problems associated with glare. Ironically, some people—like my children—react adversely to bright light, especially glare, and such glare exists all around us; in our homes, offices, and schools. It bounces off computer screens and glossy book pages. Testing procedures for visual acuity, however, have evolved to avoid interference from bright light and glare.

Third, research done to date to document Irlen syndrome and intervention through colored overlays and tinted lenses has evolved through psychology and education and does not commonly use protocols accepted by medical science. As a result, much of the work to document the existence of Irlen syndrome and successful intervention with color is discounted as poorly designed. Dr. Wilkins, now with the University of Essex, and Dr. Evans worked together to successfully design and complete a double-blind placebo-controlled study of the type and nature acceptable to medical science. Rarely, however, is this work cited by medical organizations in the United States. They cite instead studies not directly related to sensitivity to aspects of light and/or negative studies that some researchers suggest are flawed. Dozens of positive studies, reviews, and articles are seldom cited.

CONTRIBUTING TO THE BARRIER

In May 1988, six months before Katie was born, the television newsmagazine *60 Minutes* aired a story on the work of Helen Irlen. In the segment, children with reading difficulties went from stumbling over words without colored overlays to reading smoothly and efficiently when colored overlays were placed over the printed page. I remember thinking how nice it was that someone had finally found something to help below-average children perform better in school. I was embarrassingly arrogant and naive.

Children with Irlen syndrome are not below average in intelligence.

They are frequently bright kids unable to overcome an invisible barrier to learning. This barrier will not be routinely identified until four issues are addressed. They include:

- Vision screening, especially the type conducted in schools, tests only the function of the eye and excludes what happens to visual perception within the complex system of the brain.

- Assessments conducted by vision professionals are routinely conducted in dark or dimmed rooms, minimizing light and glare as factors.

- Reading materials typical to the human experience are seldom used in vision assessment.

- Vision screening continues to rely on a 140-year-old tool to determine reading capability and potential.

Since the 1860s, most public schools have relied upon one tool to measure whether children can see well enough to learn: the Snellen eye chart. This chart, with its well-spaced individual block letters arranged in spacious rows of progressively smaller size, was developed to identify children who could not see writing on a chalkboard from the back of a classroom. Over the decades, the Snellen eye chart became the standard for vision screening.

The Snellen eye chart was not designed to test a child's ability to see a page of printed text. It was developed to measure the ability of children to see letters at a distance of twenty feet—hence the term *20/20*.

The handheld reduced Snellen eye chart is a modified version of its predecessor and used by vision professionals to determine the ability to see close up, as is the case with reading. On this small chart, forty-nine letters are symmetrically arranged on a card. Patients are asked to name the letters on the card in the same way they are asked to read the letters on the larger wall chart. If a child can read the letters on the small chart, it is assumed they have no problem with reading.

The problem with both charts, however, is that they do not replicate conditions that exist during reading. With an eye chart, there is less work for the brain's visual system to perform. In everyday reading, the letters on the page are dense and crowded together. Under such conditions, a visual system must simultaneously deal with a complex set of vertical lines, crowded contours, and near equal parts of bright white (reflected page color) and dark black (text color). In any size, a Snellen eye chart does not replicate such conditions.

Two other things in our daily lives have changed significantly since the advent of the Snellen eye chart. First, the lighting conditions under which children now read are dramatically different. In the 1800s, students read by natural light from windows and/or light from oil lamps. Such sources generally provide softer and less evenly distributed light source than those now in use. Today, most classrooms in America are flooded with bright overhead fluorescent light—a form of light that tends to exacerbate problems for those sensitive to brightness, glare, the color within light, and dark/bright contrast. Second, textbook pages have changed. Many books used for learning 140 years ago used natural-colored paper with light-absorbing surfaces. In contrast, many textbooks today have bright white pages with glossy surfaces. Such paper reflects more light and glare to the visual system than the papers commonly used in days gone by. Put these factors together—overhead fluorescent light and glossy pages—and it is apparent that a tremendous amount of bright light and glare can be bounced from the printed page to our children's visual systems.

Current vision screening compensates for an overabundance of reflected light by turning off or dimming overhead room light for vision exams. Eye tests for children conducted in public schools are often administered under normal lighting conditions; but these tests typically use the Snellen eye chart. As previously stated, this chart does not create the visual work that triggers physical discomfort or perceptual problems.

Without question, the testing optometrists and ophthalmologists do to screen children and adults for eye health is of vital importance. The conditions they detect include farsightedness, nearsightedness, astigmatism, eyes that turn in or out or fail to properly align, and more. For years, optometrists and ophthalmologists alike have urged parents to identify problems with visual acuity as early as possible because they can interfere with a child's ability to learn, as well as the ability to develop positive self-esteem and social skills.

Researchers working with Irlen syndrome and families like ours, who have experienced the difference color can make, know there is another vital component in the ability to correctly perceive the printed page and the world at large. That component involves everything that happens from the eye to the brain in the process of visual perception. In this complex and overlooked system, the human eye is not like a camera sending a movie-type image to the brain. Instead, light receptors are stimulated, triggering complex biological processes that sweep through the visual system and brain. The product of this process is what we perceive and appropriately call visual perception.

What activates this complex visual system? The very thing that makes it possible for humans to see—*light*. Since the Snellen eye chart was developed, vision screening has evolved throughout the world. In that evolution, however, reaction to aspects of light continues to be overlooked as a variable in perception.

WHAT IS SENSITIVITY TO ASPECTS OF LIGHT?

Sensitivity to:

Brightness

Glare

The Color of Light (wavelengths)

Bright/Dark Contrast

Strobing

Pattern Glare

*References to light sensitivity in this book refer
to one or more of these. Physical and emotional stress
as well as fatigue can worsen symptoms.*

EQUAL PARTNERS IN HOW WE "SEE"

A growing number of professionals are beginning to test specifically for sensitivity to aspects of light. Katie and I traveled to England in April 2001 to have Katie tested by Drs. Wilkins and Evans, who are actively involved in the introduction of Meares-Irlen syndrome to optometrists.

For the most part, optometric testing procedures used by Dr. Evans were similar to those used in the United States. There was one dramatic departure. Typically, optometrists test the ability of the eyes to work together using an alignment instrument inside a stereoscope, a black box through which patients view illuminated images. In England, however, Dr. Evans also used a Mallett unit to test Katie's alignment. Through this handheld device, Katie viewed a paragraph of dense text under normal lighting conditions. In the middle of the text was the standard alignment instrument—a cross-shaped set of bars. Through a stereoscope, which removed normal room light as a factor in visual perception, Katie demonstrated no visual problems with alignment; the bars lined up properly. Through the Mallett instrument under normal room light, however, the bars did not line up. Even more significantly, when specific therapeutic colored lenses were placed in front of Katie's eyes, the bars aligned. To check this, Dr. Evans tested Katie with two sets of tinted lenses. Only the set that removed the most visual distortions for Katie helped the image properly align.

Visual acuity and visual perception deserve to be regarded as equal partners in how we see. Children are routinely tested for problems associated with visual acuity and other mechanical defects. Children are rarely tested, however, for problems associated with visual perception or aspects of light. A few school systems in a handful of places in the world are beginning to screen for it. A few others have tried it, not really understood it, and abandoned it. Families like ours have happened upon it by chance.

Like Helen Irlen's adult students with reading difficulties, millions of people may grow up believing that visual distortions, strain, and other physical discomfort are a normal part of the reading experience. They may grow up thinking that it is normal to get headaches or fidget after no more than fifteen minutes of reading.

A young friend of our family shared an interesting perspective. The eleven-year-old described her older sister as a human dictionary. To the younger sister's exasperation, her older sibling reads avidly, retains everything she reads, and can even read in the car. After fifteen minutes or so of reading, the younger sister grows physically tired. Attempting to read in the car, she adds, makes her sick.

Intriguingly, many individuals with even mild forms of Irlen syndrome fit this profile: school does not come as easily for them, reading causes them to tire quickly or fidget, and some become carsick when they try to read while riding in cars. Yes, carsickness for a small percentage of people fits the profile. No one really knows why, but there is speculation. It has to do with overloading the visual system. In a car, the human brain can perceive a rush of moving images via peripheral vision. Add to that the contrast between the soft light of the interior and the brightness outside, the physical demands of reading, a visual system so stressed it cannot help the auditory center stabilize motion, and—wham—a brain sensitive to light and contrast may become overwhelmed. The result: fatigue, headache, and motion sickness.

This example does relate to something else of profound importance: the reality that human brains, even the brains of sisters, respond differently to stimuli in the same environment—stimuli that logically include light.

John J. Ratey, M.D., is a psychiatrist and an associate clinical professor of psychiatry at Harvard Medical School. In his book *A User's Guide to the Brain*, he calls for a shift away from traditional thinking about how personalities are shaped and more investigation into the "biology" of the brain. He bases this assertion on a growing body of evidence that some human behavior is directly attributable to the biological workings of the brain. "Every brain is different," he writes, "and no brain is perfect; it is our responsibility to learn about ourselves and about what gives us each a unique way of seeing the world."

Part of this "seeing" involves the different ways individual brains perceive and respond to external stimuli. The differences may be subtle or so extreme that psychological trauma may result if physiological problems with perception go undetected.

Ratey cites an example from *Rickie*, a book published in 1990 by Frederic Flach. In the 1960s, Rickie was an energetic and joyful child. By the time she had reached the third grade, however, her school performance had declined. Rickie's struggles in school contributed to severe depression. At age thirteen, she began a ten-year odyssey in and out of psychiatric facilities. When she was twenty-three, a developmental optometrist discovered that Rickie's visual system grossly distorted what she saw.

Rickie's early life was traumatized in part because severe undetected problems associated with her visual system disrupted her life. Over time with visual training (something unrelated to color filtration), Rickie gained control of her problem—but it took another seventeen years for her to overcome the psychological devastation of those early years.

In *A User's Guide to the Brain*, Ratey devotes 380 pages to the complexities of the brain, and, from the beginning, points out the urgency to improve understanding of its biological functions. He predicts that over the next thirty years a growing understanding of the brain will transform how we see both the world and ourselves.

STRONG EVIDENCE

The impact of light on the human brain is an area of study ripe for further exploration. In the early 1990s, scientists using neuroimaging to study dyslexia found disturbances in the visual pathways that carry information from the eyes to the visual cortex of the brain. In 1998, neuroimaging specialist Jeffrey Lewine, Ph.D., made discoveries that surprised even him. As Lewine tells the story, Helen Irlen contacted him about performing a neuroimaging study on the use of color as a method of calming physical discomfort and visual distortions. Irlen and a persistent mother of one of his patients finally persuaded Lewine to do the study—but he did so with the aim of disproving Irlen's theory and methods.

In the study, Lewine and William W. Orrison, Jr., used an MEG (magnetoencephalography) scan to detect activity in the brain. Eight control subjects with no reading problems and eight people diagnosed with Irlen syndrome were shown an image intended to create high-contrast conditions—in this case, a busy black-and-white grid with a dot in the center for focusing. To Lewine's surprise, the scan revealed well-organized brain patterns in the eight control subjects and disorganized brain patterns in six of the eight individuals diagnosed with Irlen syndrome. When the six with disorganized patterns were tested while wearing their customized tinted lenses, brain patterns became organized. Lewine calls the findings objective evidence for a physiological effect of color filtration.

The findings are no surprise to Helen Irlen. Over the years, research conducted through the Irlen Institute found that 46 percent of children participating in remedial reading programs experienced reading improvement when aided by Irlen overlays or tinted lenses.

For our family, it wasn't work by Irlen, Wilkins, Evans, Whiting, Robinson, or Lewine that ultimately convinced my husband that color filtration had the potential to settle visual distortions. It was *negative* test results published in a 1993 article in *Archives of Ophthalmology* by Menacker, et al.

The Menacker study tested twenty-four children diagnosed with dyslexia, ages eight to twelve, with four basic colors (red, yellow, blue, green) in two different densities. For controls, frames with no lenses and neutral or clear lenses also were used. The study's authors reported that testing yielded no difference between the four colors, varying densities, and the placebos. Specifically, language from the study states: "There was no significant effect on the speed or accuracy of reading with the use of any colored lens, neutral-density lens, or lens density condition that was tested."

The intent of the study was to determine if a specific color would help children read more efficiently. Consequently, the study team averaged results from the specific lens results. They intentionally did not take into consideration individual improvement with varied hues among the children.

My husband is an accountant by trade and our household's expert with numbers. I asked him to look at the study's test results for each child. What he found changed his mind about tinted lenses. Paul entered the results for both reading speed and error rate into an Excel spreadsheet. By the time he was finished, he found that *ten* of the twenty-four children experienced improvement in both reading speed *and* error rate with at least one of the four colors. The average improvement among the group of ten was impressive: 49 percent.

An accountant's methods involve simple mathematics. They do not involve allowances for chance improvement, something that scientific methods typically consider. For each child, Paul simply looked for an improvement with color and calculated the results. What he found convinced him that some children experienced improvement with color. As a result, the Menacker study cannot rule out the possibility that some individuals may benefit from specific colors.

Merrill Bowan is a Pittsburgh-area optometrist who specializes in visual problems treatable through visual therapy. Dr. Bowan has personally observed individuals who struggle with reading because of an undefined phenomenon of light. He shares this insight:

"There has been great controversy about the term 'scotopic sensitivity syndrome' and its successor, 'Irlen syndrome.' It would almost do more for scientific progress to tactfully drop those names and use them only for historical reference. We need to think about labeling the neural response that these children and adults have with a new term, one that describes the actual experience to which they react. There most definitely is a brain response that occurs, but evidence indicates scotopic aspects of visual perception are not the source."

Irlen syndrome is the most widely used term for light-based reading difficulties. Literature searches on the terms "Meares-Irlen," "Irlen," or "scotopic sensitivity" will generate the most information for consumers and professionals.

Dr. Bowan may be right. If terminology is keeping children from being diagnosed and treated, then, by all means, the scientific community should be challenged to come up with a new, acceptable term.

THE DILEMMA OF LIGHT

Why is it so difficult to believe that light and modified wavelengths (color) can impact the human brain? Light is, after all, one of the most powerful forces on earth. It can change cell structure in human skin, cure dermatological conditions for some, and cause cancer in others. It can improve the processing of bilirubin in infants, and improve seratonin levels in individuals with seasonal affective disorder (SAD). It can even be focused into highly concentrated beams capable of burning and cutting human flesh. It can dry up the earth or make plants grow. The world as we know it simply would not exist without photosynthesis.

The dilemma of light and the human visual system is that each involves complex properties with aspects that remain a mystery to scientists. A multidisciplinary approach may be needed in order to understand how aspects of light may contribute to physical comfort and visual distortions. Indeed, in 1999, Kristian Donner of the Department of Biosciences, University of Helsinki, Finland, suggested that a paradigm shift is needed in how vision researchers and practitioners think about vision. In a guest editorial in the journal *Perception*, Donner points out that researchers have been well aware since 1978 that the brain plays a significant role in problems associated with how some people perceive.

Although much needs to be learned about humans and visual perception, it is clear that a diagnosis of 20/20 vision has the potential to create a false sense of security for families trying to figure out why their children struggle to read and learn. Our family's experience is proof positive of this truth. Katie supposedly had near perfect vision. Yet at the end of fourth grade, she hit a wall she could not crawl under, climb over, or go through in regard to reading. It wasn't until light was altered that she made significant gains. Jacob was showing signs of the same problem, unable to get out of first grade readers and into the busier and denser second grade texts. For both kids, it was as though an invisible barrier had been removed when they began turning the lights out or using color filtration.

The knee-deep stack of paper we have gathered in our quest to understand visual perception helps affirm, for our own sakes, that Irlen syndrome is real. It does not, however, replace what we see and experience every day—our children *reading* behind lenses of blue/blue/purple and blue/blue/gray/aqua. In eighteen months, Katie went from nonreader to voracious reader capable of reading nearly a year above her grade level. Jacob would still rather be outside riding his scooter or playing with friends, but by the middle of fourth grade he was capable of silently reading and passing tests on popular fifth and sixth grade fiction. As a family, we now understand the invisible barrier and thankfully, we have moved beyond it.

8 "KIDS LIKE US"

"KIDS LIKE US"

My children are quite specific about what they want to say in this book.

"Mom," said Jacob, "tell them light sensitivity is real."

"For kids like us," said Katie, "tell them it's real."

Okay, Jacob and Katie, I'll tell them. Mothers, fathers, educators, and other adults who care, physical discomfort and perceived distortions related to aspects of light, brightness, glare, and bright/dark contrast are real. My children know it. I know it. My husband knows it. My children insist that I tell you their grandmother knows it, too, and she is a retired schoolteacher. The "kids like us" of which Katie speaks include all children who experience physical discomfort and visual distortions, placing them at risk of emotional distress and school failure.

Imagine what life was like for James, a sixteen-year-old youth held back and eventually enrolled in an alternative high school. His reading level was low and he struggled daily with chronic fatigue, headaches, stomachaches, dizziness, and irritability. He was defiant, angry, and aggressive, and he was failing to complete his schoolwork. He felt stupid. Even playing outdoors with his friends was too stressful. James would leave a game of basketball early, go home, and go to bed. It wasn't much of a life for a teen.

James's doctors checked him for a variety of problems, including allergies, thyroid disease, and hypoglycemia. Nothing significant was found and he was diagnosed with depression. The doctor recommended that James be put on antidepressants and Ritalin, but his mother couldn't justify medication when, at night, her son was a happy-go-lucky teen.

Meanwhile, James's mother became aware that her son's uncles were using Irlen colored filters to help them with problems associated with light. When all conventional medical causes were ruled out, she decided to have her son tested. Like his uncles, James tested positive and eventually opted for tinted lenses. The change was immediate. His dizziness and headaches went away, he started playing outdoors comfortably, and he began reading at a tenth grade level.

In James's case, a lot of his symptoms were successfully treated with therapeutic tinted lenses. Some in conventional medicine will call it the placebo effect—essentially, mind over matter. But James's mother sought medical help. Nothing worked—that is, nothing but colored lenses.

Before medical science will even consider the legitimacy of sensitivity to aspects of light as a diagnosis and color filtration as an intervention, an important question must be raised: Does the intervention address a specific problem or is it promoted as a cure-all for a host of ailments?

The medical community has good reason to be skeptical of faddish cures. They have appeared throughout history. One hundred and fifty years ago they showed up in newspaper advertisements or on rolling wagons promoting "miracle tonic." Today, they appear on television infomercials at three A.M. Usually they are proffered by fast-talking salesmen promising dramatic results and eager to provide a dubious remedy for a consumer's hard-earned cash.

More than a century ago, one remedy was the subject of medical skepticism because of such claims. Over the ages its advocates have claimed its core ingredient cured scarlet fever, diphtheria, measles, syphilis, cholera, rabies, burns, eczema, freckles, anthrax, fever, rheumatism, arthritis, and the common headache. For thousands of years, people suffering from pain associated with these ailments were told to chew on the bark of a willow tree. Hippocrates suggested patients ingest the remedy as a tea. Other purported benefits included usefulness as an antiseptic, mouthwash, and water preservative.

Although this panacea could not possibly cure all it was prescribed for, its raw ingredient was eventually extracted and purified and its benefits narrowed to just a few. In the late 1800s, a German dye manufacturer became one of the world's first pharmaceutical companies and transformed the drug into what remains a trusted over-the-counter medication.

The remedy: *aspirin*. The pharmaceutical company: Bayer.

Aspirin as we know it is over a hundred years old. Bayer & Company invested years in testing, retesting, and validating its benefits. Not until the

1990s was aspirin's medicinal value expanded to include usefulness in the prevention and treatment of heart attacks and strokes.

Irlen syndrome and color filtration are controversial in part because of the long list of symptoms that researchers working in the field claim the intervention addresses. Physical strain, fatigue, headache, migraine, reading efficiency, comprehension, visual distortions, problems associated with driving and night vision, dyslexia, inattention, photosensitive epilepsy and autism, brain injury, disabilities associated with stroke, cancer treatment side effects, and more. Tinted lenses and colored overlays can appear to be a cure-all. But researchers leading the effort maintain that this is not the case.

Whether reading disability or brain injury, the only effect of wearing colored filters is to modify the wavelengths of light reaching the visual system. Light is what triggers the complex processes involved in visual perception. In certain individuals specific aspects of light appear to trigger an anomalous reaction. When this occurs, discomfort, physical stress, or visual distortions may result. In photosensitive epilepsy, seizures occur, and in photosensitive autism, some may experience a fractured world of broken images.

NEGATIVE REACTIONS TO ENVIRONMENTAL FACTORS

The visual system would not be the first area of the human body to respond negatively to environmental aspects of daily life. Most of us know people who have allergies. The range of possible reactions to allergens is broad. From those who experience no allergies at all to those who suffer from minor seasonal irritation or the misery of welting allergy-induced hives. On the far end of the spectrum are the rare few that have had their lives threatened by anaphylactic shock, an acute systemic overreaction. A friend of our family several years ago was rushed from a mountain vacation to a hospital because of a bee sting. Around the same time, a teenage girl from our community died after eating a meal that, unbeknownst to her, included peanut oil as an ingredient.

Light is not an allergen, but human beings experience a wide range of physiological reactions to things around them. For example, for some people, sage in bloom produces a sneeze, but a daisy does not. All human beings simply are not the same. The current scientific assumption about light is that all humans react to varied properties of light in the same way.

I once worked with a woman who believed allergies were all in your head. She remained belligerent in her opinion until she herself developed allergies. A respected pediatrician in our community had difficulty believing that allergies would cause Katie's rashes when she was two years old. But the subgroup of people who live with allergies, including several generations in our family, know rashes do not discriminate by age. They are real and they can be debilitating. People who lose loved ones to anaphylactic shock have absolutely no difficulty believing allergies are real.

Fortunately, few people with allergies die from them and few people who experience sensitivity to aspects of light suffer the most disruptive physiological consequences: as a factor in some autism, a trigger for epileptic seizures, or life-threatening reactions associated with a condition called xeroderma pigmentosum or XP.

A few high-functioning individuals with autism have written about improvements in the quality of their lives and ability to function with the help of therapeutic tinted lenses. Donna Williams, who has written five books on her life with autism, is one.

In epilepsy, photosensitivity is a trigger for seizures in 4 percent of those affected. Flickering and/or strobing lights, busy high-contrast patterns, and certain wavelengths of light most commonly in the red range are often sources of the problem. In his book *Visual Stress,* Dr. Wilkins notes that some individuals with epilepsy experience fewer seizures when they use custom-colored lenses as an intervention.

Without question, XP is the most devastating form of light sensitivity. Causing cancer, blindness, deafness, eye diseases, and more, XP is a rare genetic disorder typically diagnosed in childhood. Nine-year-old Katie Mahar of New York was only six weeks old when a few minutes of exposure to sunlight caused large, painful blisters on her face and arms. The culprit: ultraviolet light from the sun. Eventually, scars left by Katie's blisters likely will be cancerous tumors that will have to be surgically removed.

To avoid UV rays, families like the Mahars often develop lifestyles revolving around nighttime activity. But even at night, the fluorescent lights used in most businesses, schools, and entertainment centers restrict their freedom dramatically. Fluorescent lights are also a source of ultraviolet radiation. Fewer than 1,000 cases of XP are known worldwide.

Even though colored lenses are not an intervention for XP, the condition is a dramatic example of the effects of a small range of wavelengths of light (280–340 nanometers) on the human body.

Does everyone with autism benefit from color filtration? No. Does everyone with epilepsy benefit? No. Only those for whom light sensitivity is a trigger stand to benefit, and such sensitivity has not yet been thoroughly studied. Currently, mainstream science breaks the study of human sensitivity to light into pieces. Neurology, psychiatry, psychology, optometry, ophthalmology, immunology, oncology (ultraviolet light as a carcinogen), and molecular biology all look at different pieces of the human puzzle, leaving science fractured in its composite picture. Until the effect of wavelengths of light on the human visual system is explored exhaustively, no one can be certain why or to what extent some individuals might benefit from color filtration.

THE LIGHT SENSITIVITY CONTINUUM

With so much yet to be learned about light and the human body, there is plenty of room for hypotheses, even from a mom who has spent two years reading about such sensitivity under its many names. My conclusion: light sensitivity and Katie's "kids like us" fit logically into a pyramid of human experience, a pyramid that is, in essence, a continuum of individual reaction.

At the bottom of the pyramid are people who thrive in any kind of light, the largest group of individuals. These people read comfortably anywhere and at any time.

At the center of the pyramid are people who find fluorescent and other specific lighting conditions mildly annoying or irritating. They, too, have no trouble with the written word, but may dislike working in certain types of light.

Further up the pyramid are individuals who experience fatigue or headaches after reading for no more than fifteen minutes, or others who experience migraine headaches under certain lighting conditions.

As the pyramid narrows to its point, we find those who experience visual distortions regularly, including the few who perceive visual distortions in everything they see. This group may be most academically impaired by sensitivity to aspects of light. Many compensate by developing other methods of learning, such as acute listening skills, or by developing talents and skills in areas not heavily reliant upon reading. Others, however, develop coping strategies and habits—daydreaming or restlessness, for example—that further impede their ability to function in a classroom.

The greatest dilemma for these people may be that they are expected

Light Sensitivity Pyramid

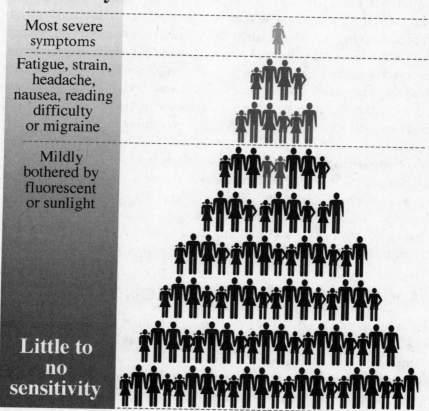

Extreme Sensitivity

Most severe symptoms

Fatigue, strain, headache, nausea, reading difficulty or migraine

Mildly bothered by fluorescent or sunlight

Little to no sensitivity

to function like those with no sensitivity at all. Like Katie and her innovative pet cage design, they demonstrate talent and intelligence that does not correspond to their struggles with reading and learning. Teachers and parents may suspect such kids of too little practice, a lack of motivation, or poor self-discipline when in fact there is a physiological barrier to their academic success.

At the very top of the pyramid is the tiny percentage of individuals diagnosed with severe disorders (photosensitive epilepsy, autism, and XP). Although it is a minute fraction of the population, this group is extremely important. Understanding how light affects them may lead to greater understanding of how light affects everyone else on the light sensitivity pyramid.

From bottom to top, the light sensitivity pyramid represents a continuum of potential reactions to light by the visual system and the brain. On this pyramid, there is a place for everyone. With my husband's mild sensitivity to sunlight, his "place" is several rows up from the bottom. With an aversion to fluorescent light and photosensitive migraine, my place is in the upper middle. Near the top, Katie stands with the children and adults who experience red eyes, fatigue, and/or visual distortions under certain lighting conditions. Jacob is a step higher, with those who experience difficulty defining the edges of everything they see.

Families like ours—in which Mom and Dad both experience some sensitivity—may produce children more likely to have problems.

Sensitivity to aspects of light does not necessarily begin in childhood. In addition to children and adults challenged by learning difficulties, screeners and diagnosticians around the world are aiding individuals who developed sensitivity after sustaining head injuries or major physiological trauma, from stroke to cancer treatment to brain surgery.

ADDRESS WAVELENGTHS, ADDRESS THE PROBLEM

Light is energy. Energy is a powerful force of nature, and the human brain is a highly responsive instrument. Individuals sensitive to aspects of light simply react to problem properties within light in varying degrees, just as the range of reaction to allergens varies from person to person. Address the properties and you address the problem.

It would be nice if it were that simple. Exhaustive studies have not yet been done to prove or disprove the theory that specific wavelengths or other properties of light can interfere with human visual perception, although the anecdotal evidence comes from thousands of individuals.

Mike and Donna Horstman are the parents of a child diagnosed with Irlen syndrome. Like me, they wish medical science would hurry up and work with researchers who have done the most on the subject. In 1999, Mike was scanning the Internet for information that would help him understand how and why color filtration was helping his daughter move from Chapter I remedial programs to straight As in the regular classroom. He came upon a Harvard University bulletin board discussion on the topic. The academicians insisted that no valid research substantiated that color filtration could alleviate visual distortions. With evidence to the contrary in the form of his daughter, Mike was one of several people posting a note of respectful disagreement on the site. He began his story this way:

> When our otherwise intelligent daughter fell a year behind her class in reading by the end of the first grade, we enrolled her in Chapter I intensive reading class. For the entire next year, we worked with her teachers and counselors, had her eyes checked, did *Hooked on Phonics,* read to her, had her read to us—all to no avail. By the end of the second grade, she was two to three years ahead of grade in all subjects except reading and spelling, in which she was 1.5 and 0.5 years behind, respectively.
>
> We were all at a loss until the school counselor mentioned (without recommendation) something called scotopic sensitivity syndrome (SSS) that she heard about at a conference.

Like Katie and Jacob, the Horstmans' daughter, Annelise, hit an invisible wall in reading. Annelise had suffered from frequent motion sickness since infancy, headaches since age three, and clumsiness. She was also awkward at navigating stairs, bringing both feet to a single step before moving on to the next, and she was terrified of escalators. The Horstmans learned about scotopic sensitivity syndrome when Annelise was in the third grade. Willing to consider any possible explanation, her parents sought help from a practitioner trained in the Irlen Method. The Irlen practitioner identified a moderate problem with sensitivity to aspects of light, and soon after, Annelise was wearing special tints.

Immediately, Annelise was better able to navigate stairs. Within a year, she caught up to her grade level in reading. By sixth grade, Annelise was an A student in all subjects. Tinted lenses also removed a barrier to her ability to learn to read music—a skill highly valued in her musically inclined home.

Until I read Mike Horstman's post, I'd forgotten how Jacob used to walk up and down stairs and about his dire fear of escalators. As a preschooler, our usually adventurous son would wrap himself around one of my legs in a death grip every time we approached an escalator. Although he overcame his fear by age six, at age eight Jacob still walked up the stairs with the same halting gate as Annelise. The first time I saw him move with ease up and down a staircase was the day Dr. Lewis asked Jacob to navigate stairs while he held three layers of colored lenses—blue/blue/purple—in front of his eyes.

You would think that holding two stacks of three-deep test lenses in front of the eyes would make the process of judging distance and body position on a staircase *more* difficult. It didn't. Instead, Jacob moved one foot in front of the other with comfort and relaxed ease. Within minutes, he was trotting gleefully up and down the stairs. He didn't do that before tinted lenses.

Sensitivity to aspects of light manifests itself in certain patterns of experience and physical symptoms. The following checklist may be helpful for identifying some of those patterns. It targets reading because it is one of the most visible areas where problems arise. It was developed based upon our family's experience, the experiences of numerous individuals and families interviewed, and printed accounts from individuals identified with Irlen syndrome. It is more appropriate for older children, second grade and above. Be sure to check all that apply.

Checklist

1. Through age five, when I read to my child from picture books:

    ___ a. S/he took an interest in the words.

    ___ b. S/he could read simple words.

    ___ c. S/he ignored the words or didn't like them.

2. In kindergarten, my child:

    ___ a. Performed well at most tasks and appeared to be developing normally.

    ___ b. Performed well at some tasks, not well at others (list these).

    ___ c. Struggled with most tasks (list these).

3. When dense text such as that in textbooks was first introduced to my child:

____ a. S/he had no problems and progressed steadily in the ability to read.

____ b. S/he began to struggle; her/his reading became slow and difficult.

____ c. S/he started missing simple words like *the, was,* or *of* or began skipping whole words or lines.

4. My child's attention span while reading is:

____ a. Long. S/he reads with ease for thirty minutes or more.

____ b. Moderate. S/he grows tired or restless after 15 minutes or so.

____ c. Very short. S/he takes frequent breaks, either by looking away or briefly focusing attention on something else. (Where is your child inclined to read for longer stretches, at home or at school? What kinds of lights are available in these two locations?)

5. Through age five, my child:

____a. Was healthy, with no complaints of headaches, vision problems, or fatigue.

____ b. Occasionally complained of unexplainable headaches or fatigue.

____ c. Complained a great deal of headaches, vision problems, and/or fatigue. (What activity most often preceded complaints?)

6. Currently, my child:

____ a. Is healthy with no complaints of headaches, vision problems, or fatigue.

___ b. Occasionally complains of unexplainable headaches or fatigue. (Is there an activity that typically precedes the complaints?)

___ c. Has at some time complained about vision, but a visit to the eye doctor found no problem.

___ d. Complains a great deal about headaches, vision problems, or fatigue. (What activity most often precedes these complaints? What light sources are in your child's environment when s/he begins to develop problems?)

Complete the checklist and study the answers. The checklist's usefulness depends upon *patterns* that appear, not on any single answer. The checklist is designed to help you identify patterns. The letter "a" represents normal development. The letter "b" is marginal. The letter "c" represents traits common to sensitivity to aspects of light. If you have checked the letter "c" frequently, the pattern indicates possible sensitivity. Chapters 11 and 12 (pages 117 and 131) provide more detailed information to help you sort through issues related to light-based reading difficulties.

TAKING THE PROBLEM SERIOUSLY

There are many reasons Katie and Jacob are adamant in their desire for others to know that Irlen syndrome is real. First, they want their need for color adjustment to be taken seriously. When it is, Irlen syndrome likely will be more intensively studied, validated, and understood. Denying their need for color adjustment means my children either cannot trust their own eyes (actually, their brains) or they are living a lie. And if Katie and Jacob are living a lie, then so are thousands of other children and adults who have already been helped. How could so many all around the world be so gullible, describe experiences so similar, and report that color does indeed have therapeutic value in improving physical discomfort and visual distortions?

There is additional self-interest in my children's desire for others to know that their sensitivity to aspects of light is real. They are weary of fielding questions and dealing with skepticism. In the sixth grade Katie had been wearing tinted lenses in class for a year when she encountered a teacher who did not understand why she wore them. In the middle of class one day, Katie was ordered to take off her tints. The embarrassment of being singled out and having to explain what the glasses were for upset Katie far more than going without her tinted lenses for one class. She came home in tears.

On another occasion, at a skating rink, I observed as Jacob fielded comments or questions about his glasses at least eight times in a single three-hour session. Often the comments were as mild as "Hey, Hollywood, cool shades." Other times they were blunt: "Why are you wearing sunglasses *in here*?" Jake responded to the first two comments and retreated from the rest. Did it deter him from wearing tinted lenses? Not for a moment.

Nor did his oops-prone visit to the optometrist. One morning an optometrist's assistant prescreened Jacob for visual acuity with his colored filters first on, then off. With his tinted lenses, his vision was 20/20. Without color, his eyes had difficulty adjusting to the light and he didn't perform as well. The optometrist decided to see whether standard correction might fix the problem. He tried lens after lens with no luck. Meanwhile, Jake was convinced the optometrist really wasn't doing anything to change the power. Everything looked the same to him—wobbly and indistinct. Then before the optometrist or I knew what my son had in mind, Jacob poked his index fingers into the viewing holes of the testing device. Yep, there were lenses in there!

Both of my children hope that soon people wearing "sunglasses" indoors will not be such an oddity. More than that, they hope educators, doctors, and vision professionals will one day understand that having a brain that responds a little differently to aspects of light isn't that big a deal. Colored filters could be considered Hollywood cool—or at the very least, better than a lifetime on aspirin, Ritalin, or antidepressants. Colored filters may be unconventional, but Katie, Jacob, Annelise, James, and thousands like them are convinced they are worthwhile.

9

HOW DO WE SEE?

UNTIL YOU CAN OBSERVE A THING YOU CAN ONLY
GUESS AT ITS NATURE.

—Contemporary physicist David Park writing about light
in *The Fire Within the Eye*

A snowflake is a breathtaking phenomenon of nature and science. It begins as molecules of mist high above the earth. When conditions are right, mist freezes into amazing six-sided, crochet-like shapes. As they drift earthward, snowflakes only appear to be white. In truth, when we see a cluster of snowflakes, what we see is the white noise of all the transparent colors that occur in light reflected back to us.

We can touch a snowflake. We can put one under a microscope and see its delicate, lacy form. We can pack thousands together and toss them as a ball. We can even watch a snowflake turn from icy crystal back to its liquid form—water. Aspects of vision, however, cannot yet be physically observed. We cannot see the way others see or perceive. We cannot yet put anomalies like light sensitivity under a microscope. All anyone can do is "guess at its nature."

To shed light on vision's secrets we must also shed light on light itself. Every day we take it for granted. In the absence of light, we see nothing. When light is present, we see color and contrast, shape and motion, depth and distance. But what is light, and how does it interact with the human visual system?

If only Albert Einstein were alive today. My fingers type his name in total reverence. I am an average mom with no scientific credentials and, yet, I am wading into a pond as complex as the physics of electromagnetic radiation and the narrow band we know as visible light. If any of us is to understand how light or wavelenghths might possibly affect visual perception, we must put a toe in Einstein's pond. Trying to understand sensitivity to aspects of light without a basic knowledge of light and related physics is like building a bridge that ends in midair.

There are five important parts to any discussion of light: the composition of light; wavelengths; the interrelationship of luminance, reflected light, and extreme bright/dark contrast; color within light; and the human visual system.

THE COMPOSITION OF LIGHT

In 1905, Einstein was a vastly underappreciated patent officer advising young inventors on forms and legal concerns in an office in Bern, Switzerland. I can almost picture him working under the crude lighting of the day; high ceilings above, plank floors or tile below, files and paperwork all around. Back then, universities weren't interested in Einstein. As a student brilliant in some subjects but struggling in others, he asked too many questions that confounded and frustrated professors. He was hungry for new ideas—not academic conformity.

Einstein was only in his mid-twenties when he wrote and published twenty-six theory-packed papers on physics. His theory of "packets of energy"—or photons—came about because of the work of many other scientists (for example, James Maxwell's 1865 theory of electromagnetic radiation and Max Planck's 1900 theory of energy as composed of quanta).

Photons, Einstein theorized, are released when electrons within atoms fall to a lower energy level. In the process of losing that energy, the electron sends it out into the world as a photon, and photons group together to form a packet of electromagnetic waves. These waves come to us as visible light. These can increase in number and volume at a wide variety of frequencies and wavelengths, like ocean waves that meander to the shore fewer and farther between in fine weather or beat one after another in times of storm. There is a slim range of wavelengths that humans can perceive as visible light. At longer or shorter wavelengths, these "packets of energy" cannot be absorbed by the human visual system.

It took at least eight years for Einstein's theory that light was made up of photons released from electrons to gain respect. In 1913, American physicist Robert Millikan conducted experiments validating the theory. Eight years after that, Einstein was awarded the Nobel Prize for his work. Light, Einstein eventually taught us, is about photons.

Even with the knowledge of photons, however, the nature of light is not fully understood. What role waves and photons have in visual perception continues to hold many mysteries. If physicists and vision experts have not yet sorted through it, a nonscientific mom certainly won't. It is an achievement to have made it this far without collapsing into a heap.

WAVELENGTHS

To understand light, it is necessary to wade a little deeper into Einstein's pond. Visible light makes up a narrow band of wavelengths within a range of mostly invisible light. Ultraviolet light, X rays, and gamma rays are invisible because their wavelengths are too short and energetic for us to perceive. Infrared light, microwaves, television and radio waves are also invisible, but it is because their wavelengths are too long for human perception. Rods and cones in the human eye don't absorb these wavelengths.

Between the infrared and ultraviolet wavelengths is visible light. These visible wavelengths travel together and interact with the properties of the things they strike and with our visual systems to produce visual perception in the brain.

Looking at it this way, you realize there is plenty of "stuff" zinging all around us every day that we simply take for granted.

One of the wonders of visible light is that we can actually separate its multitude of wavelengths. That is basically what happens when light passes through raindrops, a prism, or a crystal in a chandelier. Light passing through any of these is both slowed and bent by the substance through which it is passing. Different wavelengths are slowed at different rates, and so what had been a coherent beam of white light breaks up into its separate components, each color bending off in a slightly different direction. The result: We see a rainbow of colors—graduated hues of red-orange to blue-green to violet.

This principle of light also explains why we can see sparkles of light and color in a diamond. Light entering a diamond slows and bends, too. When light interacts with both the cut and the properties of the stone, we see flashes of color that appear trapped inside.

A diamond sparkles differently depending upon its light source. Go from room to room and you can see this principle at work. Under fluorescent light, a diamond appears somewhat flat, with considerably less sparkle and color. Under incandescent light, however, you can see the fire inside. Jewelry stores use specific types of incandescent bulbs for a reason: such light creates the greatest variation of color and visible light within a diamond.

I had always assumed that white light was the combination of all the wavelengths of color within visible light. In his book *The Fire Within the Eye*, physicist David Park defines it a little differently. He equates white light to noise. He uses sound as an example. Every sound reaching the human ear, he explains, has a separate and distinct vibration. When many sounds vibrate at the same time, we hear noise.

Wavelengths of light are measured in nanometers (nm), or one thousand-millionth of one meter. Visible light falls within the range of 380 to 780 nm. Light in the violet-blue range is at the short end of the spectrum, closer to ultraviolet light. Shades of green are closer to the middle, in the 500 to 550 nm range. And hues of orange-red are among the longest, leading up to invisible infrared light. All of these wavelengths are the separate quantities within visible light that travel together and interact with the human visual system to be perceived as white light. They are separate, but together.

Light's primary colors are not like the primary colors for paints or dyes. They are not generic red, blue, or yellow. In light, red, blue, and green can be mixed to create *all* colors—including white—and this mixing involves the human visual system and the visual response.

Reaching the human eye every day are an unimaginable number of wavelengths of light, and these wavelengths will vary in their rate of vibration and length. From here, the process of visual perception is even more complex.

LUMINANCE, REFLECTED LIGHT, AND BRIGHT/DARK CONTRAST

Every time I walk into my daughter's room at night and find her reading, I shake my head. The amount of light she needs for reading is incredibly low. I couldn't resist the temptation to give her a book light one Christmas. This is how she uses it: She turns out the light in her room but leaves the hallway light on and the bedroom door open. A stream of light from the hallway filters into her room and onto her book page. When she starts to read a new page, Katie turns her book light off and reads by the diffuse light from the hall. When she reaches the middle of the page, she turns the book light on. Print directly under the book light, she explains, bothers her eyes. When she is at the top of the page, she turns the book light off. She turns it on when she is beyond the light's direct beam.

So much for giving Katie a book light for Christmas.

Three factors are at work in this example: *luminance*, or the brightness of available light; *reflectance*, the amount of light bouncing back to the eyes after objects have been struck; and *illuminance*, the quantity of light reflected from a source or surface. Most of us don't think much about luminance, reflectance, or illuminance as we go about our days. That is, unless they cause us problems. And occasionally they do. Some people, like my husband, reach for a pair of sunglasses every time they head outdoors because the combination of bright sunlight and reflectance is bothersome. Those in the throes of a nasty headache will turn off the lights and close the shades because light and reflectance make the pain worse. We recognize these forms of sensitivity to light because most of us, at one time or another, have experienced them.

Another complication is involved for light-sensitive individuals. It is called pattern glare.

Moving and stationary geometric patterns involving near equal amounts of bright and dark are proven to be a trigger for migraine headaches and epileptic seizures. Black-and-white checkerboard patterns or striped line patterns are especially problematic for some individuals with epilepsy. Disturbances in the brain associated with what researcher Arnold Wilkins calls pattern glare or pattern sensitivity have been verified among those with photosensitive epilepsy using EEG scans (electroencephalogram).

If light sensitivity is indeed common, then pattern glare likely impacts people in a variety of ways (strain, headache, fatigue, nausea, etc.). And pattern glare occurs frequently in our homes, offices, and schools in ways and places we take for granted: TV screens, computer screens, and the printed page.

Most television sets and computer screens use cathode ray tubes. Within such tubes, images are received and beamed courtesy of photons and electrons onto a phosphor screen. Although the resulting images appear

WARNING:
Patterns may cause physical discomfort or seizures.

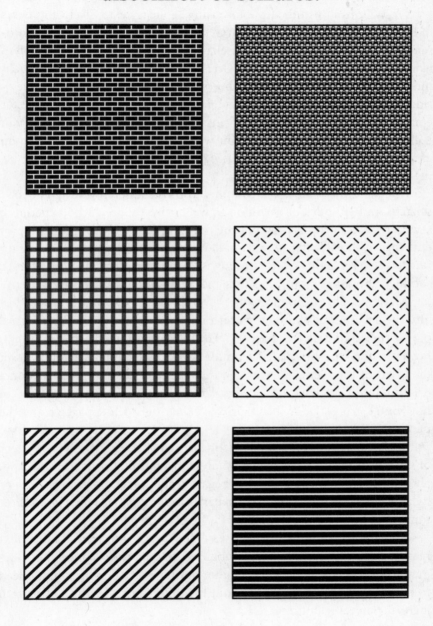

stable and solid, they are not. Instead, they are represented by rapidly flickering horizontal lines, refreshed 60 times per second, that we assume the brain does not perceive. If you take a photograph of a working television using a fast shutter speed, you can see the horizontal lines on the screen.

Dr. Wilkins has studied photosensitive epilepsy extensively and notes in his book *Visual Stress* that "a large proportion of patients with photosensitive epilepsy suffer their first seizure when watching television, often when they are close to the screen." On December 17, 1997, 685 individuals, mostly children, were admitted to hospitals in Japan as the result of television viewing. Later investigation revealed 560 of these admissions were for epileptic seizures, although 76 percent of patients had no prior history of epilepsy. Affected viewers had been watching an episode of a Pokemon cartoon when they began experiencing irritated eyes, convulsions, vomiting, and more.

The similarity of these symptoms to those suffered during epileptic seizures and episodes of migraine as well as by children who experience severe visual distortions is significant. In Japan, children's symptoms apparently began shortly after the cartoon aired five seconds of strobing or rapidly flashing red lights. Such strobing is a kind of pattern glare that can be produced by either rapidly flashing light or a symmetrically busy pattern.

Many people experience some level of visual discomfort when they observe an unusually intense pattern of geometric lines with near equal parts bright and dark (see page 95). For those sensitive to aspects of light, however, the threshold of discomfort and distortions is simply lower than that of the average person. To these people, dense lines of text on a bright white page have the potential to appear as a complex pattern of horizontal stripes. Dense black print on the bright white page creates the pattern.

Dr. Wilkins's explanation of such sensitivity helped me solve a mystery of my own. In 1998, I started a new job with a hospital and its foundation. Shortly after I took the position, I began to suffer from migraines once or twice a month. Before this, I had experienced migraines only two to three times a year.

Shortly after Katie and Jacob were diagnosed with Irlen syndrome, I read about photosensitivity's potential link to migraine. I found the information interesting, but couldn't figure out how or when light might lead to my headaches. When I read about the high contrast nature of pattern glare, the pieces fell into place.

Katie's Perplexing Print

words on the rest of the page
spaces looking like
lime green, I thought,
about how the brain
the more what she told us made

words on the rest of the page
spaces looking like
lime green, I thought,
about how the brain
the more what she told us made

For Katie, different types of light create different types of distortions. She has experienced both of these. "Wash-outs" appear hol-
low in the center. In Katie's "shimmer effect," only the words in the
center of focus are clear. The others shimmer with color.
(Print re-creation by Kirill Federspiel.)

The Color of Light

A camera easily captures the color that exists within light.

To produce crisp white, a photographer "color corrects" with magenta and blue plates over his camera lens. This shot was taken in Room 3, the classroom where Katie experiences the most visual distortions.

Room 3 without color correction. The page appears green because of poorly balanced light.

Room 6 was rich in blue light. A camera without color correction easily detects it.

(Photos by Rich Villacres/Red Sky Photography.)

Jacob's Wavy World

Without tinted lenses, Jacob perceives everything with wavy edges. A similar effect is documented in the July 1999 issue of *National Geographic* ("Lost in the No-Fun House," page 84, a computer-enhanced photo by Cary Wolinsky and Brian E. Strauss depicting how Alex Michaels sees the world).

Calming the Visual System

Properly chosen tinted lenses prevent an under- or over-reaction from occurring in Jacob's visual system. This form of sensitivity to aspects of light is less common. Physical discomfort, fatigue, and visual distortions perceived with dense text on a bright white page are more common.

(Photos by Rich Villacres/Red Sky Photography. Computer enhancement by Kirill Federspiel.)

Different Colors For Different People:

family's journey to understand light
it was first suggested that our daught
husband and I took opposing positio
it first, ask question later". Paul was
what ensued was a two-year journey
barrier preventing our children from
we found ourselves knee deep in res
all the paper made, it was not the mo
our children. The paper came to us v
the telephone, and selective sources
gather": seek all you can find, and se
family with experts and resources in

Yellow

contrast sensitivity was not an easy
ould benefit from color filtration, I
willing to give it a try; I figured "do
more conservative. He feared that bo
to understand the apparent invisible
being successful in the classroom. A
and other "paper". As logical and str
convincing factor. That distinction b
books, articles, journals, the local me
Internet. It was a process of "hunt an
for more. Ultimately, the journey co
England, Finland, and individuals in

Peach

locations throughout the United Stat
if I could find just one definitive stu
sensitivity and color filtration as its t
supporting color filtration and a trail
and light and contrast sensitivity as i
Katie and Jacob were wearing color
and bounds. In 1980, long before ou
named Olive Meares described visu
was the first to publicly suggest that
white page and black text had the po
reading. In the early 1980s, the direc
California State University-Long Be

Mint Green

Times, from exhaustion, I resolved t
Wrong the theory of light and contra
, one after another, I found evidence
studies used to discount color filtrat
mate concern. While all this was goi
and their reading was improving by
ren were born, a New Zealand schoo
untered by some of her students. Sh
amount of contrast between a bright
aid some children with the process o
tor of a learning disability program a
undertook a multi-year, government

Rose

research project to identify types of
possible solutions. Helen Irlen focus
had struggled to learn most of their
had no difficulties learning. Over fi
disabled students to document an ar
students, including those diagnosed
distortions and/or physical discomfo
they reported were vastly different
dyslexia – such as "b" appearing as
would dominate a page and cause w
pulsate, jiggle, shift, shimmer, move
that appeared to slide off the printe

Lime Green

issues adults experienced and develo
the study on an experimental group
lives and a control group of graduat
years, Irlen worked with over 1,600
array of perceived visual distortions
20/20 vision, had come to believe th
just a normal part of reading. The dis
the stereotypical letter reversals asso
Their distortions ranged from white s
more. other distortions they reporte
page of text with the words washed
words crowded together with little t

Purple

Colored overlays modify light reflected from a page of text.

family's journey to understand light
it was first suggested that our daught
husband and I took opposing positio
it first, ask question later". Paul was
what ensued was a two-year journey
barrier preventing our children from
we found ourselves knee deep in res
all the paper made, it was not the mo
our children. The paper came to us v
the telephone, and selective sources
gather": seek all you can find, and se
family with experts and resources in

Turquoise

contrast sensitivity was not an easy
ould benefit from color filtration, I
willing to give it a try; I figured "do
more conservative. He feared that bo
to understand the apparent invisible
being successful in the classroom. A
and other "paper". As logical and str
convincing factor. That distinction b
books, articles, journals, the local me
Internet. It was a process of "hunt an
for more. Ultimately, the journey co
England, Finland, and individuals in

2 Layers Turquoise

locations throughout the United Stat
if I could find just one definitive stu
sensitivity and color filtration as its t
supporting color filtration and a trail
and light and contrast sensitivity as i
Katie and Jacob were wearing color
and bounds. In 1980, long before ou
named Olive Meares described visu
was the first to publicly suggest that
white page and black text had the po
reading. In the early 1980s, the direc
California State University-Long Be

Blue-Gray

times, from exhaustion, I resolved t
wrong the theory of light and contra
, one after another, I found evidence
studies used to discount color filtrat
mate concern. While all this was goi
and their reading was improving by
ren were born, a New Zealand schoo
untered by some of her students. Sh
amount of contrast between a bright
aid some children with the process o
tor of a learning disability program a
undertook a multi-year, government

Blue-Gray and Purple

research project to identify types of
possible solutions. Helen Irlen focus
had struggled to learn most of their
had no difficulties learning. Over fi
disabled students to document an ar
students, including those diagnosed
distortions and/or physical discomfo
they reported were vastly different
dyslexia – such as "b" appearing as
would dominate a page and cause w
pulsate, jiggle, shift, shimmer, move
that appeared to slide off the printe

Gray

issues adults experienced and develo
the study on an experimental group
lives and a control group of graduat
years, Irlen worked with over 1,600
array of perceived visual distortions
20/20 vision, had come to believe th
just a normal part of reading. The dis
the stereotypical letter reversals asso
Their distortions ranged from white
more. other distortions they reporte
page of text with the words washed
words crowded together with little t

2 Layers Purple

Making the Process of Reading Easier

Tinted lenses, like those worn by teacher Jeanne Noble, and colored overlays lessen physical discomfort and/or visual distortions for individuals sensitive to aspects of light.
(Photos by Rich Villacres/Red Sky Photography.)

In pattern glare, there are two issues: the competition between dark and bright, as well as the busy, repetitive pattern. One day, while I was sitting in a bimonthly staff meeting at our office, it hit me. These meetings are held in what was once the living room of an old Tudor house. A half-dozen people attend. The primary source of light for the room is a south-facing picture window. A couple of small incandescent lamps and smaller east-facing windows add a little more light to the room.

At nearly every meeting, one of our organization's department heads sits in a chair in front of the picture window. The person sitting in front of the window is back-lit, or to the average observer they are a dark silhouette sitting in front of a mass of bright light. Of course, the light in the room is the same, but our eyes instinctively adjust to the brightness beyond the window rather than light inside the room.

What I realized that spring morning was that the extreme contrast between the shape of a co-worker sitting in front of the window and the bright cloudy sky outside caused stress to my visual system. My eyes burned slightly as my brain tried to decide which part of the composite image to choose for light adjustment—the co-worker's dark silhouette or the bright light behind her. Within minutes, I felt a migraine coming on. Within an hour I was sick.

It was the last time I ever forced myself to look at anyone or anything for more than a few seconds in front of a window or other bright light— no stress on the visual system, no problem with migraine. I have only had one migraine since, the result of a business meeting for which I could not change lighting conditions.

The interrelationship of luminance, reflected light (including problem wavelengths), and extreme bright/dark contrast likely is at the heart of why children and adults sensitive to aspects of light experience discomfort and visual distortions while reading. If the most severe forms of reaction (such as epileptic seizures and migraine) are any indication, the effect for individuals can at times feel toxic.

COLOR WITHIN LIGHT

From source to source, light is different. Photographers and cinematographers know this perhaps as well as anyone. In color photography, light source will determine whether an image is washed out, murky green-gray, or rich in color. Under a midsummer afternoon sky, for example, a photo snapped by an instant camera is often washed out. A photograph shot by the same camera shortly after sunrise or near sunset will have warmer tones with more golden hues.

Why is it that humans do not readily perceive these color differences? Gordon Legge, director of the University of Minnesota's Center for Cognitive Sciences, explains: "Unlike cameras that need color filters, human vision somehow adapts to changes in lighting." The phenomenon is called "color constancy" and it is performed automatically by the brain.

Fluorescent and incandescent lights differ in color because they are very different in means. Incandescent light is the result of heat. When a filament is heated, light radiates from it and this light is normally warm, in the yellow and yellow-orange hues. Fluorescent light, however, involves a different kind of energy. It is produced by the excitation of phosphor (a gas) within a vacuum-sealed tube, resulting in a variable range of cool colors—often, but not always, richer in blues and greens. Less frequently, they appear as pink. A charge from a magnetic or electronic ballast keeps the phosphor excited, and the phosphor must be recharged many times per second in order to create what appears to be a steady stream of light. It is this recharging in fluorescent tubes that causes flicker or strobing. Think about how fluorescent tubes flicker when a ballast wears out. As the ballast's rate of recharging slows, flicker becomes easy for our eyes and visual systems to perceive. Studies have shown that some people perceive flicker more readily than others and this lower threshold can be a nuisance.

Apparently, fluorescent light causes problems for other species as well. Professor John Endler's guppies are a good example. A researcher in the Department of Ecology, Evolution, and Marine Biology, at the University of California–Santa Barbara, Dr. Endler was studying the sensitivity of guppies to light and color when he noticed a significant difference between the behavior of guppies raised under fluorescent light and those raised under natural or incandescent light. Guppies raised in tanks under fluorescent light demonstrated erratic behavior under certain light and color conditions. Guppies raised under daylight or incandescent light did not. The phenomenon has not yet been studied in detail.

Years before Endler's observation, self-trained photobiologist John Ott discovered fluorescent light's peril to pumpkins. Ott was performing a time-lapse photographic study of the growth of pumpkin plants for the master of animation himself, Walt Disney, when he discovered plants could not sustain both the male and female blossoms needed to produce pumpkins if they were raised under early fluorescent light. Ott solved the problem by moving the study, intended to help animators develop the pumpkin-to-coach sequence for *Cinderella,* to a natural light source. Ott then devoted much of his life to the study of fluorescent light and its effects on living things. His work contributed to the development of full-spectrum fluorescent light—much closer in color quality to mid-day sunlight than early fluorescent tubes.

Photographers work with light every day and know well that all light is not the same. Rich Villacres is the type of professional photographer who needs a trolley to pack around his camera gear. In a casual conversation one afternoon, he and I discussed how to measure the color that exists within light. He pointed out that photographers do it all the time. They use a handheld color meter to determine what type and number of colored glass plates to place over a camera lens in order to produce true colors on film. The two aspects of light measured involve degrees Kelvin (color temperature) and green/magenta color correction. Calibrated to the type of film photographers use, Kelvin measurement tells how many points blue to add in order to achieve light that is well-balanced, while green/magenta color correction, or cc, measures an entirely different aspect of light. This measurement tells photographers how much purplish-pink to add when greens and reds are out of balance.

We decided to use a Gossen Color Pro 3F meter to measure the color of light in Katie's five classrooms. We were curious to see how color readings might correlate with her physical discomfort and visual distortions. What we found was most interesting.

Color meter readings of the classrooms revealed that Katie feels most comfortable and experiences the fewest distortions in blue-rich light. Furthermore, red-rich light appears to be the source of Katie's problems.

Of the five classrooms, the two where Katie experiences the most difficulty have the greatest amount of red-rich light, as evidenced by their need for the least amount of magenta color correction (15 cc and 20 cc). The room where she feels most comfortable is the one needing the most magenta color correction (25 cc) *and* the least blue correction (42 points) to produce true color on film.

The color of tinted lenses Katie uses to address discomfort and visual distortions in rooms with red-rich light: blue/blue/gray/aqua.

Rank (Most to Least Comfortable)	Room	Lighting Type	Magenta Correction (red-rich light)	Blue Correction (blue-rich light)
1	Room 6*	Fluorescent	25cc	42 points
2	Room 5	Fluorescent	25 cc	45 points
3	Gym†	Sodium Vapor	25 cc	152 points
4	Computer	Fluorescent	20 cc	66 points
5	Room 3‡	Fluorescent	15 cc	45 points

Magenta Correction: *Smaller* numbers indicate the presence of a greater amount of red-rich light.

Blue Correction: *Smaller* numbers indicate the presence of a greater amount of blue-rich light.

*Katie's most comfortable room for working without tinted lenses is Room 6, the room with the most blue-rich and least red-rich light. Her second favorite room is Room 5, which has slightly less blue-rich light than Room 6, but the same amount of red-rich light.

†Katie considers the gymnasium the brightest room. Intriguingly, it requires the most blue correction.

‡Katie's least comfortable room for working without tinted lenses is the room with the most red-rich light, Room 3. Her second least comfortable room is the computer lab, which also has a higher degree of red-rich light.

The rooms Katie considers the brightest are the computer lab and gymnasium. It is an intriguing observation. To me, neither room is bright. I would describe them as murky, like looking through a glass of slightly dirty water. Color meter readings indicate that these rooms have the greenest light, requiring the most blue correction (66 points and 152 points). From these readings, it appears Katie perceives light rich in greens and lacking blue wavelengths as bright.

In the gymnasium, the lights are not fluorescent. They are sodium vapor, a type of lighting frequently used in factories and, when operating at lower frequencies, capable of producing a nearly perceptible strobing effect. The light in this room requires three times the amount of blue correction as Katie's two favorite classrooms. But the gym yielded yet another problem with visual perception for Katie. She couldn't find words to explain it, so she drew a series of stick people instead. The first stick figure was drawn full-size and in a heavy line. The next was slightly smaller and the line lighter. She drew more stick people, each becoming lighter and smaller until they disappeared. What she illustrated was a ghost-like strobing effect she could easily perceive with movement in the gymnasium.

I have been in the school's gymnasium many times and had never noticed the strobing effect. Days before Katie drew her stick figures, however, Villacres and I took color meter readings of the gym while Katie attended classes in another part of the school. He told me then about the strobing effect—which causes an additional complication for photographers—and demonstrated it by waving his hand rapidly in front of my face. Doing so made it easy to see the ghost-like effect. I found it fascinating, but never mentioned it to Katie.

When Katie drew her stick figures, I recognized the effect. We talked a bit and she convinced me that she has a heightened awareness of the ghost-like motion associated with the strobing effect in the gymnasium.

The objective color meter readings convinced me that Katie is more sensitive to aspects of light in her environment. Red-rich color correction readings and Katie's classroom preferences were an uncanny match.

Measuring light in Katie's school environment demonstrates that:

- Indoor lighting does vary by range of wavelength (light "color") from location to location.

- Katie's problems with light follow a pattern. Specifically, she experiences the most physical discomfort and/or visual distortions in the presence of red-rich light, and she may interpret light rich in green wavelengths and lacking hues of blue as bright. Additionally, it appears she is more sensitive to strobing than the average person.

- It is possible to take wavelengths of light for granted.

We assume that everyone experiences light in the same way. What if we don't? What would it mean for those who are more sensitive to specific wavelengths and other aspects of light?

There is an amusing personal twist for me to the question of how light is perceived from one person to another. In 1988, in the process of gathering historical information for the hundredth anniversary of the school district for which I worked, a colleague and I came across an old yellowed newspaper clipping that dated back to the early part of the last century.

In the newspaper article, the county superintendent of schools at the time expressed concern about the potential hazards of the brand-new technology being introduced to the schools—electric lights. She worried that the bright light would harm children's eyes. I had known the woman in the article very well when I was a child. She was my great-aunt Pearl, a wispy, self-disciplined, and perfectly straight-backed schoolmarm who lived to be nearly a hundred.

In 1988, Aunt Pearl had long since passed away and my colleague and I laughed at the thought of electric lights being harmful to children's eyes. Surely strong and wise Aunt Pearl couldn't have believed such a thing. Secretly, I was a little embarrassed by the notion.

Today I can't help but wonder whether Aunt Pearl experienced an adverse reaction to the brightness of electric lights. Early incandescent bulbs were extraordinarily bright. Why else would she suggest such a thing? More than a dozen years after finding that clipping it occurs to me that Aunt Pearl may have been light sensitive. Indeed, she may have the posthumous last laugh when it comes to lighting being problematic for some children's eyes.

THE HUMAN VISUAL SYSTEM

Cornea, iris, lens, retina, rods, cones, optic nerve, neural fibers, visual pathways, optic radiation, visual cortex, occipital lobe, temporal lobe . . . *now* I'm collapsing into a heap. While light is a provocative mystery, the visual system of the human brain is nothing less than confounding. The opportunity for variation appears infinite. It is more symphony than single note, with its analogous strings, woodwinds, and percussion instruments numbering in the hundreds of millions.

Visual acuity—or 20/20 vision—is the easier part of vision to understand. It typically involves focus, vergence, color perception, depth perception, and general ocular health.

But visual perception begins when wavelengths of light reach the eyes. The brain knows that too much light can overload the visual system and too little light can cause us to strain to see. Consequently, when reflected light reaches the eyes, the muscles of the iris cause our pupils to constrict or open wider. Which direction and to what degree depends upon the amount of light and our sensitivity to that light. Recent research indicates that the narrowing of the pupil is influenced by scotopically rich light, involving colors with more energy—specifically blues and greens.

When Katie and Jacob last visited the optometrist's office, neither had to have their eyes dilated. Both have irises that naturally open wide in a dimly lit room. Not all light-sensitive individuals react in this way, but my children do.

Wavelengths of light continue through the corneas, the lenses (which turn images upside down), and then the orbital cavities to the backs of our eyes. Toward the back, our eyes are made up of the "satellite dishes" that receive light—our retinas. These are composed of seven basic layers and millions of cells. Behind the cells are 100 million rods, which are more actively involved in the processing of low or scotopically rich light, and 7 million cones that form the basis for color vision. Cones that are equipped to stimulate the perception of blue, green, and red receive and respond to wavelengths. To the surprise of most people, red and green cones activate to different degrees to create the perception of yellow. All three colors are activated in the perception of white. The degree to which the cones and rods are activated depends upon wavelengths of light.

As the noise of what we perceive as white light reaches the eyes, it stimulates millions of photoreceptors into action. This noise is translated into "music" or a visual image as the photoreceptors react to light and send neural impulses down the optic nerve, the beginning of the visual pathway, on their way to the visual cortex of the brain.

The hypothesis associated with visual stress related to light sensitivity is simply this: some human visual systems can be improperly activated by wavelengths of light and/or photons, initiating a reaction that creates stress for the visual system. When this occurs, children and adults experience mild to severe physical discomfort, visual distortions, or, in a severe reaction, seizures.

The visual pathways are a complex system of nerves, fibers, tracts, and cells that shuttle rapidly firing neural impulses to the center of the brain. The information comes together in the thalamus before continuing to various areas of the cortex, sweeping through appropriate regions like electrical storms. As this information is distributed at something less than the speed of light, our brains make sense of what is being received and a visual image is perceived.

Not exactly like a "movie" in the mind, is it?

The three classes of cones in the retina (red, green, and blue, designed to capture long, medium, and short wavelengths) are not the only factors that produce the brilliant and muted colors we perceive. A region called the lateral geniculate nucleus, or LGN, located in the center of the brain and on either side of the thalamus, is also involved. Intriguingly, in the 1990s this region's magnocellular and parvocellular channels were identified as a potential culprit in some dyslexia. The magnocellular pathways are believed to be involved in bright/dark processing and the parvocellular pathways in red/green processing. Neuropsychologist Karen R. Dobkins, of the University of California at San Diego, pointed out in a 2000 article in the journal *Neuron* that there is a third channel that receives little attention, and this one is most interesting. Called the koniocellular pathway, this one appears to be linked to color modulation related to the cones of the eye that receive short wavelengths (blue and blue-yellow).

What is significant about all three—the magno-, parvo-, and koniocellular pathways—is that each is believed to be involved in some way with motion processing, or how we detect movement. Why is this important? One of the chief complaints of many individuals who experience visual distortions related to Irlen syndrome is that they perceive printed text as rising, falling, sliding, swirling, jiggling, and/or otherwise moving. Scientist as yet have been unable to explain why. Most remain skeptical of individuals who report such distortions.

If, indeed, these three pathways work together to help us perceive both colors and motion, what would happen if a visual system were hypersensitive to the volume of light (brightness) and/or a narrow range of wavelengths (color), or if one or more of the pathways functioned out of sync with the others? What would an individual perceive? Would stable visual perception be harder to maintain when the visual system was bombarded with problem wavelengths? Would such individuals also have a problem with the combined effect of depth perception and movement, another common issue in Irlen syndrome? Might this explain why my daughter sees ghostlike after images in certain rooms or buildings, in which she may be able to perceive the flicker of fluorescent or industrial lights more easily than other people?

Arnold Wilkins favors a different explanation for the cause of instability in visual perception: "cortical hyperexcitablity." He draws this conclusion directly from his research with individuals who experience photosensitive migraine and epilepsy, as well as children who experience visual distortions while reading. He has published his theory in a new book called *Reading Through Colour* (John Wiley & Sons, May 2003).

In chapter 16 of his book, Dr. Wilkins proposes that cortical hyperexcitability occurs when cortical neurons fire inappropriately as the result of problems associated with visual stimulus, including light source. This excitation spreads throughout the cortex and may manifest in different ways, such as migraine headache, epileptic seizure, strain and fatigue, or visual distortions.

"Changing the color of a visual stimulus is likely to alter the pattern of activity," Dr. Wilkins writes. "This is because the sensitivity of nerve cells changes with wavelength, and different cells have different sensitivities." Evidence for the sensitivity of nerve cells was documented in the early 1980s by Professor Semir Zeki, University College London, who measured the spectral sensitivity of neurons in the brains of monkeys. Other researchers have studied monkeys in an effort to better understand the function of the visual system in human visual perception.

Is Dr. Wilkins correct? Are inappropriately firing cortical neurons the cause of Irlen syndrome?

All of these questions are provocative and may be answered soon. A few scientists are investigating the importance of light and color to the brain. As a group, though, most appear to continue to overlook the fact that nearly every individual light source has inherent within it a dominant "color," and the human brain is designed to adapt to this color as we move from one light source to another in a phenomenon known as color constancy. Midday diffuse sunlight, for example, is inherently blue—but we don't "see" this blue. Incandescent lamps are inherently yellow to yellow-orange. Again, we don't "see" it. Fluorescent lights vary depending upon the type of gas, type of charging mechanism, and age of the tube. What effect *must* the inherent color of a light source have on a human brain wondrously designed to use light "color" in some way to detect motion or stimulate the firing of neurons?

There are more questions than answers—but, until the questions are asked, scientists cannot begin to explain Irlen syndrome fully.

Light's vibrations may indeed be like a symphony of plucked strings that reaches our eyes, triggering the plucking of more strings, or, more appropriately, the excitation of notes. The symphony comes to its crescendo when hundreds of millions of cells, rods, cones, neural impulses, and fibers in the brain's multiple visual pathways work together to produce the images we associate with visual perception. It is as complex a symphony or science as any on the face of the earth—and one of amazing precision and beauty.

Certainly it is conceivable that for some brains light causes notes or chords to be struck in different ways—some perhaps more or less energetically than others. If this were the case, what would a child or adult experience? Might the mildly sensitive reach for a pair of sunglasses? Could the moderately sensitive experience migraine headaches? Would the more severely sensitive perceive visual distortions when a white page reflects problem properties of light into the eyes? Could the most sensitive experience seizures or a world that appears fractured into pieces?

Just as a diamond is capable of breaking apart and flashing colors that exist within light, might the human brain, too, be capable of "flashing" those colors or, worse, bending, breaking, and otherwise distorting the symphony of a visual image?

Scientifically speaking, color used as overlays or tinted lenses modifies the wavelengths and frequencies reaching the visual system. In children like mine, color simply increases visual stability and visual perception.

Wavelengths and frequencies not visible to the human eye are beginning to be used in other ways for the benefit of the human body. In parts of the world where there is no sunlight during long stretches of winter, ultraviolet light therapy is used to promote vitamin D production and help build strong bones in young children. In doctors' offices, infrared light is beginning to be used to analyze body tissues, fluids, and body temperatures—doing so in a matter of seconds.

It appears we know and appreciate more about the implications for the human body of invisible ultraviolet and infrared light wavelengths than we know about the use by the brain of the qualities of visible light. Colored overlays and tinted lenses have therapeutic value for some children and adults. We shouldn't take light "color" for granted.

10

BRIDGING THE GAP

A couple of years after Katie was diagnosed with Irlen syndrome, I ran into a woman I hadn't seen in years. Rosemary taught a series of classes I took before Katie was born on raising children birth through the preschool years. Being the youngest of four, I can assure you I needed the classes.

The moment I saw Rosemary, my arms stretched open and my spirits warmed. I gave her the kind of hug you give someone to whom you are indebted for life. Rosemary taught me how important it is to respect a child as you nurture, encourage, consistently discipline, and mentally stimulate her or him. Love was a given. It is the other stuff that can be overlooked. From birth, Rosemary said, talk to your child. Read to her. Play with her. You'll enjoy the process—and your child's brain will grow.

I remembered all of this as I gave Rosemary that long grateful hug.

"Rosemary," I finally said, "you did such a wonderful job teaching me how to give my children a good start in the early years. I wish someone had been around to help me when Katie began to struggle in school. I didn't even know what to look for."

"Katie?" she gasped. "Oh, my!" She nodded her head and lowered her voice. "I know. There's a huge gap between early childhood and school."

Rosemary is both an early childhood educator and a literacy activist in our community. She knows that while many schools do their best to teach our children, they often don't know quite what to make of kids who do not perform up to their potential. Frankly, neither do many parents.

In the mid-1980s, focus on early brain development between birth and age three emerged as the strategy to ensure that all children entered school ready to learn.

Every family who has invested time, energy, and love in the early development of a child only to encounter rough seas as the child progresses through school knows that early brain development is not enough to guarantee school success. In 1999, John T. Bruer, Ph.D., published a controversial book challenging the all-or-nothing birth-to-three strategy that annually receives millions of dollars in private and government funding. His book, *The Myth of the First Three Years: A New Understanding of Early Brain Development and Lifelong Learning,* points out that learning occurs in cycles throughout life and that everyday issues such as vision problems, year-to-year development, and other matters related to health are just as important to the ultimate success of a child.

Bottom line: should parents and communities focus on children only during their first few years? Or should parents be vigilant until the very day we send a grown child out the door on the way to college or a career? And, should a variety of resources be available in every community to help families address children's emerging learning and emotional needs?

Of course parents should be vigilant. But how can we be vigilant if we don't know what to look for, and when we suspect there is a problem, we don't know how to get help? This was the dilemma our family faced as Katie began to slip further behind her peers in school. From year to year, our daughter's teachers did not appreciate that her learning had stalled. The signs were there. Reading grew no easier for her from year to year. Her printing and handwriting looked nearly the same from second grade on. Homework took nearly three times the energy and effort required by other children her age. When Katie was a toddler, I knew exactly how she was progressing. I could pull from a shelf a birth-to-six development book and be comforted by the milestones she'd reached. When Katie began to struggle in school, however, there was no book on my shelf to turn to. I sent her off to school thinking I didn't need one. I assumed her school would tell me all I needed to know about my child. It didn't happen that way.

THE SUBTLE BUT PROGRESSIVE STRUGGLE

We aren't talking about obvious developmental issues here, such as an inability to tie shoelaces or learn the alphabet. We're talking about subtle and progressive school failure. Katie's early school experience was like a snowball rolling down a hill. My little snowball progressed quickly and gathered new snow during the first two years. In second grade, she appeared to reach the bottom of the hill and began to coast slowly on flat ground. In third grade, my snowball gathered little snow and needed a constant push to make it up the next hill and, by fifth grade, it felt as though we were pushing our precious ball of snow up Washington's Mount Rainier.

All Katie's teachers told us was "she needs to read more; she needs to pay more attention." The few times we mentioned how hard she worked at home, it didn't seem to register with anyone as important.

In retrospect, I realize now that Paul and I were lulled into a false sense of security by Katie's early developmental milestones. In elementary school, it didn't occur to us that her problems with reading and printing might be symptoms of a physiological problem. Why would they? We were told, "She'll catch up." Also, all the information on child development we received as young parents focused on the early years. Little was available about spotting developmental problems in the school-age child.

Even though Dr. Bruer has stirred the ire of many birth-to-three organizations, he makes a valid point. Focus on birth to three is very important, but it alone is *not enough*—and every parent of a child who passes birth-to-three milestones with flying colors only to watch that child struggle in school knows it.

THE GAP IN CHILDHOOD DEVELOPMENT

A gap of developmental milestones and warning signs exists between early childhood and the fifth grade. And ironically, this gap led our family to discover that both of our children have problems with the ability to perceive the printed page—one of the most important building blocks of learning.

It was the gap that led to my conversation with Jean Hawkins, my old colleague and a school principal in a neighboring district who first suggested that light sensitivity might be involved in Katie's reading issues. Desperation caused me to unload all my concerns about Katie's progress on Jean's tender ears. It was just a stroke of luck or divine intervention that Jean knew about Irlen syndrome. Katie's optometrist didn't. Her pediatrician didn't. Her teachers didn't.

Light sensitivity is not the reason every child struggles in school. Far from it. It is only one potential barrier to learning in what may be, for some children, a long list. If symptoms are severe, however, Irlen syndrome alone will stop a child in his or her tracks. And if moms, dads, educators, and pediatricians don't know about this syndrome or deny that it exists, we can't help those children whose lives will be shaped by its negative side effects.

If you still doubt that sensitivity to aspects of light impacts some children, consider this. Two years after our family decided to go against the recommendation of medical associations and try colored overlays and tinted lenses, physicians from two prominent organizations acknowledged to us that color filtration *does* help some children.

The first acknowledgment came as the result of an error. I was checking Internet sources to see whether any of the nation's prominent vision organizations had changed their positions on Irlen syndrome, overlays, and tinted lenses when I came upon a newly updated statement from the American Association of Pediatric Ophthalmology and Strabismus (AAPOS). It referred favorably to the benefits of photo screening, or in non-medicalese, light screening. In a moment of misplaced hope, I assumed this reference was to screening for sensitivity to aspects of light. I was so excited at the thought that a medical organization would finally affirm my children's problem with light that—I'm embarrassed to admit—tears of relief started to stream down my face. Actually it was more like a crack in a dam.

I immediately sent off a grateful e-mail thanking the AAPOS and asking their Web master, identified as an M.D., what had caused the organization to modify its opinion. Then I returned to the published online opinion to bask in its glory. Within minutes I figured out that the photo screening they referred to was not at all related to screening for sensitivity to light. It referred instead to early detection of vision problems in very young children. I sent off an apologetic e-mail for jumping to conclusions and couldn't resist asking the inevitable question. I wrote:

The AAPOS opinion is of tremendous value, both to me personally and professionally. Yet neither of my children would willingly give up their tinted lenses, and on those days when my daughter forgets her glasses at home, the bright red eyes, headaches, and fatigue return. My mother's heart longs to understand why my children have been successful with color filtration in spite of authoritative medical opinion.

Best wishes,
Rhonda Stone

A response came from the Web master. He wrote:

The Irlen lens do work in some instances, but so do eye exercises, vit[amin] B12 shots, antihistamines, and a whole variety of other "remedies." It is well known that virtually anything you do with children with learning and/or reading disabilities will help them. I would encourage you to continue to use the Irlen lens since they are helping.

There are many parents of children who struggle to learn who would challenge the assertion that "just about anything" will help. In an effort to help her son, Beth, the Australian mom and Ph.D., spent four years and thousands of dollars on conventional remedial methods American pediatric and ophthalmology associations would support. Those interventions produced little benefit for her son. What did work was colored overlays and tinted lenses. Mike Horstman's daughter, Annelise, was enrolled in Chapter I remedial reading programs that produced no significant improvement. Her parents had her eyes checked in the standard way and were given a good report. They also tried working with Annelise at home with a commercial phonics program. Progress was minimal until she was given colored overlays and tinted lenses.

Also in his e-mail, the AAPOS Web master cautioned me that a study I mentioned (Wilkins/Evans) was not as good as it looked. I had inquired as to why the study was not referenced in a joint opinion issued by organizations including the AAPOS. In his return message, the Web master called the Wilkins/Evans study flawed. When I politely asked him to educate me as to the flaws, he did not respond. Nor did Dr. Wilkins receive a response when he politely inquired as to how his research was flawed.

The Web master's acknowledgment that colored overlays and tinted lenses help some children surprised me. I didn't expect it. My curiosity piqued, I decided to see what would happen if I wrote to QuackWatch, a leading consumer Web site devoted to safe and effective medicine (**www.quackwatch.com**). In the United States, physicians frequently refer patients to this online resource when they inquire about unconventional medical treatments. QuackWatch is a valuable resource, genuine in its mission to protect consumers from unsubstantiated and profit-driven medical quackery.

My question:

I have tremendous respect for the mission and protective role QuackWatch plays in relationship to consumers and medicine. For over a year now, though, I've been holding back asking a question that continues to baffle me. If, indeed, tinted lenses are "quackery," as they are listed on QuackWatch, why are they working for my children?

The response:

Read more carefully. Our article does not say they are quackery. It says that the research supporting their use is not very good and that the percentage of people who will benefit is not large.

The e-mail message continued by citing studies, many of which I'd already read. I have about seventy-five study summaries and articles on sensitivity to light, color filtration, dyslexia, and learning disabilities in the pile of references I used to educate myself in order to write this book. I am grateful to QuackWatch's Web master for taking the time to be so thorough. The message concluded with this observation:

Overall, these studies indicate that fewer than 5 percent of readers who experience discomfort benefit from a change in contrast, brightness, or color on the page beyond what would be expected from a placebo treatment alone. Remember that even if a treatment makes the print more comfortable to look at, proper reading instruction is still needed to improve reading skills.

Yes, proper instruction *is* still needed. All colored overlays and tinted lenses do is calm the visual system, thereby easing visual perception and removing a barrier to learning. QuackWatch's Web master is correct about reading instruction, and correct in one other thing—colored overlays and tinted lenses do help some children. Researchers could disagree for decades about the percentage. But the fact remains, some children benefit and many of those children are not getting the color filtration they need. This is partly because medical opinion-makers are telling parents it doesn't work, when there is sufficient evidence to indicate for some children it does. And contrary to what the QuackWatch Web master thought at the time, tinted lenses were listed in an article entitled "Eye-Related Quackery" on the Web site. Unfortunately, headlines tend to be what people remember most.

WHOSE BEST INTEREST?

In general, doctors do have consumers' best interests at heart. But I think the opinion-makers may be misguided about one other controversy regarding tinted lenses. In journal articles and published opinions, colored overlays and tinted lenses have been repeatedly labeled as expensive.

In schools and classrooms where it is accepted that color makes a difference in reading performance, light-sensitive children typically receive overlays at no cost. In North America, when parents must seek screening on their own, they most often encounter Irlen-certified practitioners. There are two types of such practitioners, screeners and diagnosticians. Certified screeners identify Irlen syndrome and assess children for overlays. Irlen diagnosticians are trained to determine lens color, a process requiring a great deal more education and training. In 2002, the cost of testing through a screener, commonly requiring two hours of evaluation, was around $80. If this test is performed by a certified diagnostician, it usually costs more. The diagnostician in our region charges $125. Through either practitioner, the cost comes to between $40 and $62.50 per hour if the appointment takes two full hours. In comparison, Katie's and Jacob's last visit to the optometrist cost $163 per child for no more than thirty minutes with the optometrist and thirty minutes with the technician.

The cost of tinted lenses—including an average two-hour diagnostic appointment, frames, and lenses—is about $500.

Total cost of testing for overlays, $80 to $125. Average cost for testing and tinted lenses, $500. If your child has more complex needs, it could cost more—as much as $650, if a child needs an extra clip-on filter because of varying needs associated with different types of light.

Sound expensive? Then you need to meet "Diana."

Diana's parents followed a conventional path recommended by medicine when their daughter began to struggle in school. A doctor's referral allowed Diana to be tested in one of the best learning disorders clinics in the country, an opportunity few children with reading disabilities receive. Comprehensive testing led to a fairly routine diagnosis of dyslexia. A variety of learning interventions were recommended, from speech therapy to specialized reading instruction, to help Diana improve her skills.

I asked Diana's mother if she would mind adding up the total cost of and hours invested in assessments, therapies, tutoring sessions, and all other activities recommended to help Diana with her reading problem. She gathered up all the paperwork she could find and assessed the amount of time required over several years. The total cost: more than $6,550. Total hours: 2,350+.

Diana and her parents invested a tremendous amount of time and money to help their daughter increase her reading skills. Did it work? To some degree. Diana is doing much better, but homework still takes her longer than most students.

But $80 for colored overlays and/or $500 for tinted lenses hardly compares with $6,550. Nor does up to two hours of screening compare with what Diana and her family went through to make progress. Six hours of reading tests, twelve hours of learning disability assessment, fifty hours of Individualized Education Program meetings, 252 hours of language acquisition program, sixty hours of speech therapy, and hundreds of hours at the dining room table working with her parents. Do most doctors know that this is what many children endure to overcome barriers to reading and learning?

Eventually Diana was tested for sensitivity to aspects of light. It took less than 90 minutes. She was one of four individuals struggling with reading for whom I arranged testing. Three of the four tested positive for Irlen syndrome to varying degrees. Did Diana? No, she did not. But her mother, seated at her side, confided that while her daughter performed well with the testing instruments, she could hardly tolerate looking at the dense text and busy patterns.

Around the world, millions of families know how much it hurts to watch a child struggle in school. They know what it's like to have a happy, bright child encounter an invisible barrier to academic success. They've experienced what our family did—hour after hour of help, support, and frustration at the kitchen table. They've seen otherwise bright children that, no matter how hard they tried, struggle to read and learn. These children don't want to fail—but they do.

In 2001, Wilkins and his colleagues tested 426 children from twelve schools in England. They found that 5 percent experienced significant gains in reading using colored overlays.

If there is a chance that we can make the process of reading easier, shouldn't we try? Before children and families are put through hundreds of hours of testing and remediation and thousands of dollars of expenses, shouldn't we first make sure that aspects of light, the most pervasive factor in all of our daily lives, aren't in some way interfering with the process of what children perceive? For some children, the bridge between success and failure in school is light modified by color.

SIGNS, SYMPTOMS, AND, AND

11

SIGNS, SYMPTOMS, AND COLOR FILTRATION

Children like mine can be easy to spot. Often they can be identified by body language alone. With a page of dense text in front of them, some will tilt their heads, wriggle in their seats, and shade their eyes in an unconscious attempt to find a way to see the page comfortably. Sometimes such children are mislabeled as inattentive, unable to hold still, or even suspected of attention deficit/hyperactivity disorder (ADHD). It is easy to confuse Irlen syndrome with other learning problems.

Helen Irlen's observations and research led to the screening methods now used to diagnose sensitivity to aspects of light in more than thirty countries. The identification of signs and symptoms and the use of colored overlays and tinted lenses are based on over twenty years of work beginning with her government-funded research project at the University of California at Long Beach. The method is now used at a number of school and college campuses throughout the United States.

So how are children, men, and women who struggle with the cluster of symptoms known as Irlen syndrome identified? Practitioners begin with a personal history and a list of questions designed to identify problems with reading. Examples include:

"Do you misread words?"

"Do you look away or take breaks?"

"Do your eyes bother you?"

"Do they get red or watery?"

"Do you find yourself blinking frequently?"

"Is it harder to read in bright lights?"

Once the questions are completed, assessment begins. This process includes a number of graphics and charts designed to stress and fatigue the visual system. Individuals with Irlen syndrome routinely experience discomfort and/or visual distortions when viewing these busy, high-contrast images.

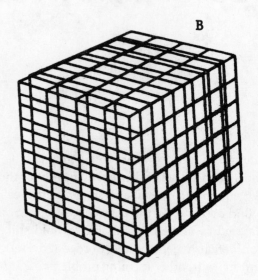

Counting the Squares
Following a line of squares by counting across the top and down the side is difficult for individuals bothered by aspects of light.

Through it all, Irlen certified practitioners listen to what children and adults say about how they perceive the printed page and how they feel during the process of reading. They also observe physical behavior during testing. For the most part, these types of questions and observations are not a part of standard vision testing. Surprisingly, they are seldom even a part of testing for perceptual problems, dyslexia, or learning disabilities.

The following Reading Inventory and Inventory of Physical Symptoms developed for this book may help you determine whether sensitivity to light, brightness, glare, or bright/dark contrast is a problem in your family. Once again, its usefulness lies in the patterns it may help to identify.

As you complete the inventories, keep in mind that the common symptoms of Irlen syndrome are shared by other barriers to learning, and that Irlen syndrome is only one possible cause of reading problems.

Reading Inventory

Check the item that best applies for a specific individual:

____ 1. School was easy.

____ 2. School was never easy.

____ 3. School became more difficult when dense reading was introduced (usually third grade, sometimes earlier—for my children, it was second grade).

____ 1. Attention span is not a problem.

____ 2. Attention span was always short.

____ 3. Avoids reading.

____ 1. Mastered short words easily (*the, was, saw,* etc.)

____ 2. Had a hard time mastering short words.

____ 3. Could read short words until they were introduced in dense text.

____ 1. Never skips words or sentences.

____ 2. Skips words or sentences once in a while.

____ 3. Skips words or sentences frequently.

____ 1. Reads long words well.

____ 2. Makes an effort to read long words.

____ 3. Intentionally looks away from dense text.

____ 1. Is capable of neat and uniform printing and/or cursive hand-writing.

____ 2. Printing or handwriting is improving steadily.

____ 3. Printing or handwriting is erratic or not progressing.

____ 1. Loves to read.

____ 2. Has a neutral attitude about reading.

____ 3. Digs in his/her heels and resists reading.

Inventory of Physical Symptoms

____ 1. Experiences no problems with headache, stomachaches, or fatigue.

____ 2. Experiences occasional problems, but there is no pattern.

____ 3. Frequently complains of physical discomfort with reading at school or at home. Log the complaints by noting dates.

____ 1. Experiences no eye soreness or red eyes.

____ 2. Occasionally has sore or red eyes, but there is no pattern.

____ 3. Frequently complains of eye soreness and/or has red eyes, especially after reading. Log the complaints by noting dates.

____ 1. Can read for long stretches of time

____ 2. Reads for thirty minutes or more without a break.

____ 3. Tolerates reading for only fifteen minutes or less and frequently looks away from the page. Log this pattern by noting dates.

____ 1. Has never complained about the ability to see.

____ 2. Has asked to have vision checked.

____3. Has complained more than once about trouble seeing print when reading or copying from the board in spite of checkups indicating no problem. Log this pattern by noting dates and specifics of complaints.

____ 1. Is bright-eyed most of the time.

____ 2. Occasionally rubs eyes, squints, or shades eyes, with no pattern.

____ 3. Frequently rubs eyes, squints, or shades eyes, especially during reading. Log this pattern by noting dates and specific action.

____ 1. Never becomes restless or agitated.

____ 2. Occasionally becomes restless or agitated, with no noticeable pattern.

____ 3. Frequently becomes restless, agitated, or tired, especially after working under fluorescent lights.

____ 1. Comes home from school rested and energetic.

____ 2. Comes home mildly tired on occasion, but rebounds.

____ 3. Comes home frequently exhausted and cranky, in spite of a good night's rest. Log this pattern by noting dates.

In these inventories, Katie was a mix of 1s and 2s in the first grade. Between second and fourth grade, the pattern shifted to mostly 3s. Jacob was just beginning to move into a few of the 3s when he was tested for Irlen syndrome and began to wear colored lenses.

Irlen certified practitioners report a variety of results for children and adults experiencing different types of sensitivity to aspects of light. There are children, for example, who perform fairly well in school without colored overlays, but who can tolerate reading for only fifteen minutes or less. These children experience no visual distortions per se, just fatigue or mild discomfort. Helen Irlen says color filtration helps these children increase the amount of time they can tolerate reading, so they make even greater gains in academic performance. On the Reading Inventory and Inventory of Physical Symptoms such children might score all 1s, except for questions concerning the amount of time they are willing to read.

Other children may have more serious disabilities, with Irlen syndrome as one factor among many. Observing how these children respond under different lighting conditions may help you determine whether sensitivity to aspects of light is an issue.

Without the tools to identify patterns, it is difficult to communicate your concerns about your children's health and learning issues to doctors, educators, and others who can help you sort through them. If you complete the inventories and see a pattern that concerns you, take it with you to visit a health care professional. Keep in mind, though, that many are not knowledgeable about or receptive to Irlen syndrome.

The Irlen Institute encourages all parents to have children tested by physicians and vision professionals first for potential health concerns. This is a wise and necessary first step. It is not the intention of Irlen-certified practitioners to identify overlays or tinted lenses as a solution when the problem is related to visual acuity or some other health issue. On the contrary, the objective of practitioners is to see that individuals with problems associated with visual perception get the proper help they need. For colored overlays and tinted lenses to be effective, issues related to general health and the eyes must be addressed first.

Another important consideration: if you take the inventories with you to visit an optometrist, keep in mind he or she may see a pattern calling for vision therapy, optometry's solution to problems with visual perception. Accounts by individuals who have experienced success with vision therapy lead me, as a parent, to believe there is a place for it in the treatment of problems associated with visual perception. A few of the many individuals with sensitivity to aspects of light interviewed for this book, however, tried vision therapy and had little success with it. Does this mean that one should replace the other? No. It means that different problems likely respond to different treatments. Parents need plenty of tools in their toolboxes, and the tools need to be diverse, not of only one type or nature. Ultimately, parents must decide what is right for their children. Given enough information and the appropriate tools, parents will make good decisions.

SORTING THROUGH THE ISSUES

Issues related to aspects of light are very similar to issues associated with dyslexia, a general term that often is applied to multiple forms of reading disability. Visual perception is one possible issue in dyslexia, although perception within the auditory processing center of the brain is more commonly associated with the condition. In general, individuals with auditory processing problems have trouble equating and arranging sounds to printed and spoken language.

Some individuals struggle with both auditory processing and visual perception. Imagine what it would be like to have a brain that encounters miscues and misperceptions with both the spoken and the printed word. For such a child, school would be a most unhappy place. Imagine, too, the benefit such a child would receive if at least one of the problems could be solved.

That is what happened for Katie. Modifying light in her environment or wearing tinted lenses made a huge difference in her ability to interpret printed language.

The day Katie received her second set of tinted lenses—the pair that removed the last of her visual distortions—I asked her what reading was like *before* all the words were clear and distinct. This is what she said: "It was like being in a prison. I'd be in this jail [she pointed to a block of text] and suddenly I'd be in this jail. And I couldn't remember how I got there or anything in between."

Katie was describing seeing two or three words at a time scrunched together without benefit of breaks or white space. She could read the words, but the difficult process of separating one word from another and then deciphering them consumed her. She couldn't remember the content of what she was reading because all of her energy was spent deciphering. Consequently, Katie's comprehension was poor.

Then I asked Katie what her new and improved glasses were like. Her response: "Well, I start in this part of the prison and I find my way from jail to jail until I end up down here. I remember everything in between and I remember how I got from place to place."

Katie's ability to process information with the new lenses fit her description. The very day she received the additional filter, she was able to complete a social studies assignment in one-third the time it normally took her. Why? Because she could read the chapter once, efficiently and quickly, remember what she read, and then scan through the text without hesitation. She could find answers to chapter questions that were once very difficult for her to find. The difference was indisputable.

It is interesting to me that Katie chose the metaphor of a prison—a bleak, empty place from which there is no escape—to describe her experience. It is a place you have to be, whether you want to or not. A place where you serve your time; then when the bell rings, you are free. It seems an appropriate metaphor for a child forced into a visual world of print that is full of dead ends and blind alleys.

Katie's response to this kind of confinement was daydreaming and a quiet reluctance to do seatwork—classic symptoms of attention deficit disorder. It stands to reason that a more energetic and demonstrative child might act out with restlessness and physical activity—traits commonly associated with attention deficit/hyperactivity disorder. Interesting dilemma, isn't it?

COLOR FILTRATION

So what can colored overlays and tinted lenses do for a child?

Colored overlays modify the bright light reflected from a page of text. Tinted lenses filter wavelengths of light as they pass through lenses and into the eyes.

In reading, a color carefully chosen for a light-sensitive child appears to help calm and restore order to the neural impulses flashing through the brain. Problems appear to be triggered by aspects of light reaching the visual system. Because white is the most reflective color, it sends the most bright light to the brain. If sensitivity to aspects of light could be resolved by simply reducing the amount of brightness or bright/dark contrast on a page, however, a gray overlay alone would solve the problem. This is not the case. The specifically chosen color used to reduce brightness also appears to restore order to visual perception—and the brain can be very picky about what color it requires.

The color of overlay a child uses and the color of tinted lenses she or he may require will not be the same. According to Irlen practitioners there is a logical reason for this. Overlays affect only page color. Tinted lenses affect nearly all light reaching the visual system.

Tinted lenses worn as glasses affect most light reaching the visual system because it would take tightly fitting goggles (or contact lenses) to alter *all* of the light reaching the eyes. Intriguingly, that is nearly what Katie prefers. She uses wrap-around frames similar to goggles because they alter the most light reaching her eyes. If there is too much white light getting to her visual system around the edges of her tinted lenses, she becomes easily distracted and vulnerable to headaches. This is because Katie's visual system is highly reactive to extreme contrast—in this case, contrast between the bright white around the outside of her lenses and the dark tinting in front of her eyes.

Jacob, on the other hand, is not bothered by bright light reaching his eyes from around the edges of his glasses. Remember, Jacob and Katie experience different things related to their sensitivity to aspects of light. Jacob does not have a problem with high contrast, but instead sees slight distortion and instability in everything he sees (for a visual example, see the July 1999 issue of *National Geographic*). For Jacob, color filtration helps the edges of everything he sees remain stable and sharp.

Two different problems, two different needs.

Many factors influence how well colored overlays and tinted lenses work. The following issues in particular need to be kept in mind as families consider color as a solution for sensitivity to aspects of light.

- *Colored overlays can be a source of glare, and glare is a major source of problems for some children sensitive to light.* Consequently, children using colored overlays must be monitored closely. If glare occurs on an overlay, it needs to be repositioned or the child needs to be moved to another location so that glare is minimized. It is important to teach children to spot problem glare. Several individuals interviewed for this book noted that colored overlays created too much glare to be helpful to them. Tinted lenses worn as glasses, however, create no problems with glare. These individuals choose to use *only* tinted lenses.

- *Color of filtration must be specifically prescribed, just as lenses for nearsightedness or farsightedness must be specifically prescribed.* Science may not fully understand why this is the case, but our family tested this idea to the limit and found it to be true. We explored both the Irlen and Wilkins methods. Each has developed a different set of colors for testing. Dr. Wilkins produced a lens color that Katie absolutely loved. It was similar to the cumulative color of her Irlen-tinted lenses, but it did not require the extra clip-on filter Katie used under fluorescent lights.

  We returned home from England and completed all the arrangements for the new tints and Katie waited expectantly every day for the arrival of the lenses, a dark shade of mostly blue and gray, with just a hint of aqua. I didn't have to worry about the mail getting into the house during those weeks. I'll never forget the day the lenses finally arrived. Katie tore open the package and found them nestled in several layers of bubble wrap and plastic. I didn't say a word to her or even change my expression, but I suspected immediately that the color wasn't right. They appeared far too blue. I hoped it was only faulty memory on my part. Katie lifted them to her eyes and dejection immediately spread the length of her frame. "They're too bright, Mom. Way too bright."

  We immediately contacted Arnold Wilkins, who contacted the company responsible for tinting the lenses on our behalf. They offered to tint them again. Rather than risk months of mailing back and forth, Katie and I decided to see what we could do closer to home. We found an optician who felt he could add an extra color to the blue tints; then we visited optical shops throughout town in search of the right color to modify the blue. It took four shops, but we finally found a tint. The lens color was called pewter, and it was a yellow-green shade of gray. It was the only lens like it in town. We delivered the pewter-colored lens and the lenses from England to the optician. It took several tries, but he finally produced a color that removed all of Katie's distortions.

The story doesn't quite end there. Four months later, after standard vision screening, Katie needed a slight prescription for nearsightedness, which meant a new set of lenses and new tinting. This time, we were not so lucky. The tint the optician produced was blue-gray, all right, but it was not the right kind of gray. Under the optical shop's fluorescent lights, the lenses looked fine. When we got them home, under incandescent light, the lenses looked red. In fact, Katie put them over her eyes and immediately reacted to red streaks she could perceive in the room's incandescent lights. We took the lenses back to the optician who confirmed that yes, indeed, the lenses would appear to be different under fluorescent and incandescent lights because of the properties within light (fluorescent lights lean toward short wavelengths; incandescent lights lean toward long). The gray he used had some red in it and incandescent light picked it up. Fluorescent light didn't. The lenses went back to the optician for several more tries. Finally they were right.

Without question, tinting is tricky business. For individuals with sensitivity to aspects of light, it requires educated selection and careful translation to actual tints worn as glasses. With his Irlen tints, Jacob has only ever needed a single, reliable color.

We tried to get around careful application of color, and we couldn't. It doesn't work. It needs to be left to those who have been trained, certified, and have experience with color as an intervention for issues associated with reading.

· *Lighting varies from location to location, and so may the effect of tinted lenses.* Both of my children tell me that under some lighting conditions, their tints are too dark. Because he wears them all the time, Jacob encounters this problem more often than Katie. Jacob switches from looking through his lenses (for clarity) and over the top of his lenses (to compensate for lack of brightness) to perceive his surroundings when a light source is too dark. He uses his lenses as he needs them.

My daughter has become very clever in how she compensates for light. When she does not have her tinted lenses in class (she sometimes forgets them in her locker or at home), she modifies bright light by resting one arm across a page to cast a shadow across the text. With her face tilted down, Katie's chin-length bobbed hair sweeps across the sides of her face and prevents the overhead light from directly reaching her eyes. In computer classes, rather than wear her glasses, she prefers to turn down the brightness on her computer screen. It is another modification recommended by Irlen practitioners. And I know just exactly how dim she likes it. I am frequently reminded of this when I sit down at the computer in our house and, after fifteen minutes or so, begin to develop my own symptoms of visual stress— tired eyes, headache, a little nausea. When I finally realize Katie has been using the computer, I check the brightness. It is almost always set around 50 percent.

- *Twenty-five percent of the time, children who receive tinted lenses need to have their tints adjusted within the first year.* If required, retinting adds another expense for families. Katie had to have her tints adjusted the first year, but Jacob did not. A typical recheck and color change can cost $140: $80 for the appointment, $40 to modify the color, plus tax and shipping. Was it worth it? To see my daughter finally be able to do homework in the time it took other children—you bet. Would I do it again? Absolutely. Will it work for your child? I can't say. Whether or not to try it is a decision only you can make.

- *Some children resist overlays and tinted lenses.* With twenty-five to thirty children in a classroom, it may be too much to expect teachers to remind a student to pull out colored overlays every time it is time to read. Yet that is what is takes for many children to get into the habit of using overlays. Children resist for several possible reasons. First and foremost is that using a colored overlay is different. It is something a child does and every other child in the classroom can see him or her do. Second, some children are particularly sensitive to glare, and glare is a common problem when light reflects off of the plastic surface of overlays. Third, using overlays is something children have to remember to do. When not in use, an overlay is tucked inside of a desk. Out of sight, out of mind.

Some Irlen practitioners have observed that resistance to colored overlays or tinted lenses peaks between the ages of twelve and eighteen. At age nineteen, individuals diagnosed years before with Irlen syndrome often become more willing to wear and use tinted lenses.

Putting colored overlays in front of a child or giving them tinted lenses is not an effortless prospect. There are lots of variables, some of which depend upon the child. I have one child who never goes without tinted lenses and another who wears them only when needed for reading. Would either give up their tints? Absolutely not. Their lenses are tools available to them every day, tools they want and need.

• *Not all children benefit from colored overlays and tinted lenses.* Sensitivity to aspects of light is only one of many reasons children struggle in school. Some children will benefit from color filtration, and some will not. Those who benefit divide into two subgroups—those who need color filtration and nothing more to be successful in school, and those who need color filtration and other interventions to address all of their learning needs.

Sorting through the many potential sources of a child's learning difficulties is likely the most complex part of helping a child who is struggling to read and learn. Helen Irlen cautions parents that color filtration is not related to reading instruction, nor does color correct all problems associated with reading. Colored overlays and tinted lenses modify the light reaching the visual system, thereby making the reading process more comfortable and efficient.

MILDLY SENSITIVE CHILDREN

Will all children need colored overlays and tinted lenses forever in order to read? Not necessarily. According to Dr. Wilkins, it appears colored overlays help some mildly to moderately light-sensitive children acquire enough reading skills to discontinue use of overlays after a brief length of time. However, such children may continue to tire after brief periods of reading and struggle with other issues, such as headaches, later in life. Parents need to observe this carefully in order to determine whether overlays truly are no longer needed.

Some children learn to compensate in other ways. Since Katie has learned what dense text is supposed to look like (stable and unmoving), she works a little harder to get her brain to settle the distortions. In combination with strategies she uses to modify light in her environment (shading both the page and her eyes), she functions better for short periods of time without tinted lenses in classrooms where the light source is a problem. She also has learned, wherever possible, to sit near a window.

Helen Irlen estimates that 46 percent of all children with reading disabilities benefit from colored overlays or tinted lenses. Dr. Wilkins places the percentage closer to 12 percent, and a QuackWatch representative, who has reviewed the literature but not conducted studies of his own, acknowledges a number under 5 percent. The National Institutes of Health estimates there are 10 million American children struggling to read. By the aforementioned estimates, the number of children in the United States alone who could be helped by color ranges somewhere between 460,000 and 4.6 million.

Any way you look at the numbers, this is a lot of children. And what do the percentages matter if one of those children is *yours*? Clearly, there is a place for colored overlays and tinted lenses in a parent's toolbox of strategies for helping a child succeed in the classroom and in life.

12

NOT DYSLEXIA AND
NOT ADD/ADHD

Some of the most profound words I read during my study of Irlen syndrome and color filtration came from an unexpected source—an article in a government newsletter. The author was G. Reid Lyon, an insightful research psychologist and chief of the Child Development and Behavior Branch at the National Institute of Child Health and Human Development (NICHD). It was somewhat of a shock to see a government official come out and admit that for decades the teaching of reading in many locations of America has been all wrong.

In the April 2001 issue of *Community Update*, a publication of the U.S. Department of Education, Dr. Lyon writes: "As a brand new third-grade teacher in the mid-1970s, I was responsible for teaching 28 students of varying abilities and backgrounds. Unfortunately, many of my students had not yet learned basic reading skills and were clearly floundering in almost every aspect of their academic work." He continues by explaining that as a student teacher, he was taught to believe that reading skills are acquired naturally when children are ready. "Thus," he writes, "children did not need to be taught basic reading skills in a systematic or direct manner."

He closes his story by acknowledging that the students in his charge during that first year learned little about reading or writing—an honest and gutsy admission for an educator to make.

Few parents are aware that reading experts readily admit that they do not yet know exactly what the human brain is doing when it reads, nor do they yet know all that a child requires in order to develop excellent reading skills. Most of us assume that experts know, but recent books published by the International Reading Association (*Reading Researchers in Search of Common Ground*, published in 2002, edited by Rona Flippo; and *What Research Has to Say About Reading Instruction*, 2002, edited by A. E. Farstrup and S. J. Samuels) make it clear that the mystery has not yet been solved.

Additionally, in the mid and late 1990s, the federal government charged a group called the National Reading Panel with the task of reviewing thousands of studies and articles on reading in order to make specific recommendations as to the best methods for reading instruction. Ultimately, the group determined that a balanced approach to reading instruction involving phonemic awareness, phonics, vocabulary fluency, and comprehension was preferred for kindergarten through third-grade children. The group acknowledged that phonemic awareness and phonics appear to have little benefit for children who continue to have significant reading problems beyond the age of nine.

In 2003, the United States government is preparing to invest millions of dollars in research that might shed light on what has come to be known as the "fourth-grade slump," or reading development that plateaus at a fourth-grade level for literally millions of American children. From this research it is hoped that new solutions will arise for an epidemic of poor readers.

Of the 10 million children in public and private schools across America experiencing reading difficulties, many eventually are suspected of dyslexia, although many are never officially diagnosed. The International Dyslexia Association (IDA) estimates that 85 percent of children who experience reading difficulties have dyslexia. More concrete data is available on the number of children in the United States diagnosed and treated for ADD and ADHD, attention deficit disorders that also impact reading ability. In the October 5, 1995, issue of *The New England Journal of Medicine*, Swanson, Lerner, and Williams reported that visits to the doctor for ADD/ADHD grew from 1.7 million to 4.2 million between 1990 and 1993 alone. The treatment is psychostimulants. Beginning in the early 1990s, a couple of million children in the United States were being prescribed stimulants each year.

What has any of this to do with sensitivity to aspects of light, aka Irlen syndrome? Plenty.

Parents must sort through a host of issues in order to determine the best course of intervention for their children. If reading instruction is the problem, then children need opportunities for alternative reading instruction. If Irlen syndrome is the issue, then children need to be properly tested for overlays or tinted lenses and they need to be encouraged to use them correctly and consistently while they catch up to their peers.

But there's a catch. If sensitivity to aspects of light is not universally acknowledged as a legitimate diagnosis and tested for, children are at risk of being assumed to have dyslexia or ADD/ADHD, when in fact they have Irlen syndrome. As yet, doctors do not readily have at their disposal definitive diagnostic tools that will confirm dyslexia or ADD/ADHD. Instead, they analyze a cluster of symptoms to make a diagnosis, prescribe treatment, or make a referral. If Irlen syndrome isn't on a doctor's radar screen at all, it will be completely overlooked as a possibility. And that's unfortunate, because sensitivity to aspects of light is more easily addressed than dyslexia and requires no psychostimulants.

There is tremendous room for confusion, as well as misdiagnosis and misdirection. Parents of children struggling to read must be vigilant and actively involved in the gathering of information and observations that may help professionals properly identify the barriers to reading and learning. Parents are in the best position to advocate for their children and observe telltale patterns. This is why we need that handy toolbox of resources at the ready.

So let's add a few more tools. This time, let's compare the classic symptoms of Irlen syndrome, dyslexia, and ADD/ADHD. A Chart of Common Traits of the three (pages 134–36) can help parents make an informed decision concerning how to proceed. Keep in mind that many of the symptoms listed may also be associated with conventional vision problems. It is essential that parents have their children tested by an optometrist or ophthalmologist first to rule out issues related to the function of the eyes. Also, headaches may have another, more serious source. If headaches are a problem, consult with a pediatrician or a family physician first to rule out serious health concerns.

If conventional examinations yield nothing, then the Chart of Common Traits is ready and available to help parents consider other possibilities. This is not medical advice. This chart provides traits parents can look for; that is its sole purpose. Also, a variety of circumstances may cause crossover in the traits. For example, a child who becomes physically uncomfortable after reading for fifteen minutes (a common trait of Irlen syndrome) may appear distractible (a common trait of ADD/ADHD). Once again, look for patterns, not absolutes. Also, children will manifest sensitivity to aspects of light and other learning issues differently. Whether the problem is Irlen syndrome, dyslexia, or ADD/ADHD, children will exhibit several of the traits in any given area, not necessarily all of the traits.

Chart of Common Traits

Trait	Irlen Syndrome	Dyslexia	ADD/ ADHD
PHYSICALLY OBSERVABLE			
Eyes burn, itch, or water	✓		
Experiences headache, stomachaches, or fatigue	✓	✓	✓
Rubs eyes frequently	✓		
Shades eyes while reading	✓		
Squints or blinks excessively	✓		
Tilts head to read	✓		
Physically fatigues quickly during reading (15 minutes, more or less)	✓		
Reads in dim light	✓		
Family history of strain with reading, light sensitivity, headaches, or migraine	✓		
READING PATTERN			
Skips words or whole lines during reading	✓	✓	✓
Loses place easily	✓	✓	✓
Is a slow reader	✓	✓	✓
Comprehension is poor	✓	✓	✓
Avoids reading or takes frequent breaks	✓	✓	✓
ISSUES OF VISUAL PERCEPTION			
Sees print as fuzzy or unstable	✓		
Mixes up numbers in math problems	✓	✓	

Trait	Irlen Syndrome	Dyslexia	ADD/ ADHD
Perceives visual distortions on the printed page	✓	✓	
Reads words that are upside down	✓	✓	
Experiences letter reversals	✓	✓	
Difficulty learning to tell time		✓	
ISSUES OF AUDITORY PERCEPTION			
Slow to learn connection between individual letters and sounds		✓	
Difficulty sounding out words and blending words together		✓	
Jumbles up syllables in spoken and written words		✓	
Was slow to learn to speak		✓	
Struggles to follow verbal directions		✓	✓
Talks excessively			✓
PRINTING/HANDWRITING (Issues commonly related with dysgraphia)			
Unequal letter size or spacing	✓	✓	✓
Difficulty writing on the line	✓	✓	✓
Poor handwriting; avoids cursive	✓	✓	✓
Awkward pencil grip		✓	
Prone to mirror writing (writing backwards)		✓	

Trait	Irlen Syndrome	Dyslexia	ADD/ ADHD
ACTIVITY			
Impulsive			✓
Energy is difficult to contain / in constant motion			✓
Blurts out answers before questions are finished			✓
Difficulty taking turns and with self-restraint			✓
Restless or daydreamy	✓	✓	✓
Struggles to complete homework	✓	✓	✓
PSYCHOSOCIAL			
Depressed, frustrated, or angry	✓	✓	✓
Poor sense of self and/or predisposition to depression or anxiety	✓	✓	✓
Difficulty making and keeping friends	✓	✓	✓

Where do most of your child's traits fall on the chart? The chart is designed to cluster traits in two ways—first, by type of trait, and second, by relationship to Irlen syndrome, dyslexia, *or* ADD/ADHD.

On the chart, it is easy to see that traits of Irlen syndrome frequently have observable characteristics—either physical symptoms or behavior. Arnold Wilkins notes that this is not always the case; sometimes children will test positive for visual stress yet communicate no physical complaints. In keeping with the International Dyslexia Association's definition, dyslexia typically affects both oral and written language. The traits related to ADD/ADHD center around an inability to focus one's attention, and according to experts, this pattern begins before the age of seven.

With the exception of mirror writing and being slow to speak, either Katie or Jacob at one time or another exhibited most of the entries on the chart. How did we sort through them? Carefully.

In our experience, children displaying several physically observable traits (eye rubbing, blinking, squinting, etc.) can be considered good candidates for Irlen syndrome. Also, researchers in Australia, England, and the United States have found that children with Irlen syndrome occasionally have parents or other close relatives who suffer from migraine headaches. If a child experiences physically observable traits *and* has a close relative who experiences chronic, unexplainable headaches, it may be worthwhile to have that child tested for Irlen syndrome.

For Katie, modifications of the light in her environment or tinted lenses work very well to calm visual distortions. They do not, however, help her with her difficulty with word attack. By solving *one* of the two problems (settling her visual distortions) and giving Katie a relatively small amount of help with the other (fifteen to twenty minutes twice a week on word attack), we restored Katie's ability to function independently in class and with homework.

With Katie, we also had to sort through the symptoms of ADD/ADHD. Were her attention issues related to brain chemistry, light sensitivity, or habit? We will never know for sure, but there are things to consider. At one point, Katie's pediatrician tried gradually elevated doses of Ritalin to help her focus. Over a period of a year, we noted no consistent difference in her ability to stay focused. Eventually, we determined that perhaps Katie had established a habit of daydreaming when work was dull or difficult, largely related to her early struggles with print. We tackled this habit head-on when she was in sixth grade, and by seventh, she overcame it—without any medication or outside support.

Without question, some children experience coexisting learning problems. Addressing one problem may help enough to bring a child a degree of school success. Addressing another is likely to result in even more success. So it goes until all the problems are addressed. Medical and educational professionals should not assume that one intervention will help all children, and parents can contribute to the identification of issues at the heart of a child's reading and learning problems. Color and the modification of light need to be among the available interventions.

13
SOLVING THE MYSTERY
OF IRLEN SYNDROME

If Irlen syndrome is neither dyslexia nor ADD, what is it?

In summary: It is likely a long overlooked reality of human physiology. It has been assumed for decades that lighting conditions have no effect on the visual system and brain, other than to cause us to perceive our environments as bright, dim, or dark. Recent studies, however, are revealing a host of new information about the human brain, color processing, and—yes—even light. For example, scientists are learning that brightness and color are processed in different parts of the brain. What does this duality mean when "color" is inherent in the "brightness" of every light source? Also, scientists are learning that the firing of nerve cells in the brain can be altered through a change in light color. What does this mean to a human brain that is hypersensitive to such changes? Definitive answers do not exist for either of these questions yet because few scientists are investigating the implications.

The mystery of Irlen syndrome will be solved when, on a large scale, science finally begins to pay attention to what has been right in front of its eyes all along. Light is not simply "bright"—every light source is loaded with "color." The human visual system and brain are wondrously designed to do something with every aspect of light, including light color. Scientists simply have not yet figured out all the ways in which light affects humans, and this leaves children who are hypersensitive to a narrow range of wavelengths and frequencies vulnerable to being misunderstood as having learning problems when, in reality, they have an undiagnosed problem with lighting conditions.

Irlen syndrome is a physiological problem with the brain. It is not a problem of vision, per se. How can we know this? There are at least three reasons:

1. Individuals with Irlen syndrome routinely pass tests for visual acuity and binocularity with no identifiable problems.

2. Scientists are continuing to investigate the mechanisms that contribute separately to motion detection and the firing of neurons in the brain. Scientific evidence indicates that color affects *both*.

3. Just like reading problems associated with light source, some photosensitive epileptic seizures and migraine headaches can be prevented through the use of tinted lenses specifically chosen for an individual's unique visual system. Studies documenting decreased incidence of photosensitive epilepsy and migraine among individuals prone to these problems have been successfully completed and reported in peer-reviewed journals.

Emerging theories about the cause or causes of Irlen syndrome do not answer an important question relative to reading. Why do some children with Irlen syndrome become capable readers, experiencing only fatigue and headaches with extended reading, while others report odd visual distortions that make it difficult for them to develop even basic reading skills? Is greater sensitivity to blame? Maybe—but maybe not. The answer may lie in the fact that reading experts do not yet know all that the human brain does when it reads.

READING AND THE HUMAN BRAIN

The February 2003 issue of the *Proceedings of the National Academy of Sciences, Early Edition* offers an excellent example of how far we still need to go to understand exactly what the human brain is doing when it reads. Using functional magnetic resonance imaging (fMRI), researchers at Stanford and Rutgers universities documented that brain activity in twenty children diagnosed with dyslexia could be changed to be more like that of excellent readers with Fast ForWord, a computerized language program developed to help readers with auditory processing skills. Supported by the study's images comparing the brains of excellent readers with those of struggling readers researchers point out that the intervention improves function in regions of the brain associated with phonological processing and provides a little benefit to other parts of the brain.

In the February 25, 2003, issue of *Stanford Report*, one of the researchers, John Gabrieli, draws this conclusion: "We see that the brains of these children are remarkably plastic and adaptive and it makes us hopeful that the best language intervention programs in the future can alter the brains in fundamentally helpful ways."

But Dr. Gabrieli adds that Fast ForWord is not "a one-shot vaccine." In spite of the success in improvements with auditory processing, the article notes, the children studied will continue to need considerable help in reading.

Of course they will. In the accompanying fMRI images, it is possible to see that the brains of these struggling readers did not become entirely like those of excellent readers. Children's brains changed significantly in relationship to auditory processing—the system Fast ForWord was designed to affect—but other regions were not necessarily significantly changed.

This would appear to provide additional evidence against the old idea that only auditory processing is different in children with reading problems. So, why do so many researchers remain focused on this single area of reading?

One possible answer: Problems with auditory processing are easy to identify and measure. Problems with other aspects of reading—such as issues in the visual processing centers of the brain, how the brain uses all of its accumulated knowledge in the reading process, and the role of motivation in reading development—are far more difficult to understand and measure. As a result, these aspects of reading are being ignored in favor of the more easily measured aspects, such as phonemic awareness and phonics.

As early as 1986, long before neuroimaging became a widely used tool for peering into the human brain to see what it does when it reads, a number of reading researchers talked about the impracticality of knowing all the "implicit" or subconscious processes engaged by the brain for reading. One researcher in particular developed a new methodology to address reading problems based in part on the works of world-renowned learning theorist Jean Piaget. Dolores R. Tadlock, Ph.D., published her conclusions and the basis for her methodology in 1986 in the journal *Reading Psychology* (7:183–195). In that article, Dr. Tadlock notes that the brain uses a complex system to read—and this system simultaneously integrates information and processes from multiple regions of the brain. In the process of doing so, the brain also integrates all of its accumulated knowledge, encoded chemically throughout the brain.

Reading, therefore, is not dependent upon a single region of the brain, as implied by focus only on the auditory processing system. Multiple regions are involved. Reading researchers know this; they simply have not yet figured out how all of the various regions are involved, how to measure what each does, or what each contributes to the reading process.

Dr. Tadlock may be the first to put it all together. In the late 1970s, while in the process of earning her Ph.D. in education with a reading emphasis, her own son developed a significant reading problem. Extensive remedial help did little to correct it. Dr. Tadlock spent the next three years exhaustively researching learning theory, reading theory, and brain development, in search of a solution. Equipped with a new understanding of how brains learn any process, Dr. Tadlock created a new methodology to address her son's problem. Through this new methodology, her ten-year-old son's reading problem was eliminated in just three months.

Dr. Tadlock thought she might be on to something and, for the next dozen years, further developed and tested the methodology with struggling readers in small schools and a community college in Washington State. With her reputation quietly growing, she was recruited in 1991 by private industry to try the methodology on adults who had faced a lifetime of reading failure, including adults diagnosed with severe dyslexia and other learning disabilities. Dr. Tadlock's methodology worked for them, too. Word of her success spread and, over the next seven years, she was hired by thirty private companies to remediate more than two thousand adult workers at eighty plant sites. Among the companies were industry giants such as Weyerhaeuser, Boeing, Motorola, International Paper, and Johnson & Johnson. Between 1998 and 2003, interest in her work grew within public education. In 2003, her methodology was being used by sixty schools to help improve the reading ability of more than 6,500 students.

Long before Dr. Gabrieli and other prominent researchers like him came to the conclusion that the brains of children with reading difficulties are "remarkably plastic and adaptive," Dr. Tadlock was proving that they are. It isn't even necessary to know how each region of the brain contributes to the reading process. It is only necessary to know that these regions must work together and that an appropriate neural network is needed to guide the process. Reading and brain experts have begun talking more actively about neural circuitry and its role in learning and reading in recent years. Dr. Tadlock referred to a properly functioning neural network to guide reading as early as 1995, when she mentioned it in an interview published in *Industry Week* magazine.

Our family learned about Irlen syndrome and light-based reading difficulties because a good school in our home state made a decision to try innovative strategies in order to help children with reading problems. Between 1998 and 2002, this school received several state and national honors for reading achievement. The latest came in February 2002 from Washington State's governor, Gary Locke. Specifically, the honor was bestowed on the school for exceptional improvement in Washington Assessment of Student Learning (WASL) reading test scores.

Union Gap School in Union Gap, Washington, is the kind of school where it is considered difficult to produce exceptional results in reading. Eighty-two percent of all students are eligible for free and reduced-price school lunches, and minority students represent 55 percent of the student body. The school also has an annual student turnover rate of more than 50 percent. In addition to colored overlays, Union Gap was using one other program at the time to help struggling readers: Dr. Tadlock's Read Right® methodology. Before Union Gap began using these two methodologies, less than 21 percent of its fourth graders passed the state-mandated WASL tests for reading. A year later, more than 54 percent of students passed the test. By 2001–2002, the number grew to 74 percent.

In spite of Union Gap's remarkable improvement in reading development, neither of the interventions it has used to achieve significant results for struggling readers is recommended to other schools by the state of Washington. Why? Because the state's education department will not recommend any reading program that does not involve explicit instruction in phonemic awareness and/or phonics, strategies intended to improve upon auditory processing in the brain. Colored overlays available for use in classrooms do not teach phonemic awareness or phonics. By design, they are intended to improve comfort and visual stability, involving the brain's visual processing centers. Dr. Tadlock's methodology does not involve explicit instruction in phonemic awareness or phonics, either. Instead, it creates a total environment in which the brain is compelled to restructure the neural circuitry that guides reading, and this neural circuitry involves the coordination of multiple regions of the brain, not just the auditory processing center.

Sad, isn't it? Innovative strategies are *working* to eliminate reading problems in adolescent struggling readers, and reading researchers will not look to see why, primarily because their focus continues to be on one processing system of the brain!

Varying severity of problems associated with Irlen syndrome may explain why some affected children become skilled readers, complaining only of headaches and fatigue, while others experience visual distortions that prevent them from developing even basic reading skills. But how neural circuitry is constructed to guide the reading process may be involved, as well. In essence, some children's brains may become "wired" incorrectly for reading, and hypersensitivity to lighting conditions may contribute to this erroneous wiring. This possibility brings with it urgency to address children's problems with lighting conditions as early as possible—before their neural circuitry becomes influenced by physical discomfort and instability associated with Irlen syndrome.

REMODELING NEURAL CIRCUITRY FOR READING

In Dr. Tadlock's methodology, prediction by the human brain plays a key role in reading development. For prediction, the brain may be subconsciously calling upon multiple regions of the brain. From the work of Jean Piaget, she explains, we know that infants learn by developing a concept of an end product (e.g., touching a mobile dangling above their heads), making an attempt, failing, analyzing the results, and subconsciously predicting how to change the next attempt so that it is more successful. From the day they are born, infants perform this cycle of prediction intuitively in order to develop muscle control, eye-hand coordination, and every other physiological and cognitive process they eventually use. From more recent advances in neuroimaging we know that, as humans learn, we form millions of neural networks to guide human activity.

Dr. Tadlock's methodology applies the subconscious cycle of prediction to reading development. Coupled with a concept of the end product (in this case, excellent reading) and unwavering intent to become an excellent reader, the cycle of prediction can compel individuals to subconsciously remodel a neural network into one designed to produce excellent reading.

If Dr. Tadlock is right, and her success with thousands of struggling readers implies she is, what might this mean to children who are impaired by lighting conditions? Four possibilities come to mind.

1. Children hypersensitive to lighting conditions are more likely to resist reading because reading doesn't "feel good."

2. When reading doesn't "feel good," children are less inclined to engage in the mental work that is required to form an efficient and effective neural network to guide reading. Jeffrey M. Schwartz, M.D., refers to the work needed to remodel neural circuitry as "mental force."

3. Abnormalities in what children with Irlen syndrome perceive may negatively influence the development of neural circuitry. The "rivers" or "waterfalls" individuals like Katie perceive offer a good example. When a brain becomes subconsciously overly focused on white spaces between words, made even brighter and more distracting by an individual's hypersensitivity to aspects of light, the individual may be unable to tune out the white spaces. As the brain hyperfocuses on these spaces, they connect with spaces above and below on the page, creating an illusion of vertical rivers of white up and down the page. Such visual disruption would make it difficult for the brain to integrate printed symbols (graphemes) quickly and efficiently with their related sounds (phonemes) during the complex act of reading. Such disruption would logically result in chemically encoded neural circuitry that is inefficient and ineffective.

    Think of it as the difference between two distinct systems of road maps: One map uses straight roads and bridges to get to a destination. The other map shows no bridges and takes a long and laborious course of detours in an attempt to get around canyons and rivers blocking the way. In this analogy, one map is efficient and effective; the other is tiring, frustrating, and potentially unsuccessful. Children need efficient and effective neural circuitry to guide the reading process.

4. Children who struggle with lighting conditions in the classroom appear to have a reading problem. To help them, teachers assign inter-

ventions that typically focus on phonemic awareness, phonics, and decoding words. None of these interventions addresses the child's problem with lighting conditions. Additionally, all three focus on a single aspect of reading—issues related to auditory processing, further diverting the brain's attention away from all of the things that must be done simultaneously to guide reading. The neural circuitry, therefore, becomes hyperfocused on yet another single aspect of reading. This time, rather than white spaces, the brain becomes overly focused on phonics.

Our son may be a good example of the latter. Jacob took off in his reading development as soon as he received his tinted lenses in the second grade. He quickly advanced from first-grade readers to third- and fourth-grade fiction. In the latter part of third grade, his improvement in reading appeared to slow. To be sure that he received everything he needed to continue to be able to read at or above grade level, we devoted the summer between third and fourth grades to what parents and educators are being told is the fundamental building block for reading: phonics. I worked with Jacob on "sounding out" strategies for new words and even had him work with phonics workbooks.

When he started the fourth grade, Jacob hit what reading specialists refer to as the "fourth-grade slump." His reading development stalled. Toward the end of the year, we enrolled him in a community program that used Dr. Tadlock's Read Right® methodology. There, volunteers used strategies quite the opposite from what I had done with Jacob at home. Children were never asked to "sound out" words. Instead, children were compelled to figure out text using predictive strategies involving all of their accumulated knowledge—or, put another way, they were encouraged to make connections to information stored in multiple regions of the brain.

Intriguingly, to this day, when Jacob begins to read aloud in an even slightly halting way, I use a subtle cue—"Read it again so you are more comfortable, Jake"—and, because of his Read Right training, this is enough to cause him subconsciously to stop paying attention to individual syllables and words and start predicting what is coming next in the text. When he does this, his oral reading instantly becomes smooth and efficient. Why does he continue to fall back into the old pattern for reading? Because, according to Dr. Tadlock, his brain still has access to the original neural network constructed to focus on phonics, and he slips naturally into it. Such regression is more commonly known as "habit."

Some children with Irlen syndrome develop good reading skills in spite of their sensitivity to lighting conditions. Their problems simply manifest differently—in the form of eyestrain, headaches, fatigue, and slow reading. With colored overlays or tinted lenses, these children will become comfortable and efficient readers immediately. In Dr. Tadlock's paradigm, this is possible because, prior to receiving properly selected color, these children had already formed efficient and effective neural circuitry to guide reading, possibly because they learned to read in lighting conditions that were comfortable for them.

Other children, however, will not show immediate improvement in reading ability when aided by colored overlays or tinted lenses. They are, however, able to perform complex nonreading visual tasks with greater speed, comfort, and visual stability. The reason they do not instantly become better readers is that such children have not yet formed appropriate neural circuitry to guide smooth and efficient reading. They will require the right environment to remodel their neural circuitry for excellent reading.

The business of reading is highly complex. Anyone who thinks that a single "magic bullet" will solve every child's reading problem is grossly misinformed. Where color is concerned, it must be put into proper perspective—by parents, classroom teachers, and even reading researchers. Color improves comfort and visual stability; it does not teach children to read. By itself, it cannot cause a child to construct efficient and effective neural circuitry to guide the reading process.

Color *can*, however, remove a barrier to reading development in children who are hypersensitive to lighting conditions and, in young children, it may prevent neural circuitry from being inappropriately formed.

Humans are wonderfully designed to be different one from another. Not too long from now, it likely will be proven that one of the ways in which we differ is how our visual systems and brains react biologically and biochemically to the physical properties that exist within light. Solving the mystery of Irlen syndrome requires new respect for the ways in which humans differ—it *is* that simple.

part III

HELPING OUR KIDS

HELPING OUR KIDS HELPING OUR KIDS

THE RIGHT WAY
TO GET HELP

When and how is a new science born?

I've spoken to many people about Katie's and Jacob's success with color. Reactions have varied from fascination to that glazed-over look people get when they can't believe something could possibly be true.

A brief conversation caused a teacher I know to think of one of her students. She decided to try turning off a bank of overhead fluorescent lights for the boy. Weeks later I heard from both the teacher and the student's mother that the boy's reading appeared to improve. As far as I know, the child was never formally tested for sensitivity to aspects of light.

A man I talked to decided to experiment at home with a few transparent sheets of colored plastic. When he couldn't make color work for him by playing with it, he dismissed the whole thing as a sham.

A few parents I know decided to have their children tested by Irlen screeners and were brought to tears by what they learned. I remember that feeling—a mixture of confusion, relief, frustration, and awe. Another mom I met had her daughter tested and was sent home with a set of colored overlays. A few weeks later the mom shared that her daughter hadn't benefited much from the overlays, but then acknowledged that she hadn't had much time or opportunity to encourage her daughter to use them, either.

There is a lot of confusion about this color thing and perhaps it shouldn't be so surprising. In contemporary culture, color is something we play with—in how we dress, decorate our homes, and plant our gardens. It's *only* color. Slap some yellow here, dab a little red there, splash a bright spot of blue on the side. From the time we can open a jar of tempera paint, our fingers are playing with color. It is not something we would readily think of to resolve issues of perception and the brain. It makes sense, then, that we struggle to understand color for what it truly is—an important aspect of science, not just the visual paint we use to create beauty for our minds.

Indeed, if Katie had been the only child in our family who experienced physical discomfort and visual distortions because of aspects of light, it is likely we may have given up on color after the first six months. By accommodating for sensitivity to brightness, color took away Katie's red eyes and fatigue immediately (when she followed instructions and wore her tinted lenses), but the first try did not significantly help her classroom reading and comprehension. For a variety of reasons, including lack of significant progress in reading and not wanting to be different from her peers, Katie was not motivated to wear her first set of tinted lenses. At the six-month mark, there were few reasons to keep Katie in tints.

In another classroom, however, Jacob was wearing his colored lenses faithfully and making progress in reading. His "monsters" were gone and he was becoming more social again. His teacher noticed—it would have been hard not to. Jacob went from resistant reader and writer to noticeably more cooperative. Without Jacob's very different experience, we probably would have written off tinted lenses as a possible solution to Katie's problems with print. We didn't, though, and a few months later an added tint moved Katie from near failure to a homework champ.

Jacob needed to be tested only once for proper lens color. Katie required more effort. Matching color of tint to a child or adult who is sensitive to aspects of light is as much a science as matching the type and quantity of medication to someone who, say, has thyroid disease. Doctors frequently go through months of trial and error to figure out just how much medication to give patients whose thyroids do not produce enough natural hormone. It can be a delicate process. Then there is the whole other matter of getting the patient to actually *take* the once- or twice-a-day pills. I know. I was once the world's worst patient.

A tall and imposing doctor once said to me, "Your medication won't do you any good sitting on the shelf. *Take it.*" I'm embarrassed to say it took a good eight years to get into a regular habit of taking thyroid hormone, and then it was only because my thyroid had completely shut down to the point that it had to be removed. I *loathed* the idea of being only twenty-nine years old and dependent upon a drug for the rest of my life.

People are like that. We react differently to the twists and turns that we encounter in life. Whether it is a matter of physiology or psychology, we don't all react or respond in the same way.

The prescription of specific colors to calm physical discomfort and visual distortions may be every bit as much an art and science as the prescription of thyroid medication. It requires skill, a specific process, careful observation, and thoughtful analysis of information to produce optimum results. Because we think of color in terms of red, green, yellow, or blue, it is easy to forget that there are *thousands* of hues within the spectrum and that hues represent specific properties of energy when light is involved. There is plenty of evidence to suggest that individuals experiencing success with color respond best to a narrow and specific *range* of hue (often involving a mix of color)—*not* a randomly selected hue.

Practitioners who learn how to help individuals choose color are taught to ask the right questions and interpret body language as much as words during testing. What a child thinks is his or her favorite color and the actual color it takes to address issues are two completely different things. I met a nice man recently who wears tinted lenses in a beautiful shade of electric rose. Is that the color he would have chosen to complement his wardrobe? No, but it's the color that his brain needs to feel comfortable during focused visual tasks.

What about research that continues to be contradictory? Some studies say color works, others say it doesn't. You will find a list of positive and negative studies at the back of this book. They are provided for you so that you may do some reading on your own. This book is not intended to be your only source of information as you consider a decision about color. It is intended to share what our family learned about Irlen syndrome, reading, light, and color; offer a process through which you may include professionals in your decision-making; and offer resources that will help you make a decision you feel is in the best interest of your child. Color doesn't help every child, but it does help *some* children.

One factor does seem to be missing from any of the research for or against color: a sufficient respect for light source. I have yet to find a study in which subjects are tested for the lighting type that causes them the most problems (it can vary from person to person) and for that type of light to be used to test reading ability with and without color. In some studies, researchers even dimmed the lights or used full-spectrum fluorescent lights, a higher quality fluorescent tube that causes fewer problems for some light-sensitive individuals. Furthermore, full-spectrum light is not the type of fluorescent light typically used in children's classrooms.

Some skeptics express concern that colored overlays and tinted lenses are owned and sold commercially by the individuals studying them. For medicines, drug companies hold patents for the products they develop for a certain number of years. Eventually, the patents expire. Then other companies may develop products based upon their research and findings. The same could be said for the tools and methodologies developed to properly determine the tint needs of individuals sensitive to aspects of light.

We are indeed talking about a science, a unique and special science requiring knowledge and careful skill to apply. As a family, we tried to play with color; dime-store purple glasses for Jacob did not work nearly as well as specifically prescribed tinted lenses. Trying to add color to a set of Katie's lenses that were not quite right was a frustrating exercise in trial and error. Only carefully determined color produced the kind of results she needed.

There is a right way and a wrong way to explore the connection between light and color. And the right way begins with recognizing the concept as a *science*. Once it is regarded as a science, perhaps it will become widely accepted that there is a right way to have individuals tested. In the meantime, parents will want to look for the best screening options available. Before taking that step, however, it is important to rule out other possible causes for reading difficulties. It is also important to be aware that sensitivity to aspects of light may not be the only barrier facing a child.

All of this requires an organized process and involves *all* the professions we normally would expect to support us in our efforts to identify learning difficulties in a child. Here are the steps our family took.

STEP 1. A VISIT TO THE DOCTOR

A logical first step is to consult with a child's physician. Because we didn't know anything about sensitivity to aspects of light, such a label did not enter into discussions with our children's pediatrician. The physical symptoms associated with such sensitivity, however, were discussed. In Katie's case, that included frequent fatigue, headaches, and nausea. Such symptoms can be associated with serious health problems, so children with such complaints need to be examined by a physician.

Katie's medical file is almost an inch thick. In addition to off-and-on struggles with headaches, nausea, and fatigue, it details problems with allergies, asthma, and at times weight gain, but does not fully outline what our family knows about Katie. She tends to be more sensitive to everything—light, sound, allergens, smells, tastes, and touch. By the time we were introduced to Irlen syndrome, she had been seen many times by her doctor. Only allergies and asthma, an unusual pattern in her antinuclear antibodies (related to the immune system), and occasional low-normal levels of thyroid production were ever found. Most of her health complaints were related to fatigue, headaches, and susceptibility to viral and bacterial infections.

There are only a few pages in the medical file for Jacob. Except for light and occasional annoyances caused by shirt tags and sock seams, he is less sensitive than Katie and more robust. He does not experience problems with allergies or asthma and he never developed chronic problems with headaches or fatigue. Ask him to go without his glasses today, though, and he will say no—it hurts his eyes and gives him a headache.

Some may call this difference between our children a matter of personality. I don't. Katie continues to battle with occasional allergy-induced rashes and asthma, can hear sirens a second ahead of anyone in our family, and would make a wonderful chef because her senses of smell and taste are so keen. Jacob hardly even notices such things. Yet Jacob is the one we seldom see out of his tinted lenses.

Helen Irlen says such differences between individuals sensitive to aspects of light are common. Irlen syndrome can coexist with other learning issues and sensitivities, or it can be the only issue. In our family, we have one of each. Perhaps one day science will understand why.

STEP 2. A VISIT TO A VISION PROFESSIONAL

Visual acuity and general health of the eyes are vital to the ability to read and function successfully in school. Only an optometrist or an ophthalmologist, through comprehensive screening, can tell you for certain whether your child's abilities to focus and converge are up to par; vision screening in schools does not necessarily catch all issues.

In recent years, both ophthalmologists and optometrists have warned that problems associated with vision can contribute to ADD or ADHD-like symptoms. Yet this information is not widely known by parents or teachers.

In the United States, a couple of states now require thorough vision assessment for all children entering school. This is a concept worthy of support. It may, however, also open the door for misunderstanding about a child's ability to perceive the printed page.

As it relates to sensitivity to light, brightness, glare, and dark/bright contrast, those things associated with Irlen syndrome, there are several important facts to keep in mind about contemporary vision screening:

- Standard vision screening does not check specifically for problems associated with Irlen syndrome or how the brain reacts to light and perceives the printed page.

- Conditions typical of reading (dense text and normal room light) are not a routine part of vision screening.

- Some optometrists will recommend vision therapy when reading issues cannot be linked to visual acuity.

When our children's reading problems first became apparent, they passed conventional vision screening with only modest reservations. Jacob had a minor difficulty with color discrimination (pink rather than red) and Katie had a slight problem with distance vision that was so minor her optometrist recommended against correction. Additionally, although we told Katie's optometrist of her difficulties in school, she was not referred for vision therapy.

I cannot comment on the effectiveness of vision therapy. Like colored lenses, the American Academy of Pediatrics and American Association of Pediatric Ophthalmology and Strabismus recommend against it. Vision therapy's proponents say that studies documenting its effectiveness are being ignored. I have seen accounts and spoken with parents who both sing its praises and criticize its lack of effectiveness.

I can tell you approximately how much it costs. One family I know paid $80 per session. For twenty sessions, the cost was $1,600. This family saw improvement and is grateful to vision therapy for the results. But other families whose children later tested positive for Irlen syndrome did not find vision therapy beneficial.

Varied results may provide further evidence that there are multiple
issues involved in the ability to perceive a page of text. More information
about vision therapy is available at the Parents Active for Vision Education
Web site at www.pave-eye.com. Know, however, that as late as 2002, this
organization did not recognize light-based reading difficulties as an issue.

STEP 3. READING INSTRUCTION

In the United States, debate rages over the best way to teach reading. In the
1970s, "whole language," or familiarization with printed words within the
context of their meaning, emerged as the popular methodology. In 2001,
however, after a review of available studies, the National Reading Panel
issued recommendations that school-based reading programs use a balanced approach, inclusive of several key components: phonemic awareness, phonics, fluency, vocabulary, and comprehension.

So, which is right? Many teachers are just as confused by the debate. For
years, they have included phonemic awareness and phonics as part of early
reading instruction. Many teachers deeply involved in whole language even
included phonics in the early teaching of reading. With either method, a
large number of children still continue to struggle to develop reading skills.

This poses a dilemma for many parents. Are problems associated with
reading the fault of a physical barrier to reading? Or is inadequate reading
instruction the cause? This was one more issue we had to sort through to
determine the best course of action for our children.

Reassured that Katie's and Jacob's overall health and vision were fine,
naturally we began to look at reading skills and reading instruction. The
kids' schools were heavily vested in the whole language method at the
time. Limited instruction was provided in phonics. At home, I attempted
to compensate by encouraging the kids to concentrate on word parts
instead of just whole words. Even with this encouragement, Katie continued to mispronounce simple words, jump over whole words, or drift from
one word in a line of text to a word on a line directly above or below. Her
reading at the time was labored and unstable.

Jacob was doing better with grade-level reading, but he hadn't yet progressed to dense text. He was only a few months behind his peers, but
showing increasing signs of resistance to reading.

The added focus on phonics did not help. Both Katie and Jacob knew
their phonics—they knew what word sounds went with individual letters

or with combinations of them. Additionally, we spent one summer focusing on phonics with the help of workbooks. Katie's reading level did improve significantly that summer, but she will tell you it was because she started reading in dim light. Her word attack skills did not improve. Jacob showed no signs of reading improvement with the aid of phonics.

The debate over the best way to teach reading is likely to continue for years. It stands to reason, however, that whatever method is used, children who are sensitive to aspects of light need to have their sensitivity addressed in order to benefit fully from whichever method of instruction is used. Otherwise, what may be a problem with lighting conditions may be misinterpreted as a reading problem, causing children to receive more emphasis on a single aspect of reading development completely unrelated to the source of the problem. According to Dolores Tadlock, Ph.D., whose work has focused on the formation of efficient and effective neural networks to guide reading (as was discussed in chapter 13), such emphasis has the potential to cause children to believe subconsciously that reading is only about a single aspect of reading, e.g., decoding. There is sufficient scientific evidence to indicate that reading is a process involving many subconscious activities and not any single skill.

STEP 4. USING PATTERNS TO IDENTIFY BARRIERS

Once issues related to medicine and visual acuity can be ruled out as sources of a child's difficulties, four tools are provided in this book to help identify patterns in a child's ability to read and function in a classroom. These tools represent a mental process our family worked through as we tried to identify our children's barriers to reading.

The Checklist of Observations in Chapter 8 is designed to initiate thinking about how and when reading discomfort or difficulties emerge. The Reading Inventory and the Inventory of Physical Symptoms in Chapter 11 are designed to help separate the differences between skill and physical issues associated with reading. It is important to be able to identify the differences between these two in order to use the fourth and final tool, the Chart of Common Traits, located in Chapter 12.

Putting together the pattern of clues in Katie's development in elementary school could have helped us seek intervention. Because there was nothing available to help us make sense of the information, however, the clues did not come together in a useful fashion. For example, Katie's optometrist tested her for visual acuity and vergence, but not for how she perceived text on a printed page. Potentially helpful information about her trouble reading, eyestrain, and headaches had no relevance because her visual acuity and vergence were fine. Katie's teachers observed that she had difficulty staying on task, signs of delayed reading, and poorly developed handwriting and printing, but they would not have known what to do with Katie's complaints of vision problems, nor information about periodic trips to the pediatrician for concerns related to fatigue, headaches, and strain.

Back then, before we knew what to look for, all we could do was ask questions and try to make sense of answers. Of her doctor: "Why are Katie's eyes turning red? Why does she get so tired in class?" Of her optometrist: "Are you sure a problem with her vision isn't getting in the way of reading?" Of her teachers: "Why isn't Katie's handwriting progressing? Why should homework take hours instead of just minutes?" Parents can put all the pieces together, but tools are needed to help us make sense of it all and the tools must address all the possibilities. General labels such as "unmotivated" or "distractible" or vague diagnoses such as "learning difficulties" have the potential to mask a specific problem, such as light sensitivity.

I invite you to use the checklist, the inventories, and the Chart of Common Traits. If possible, do so in conjunction with your child's teacher. She or he may observe traits your child demonstrates at school that you do not see at home. Why? It all goes back to the culprit causing the problem for sensitive children—the type of light in places where we ask them to read and work.

If your child's teacher knows little or nothing about visual perception and the potential impact of aspects of light, she or he may discount the connection between color and light. An alternative technique in this case is to simply ask a teacher to watch for certain things—fatigue, attitude about reading, length of focus on reading task, eye rubbing, blinking, etc. Most teachers will gladly watch for and share this information with you.

Once the information is gathered, see if a pattern emerges. What happens next is entirely up to you. If your child shows many traits typical of Irlen syndrome, dyslexia, or ADD/ADHD, consult with the appropriate professionals about testing. Any of these conditions could mean another visit with your child's doctor or other professionals. The checklist, inventories, and Chart of Common Traits are available to take with you, but keep in mind it is possible your child's physician and vision professional may not be aware of Irlen syndrome. If they are, they may not support it as a diagnosis. Consider such a scenario an opportunity to explain in concise terms your concerns as well as to educate them about Irlen syndrome.

Becoming knowledgeable about Irlen syndrome, dyslexia, and ADD/ADHD can help you sort through the various issues and better communicate with your child's physician and vision professional. The following Web sites can help you become better informed. Some can even help to locate resources in your area for screening.

For Irlen Syndrome:

www.Irlen.com, managed by Helen Irlen and the Irlen Institute, offers information and a composite list of professionals using the Irlen method for screening available in North America and thirty other countries. A list of published studies is available at this Web site.

www.essex.ac.uk/psychology/overlays, managed by Arnold Wilkins. This Web site provides general information under the term Meares-Irlen syndrome. Information on published studies, including a few downloadable papers, is available.

www.ceriumvistech.co.uk, managed by Cerium Technologies, the company tinting lenses via the Wilkins method, offers information and a composite list of professionals using new technology available in the United Kingdom and a growing number of other countries.

www.readingandlight.com, managed by Irlen screeners Julie and Jeff Evans. This Web site was originally created for residents of the state of Minnesota, but offers plenty of basic information on Irlen syndrome. Many similar Web sites in other regions of the world are managed by other Irlen screeners. These can be located by performing an Internet search on the term "Irlen."

For Dyslexia:

www.pacer.org, managed by the Parent Advocacy Coalition for Education Resource (PACER Center), provides a listing of learning centers equipped with dyslexia resources in most states in the U.S.

www.disabilityresources.org, for residents of the U.S., provides helpful information from the DRM (Disability Resource Monthly) Guide to Disabilities.

www.ldac-taac.ca, for residents of Canada, provides helpful information from the Learning Disabilities Association of Canada.

www.dyslexia-parent.com, an international resource, provides extensive information about dyslexia, including innovations and advancements.

www.interdys.org. Formerly the Orton Society, the International Dyslexia Association hosts this site, designed to provide parents with a variety of information and opportunities for information exchange. The International Dyslexia Association does not support Irlen syndrome as a diagnosis.

For ADD/ADHD:

www.nimh.nih.gov, a service of the National Institute of Mental Health, provides excellent information in a question-and-answer format. When you reach the site, search on "ADD" or "ADHD."

www.chadd.org, managed by Children and Adults with Attention Deficit/ Hyperactivity Disorder, provides well-rounded information, including recommendations for diagnostic standards.

www.add.org. Geared more toward addressing ADD and ADHD in adults, this site is managed by the National Attention Deficit Disorder Association.

STEP 5. SEEK COMPREHENSIVE ACADEMIC SCREENING

Some families will reach this step much sooner than we did. Logically, one might think it would be first on the list, not last. There are several reasons for its position on our family's list.

It has to do with that snowball we call Katie. Academic progress in Katie's early years was fine. There were no obvious delays. But schoolwork became more difficult for her with each passing year.

We decided to do comprehensive screening for special education program eligibility in the winter of sixth grade largely because Katie was still having trouble with attention issues in one of her teacher's classes. It was one of the most insightful processes we undertook that year. The two subjects she struggled with most were math and reading. We wanted to know why Katie was capable of reading grade-level fiction and exactly where she was in terms of skill development.

The Woodcock-Johnson Tests of Achievement, Revised, are a standard evaluation instrument used to determine academic placement in special education programs. What we learned was that Katie's reading comprehension—fairly low just a year before—had become one of Katie's strengths. At mid-year sixth grade, Katie tested nearly a full year above grade level. The school psychologist also performed a brief check of Katie's reading ability with and without her tinted lenses.

"Katie performed markedly different," the school psychologist wrote, "with her Irlen filter glasses. Her rate and fluency improved significantly when she read from a textbook."

In math, Katie demonstrated mixed results. The ability to calculate was right on grade level, but she fell a year or more behind when it came to word problems.

The obvious pattern that emerged through comprehensive testing was that Katie had made great strides in reading comprehension, but continued to have difficulty with skills required to organize language and express it in print. Problems with auditory-related dyslexia could be the source. But we have considered another possibility. The core skills needed to perform math word problems and to move language from the brain to print are taught and developed in the first through fourth grades. It is possible that the three or so key developmental years during which Katie endured physical stress and visual distortions interfered with the learning normally done in those years. Such learning would include skills related to solving math word problems, as well as word attack skills.

It was agreed that Katie did not need special education services. Even so, comprehensive testing helped us pinpoint the sources of Katie's continued learning challenges and helped us understand where she needed additional support. Parents can investigate the possibility of testing with their children's schools. If a school is not supportive, parents can contact state or regional resources to find out their rights to academic screening.

15
FOR PARENTS

I love my daughter's smile. These days it lights up her face; a single dimple dotting her expression like a period on the end of a sentence. Katie grew six and a half inches in height in the two years we worked to understand her reading issues. She now stands more than an inch taller than me.

Childhood is like a favorite song—sweet, but all too brief. Children grow up, and each day we spend with them enriches both them and us. Without question, every single day *matters*.

Sometimes things don't turn out the way we think they will. My husband and I never expected Katie to have difficulty with school. We encouraged Katie from the time she was small to think big about her future. We encouraged her to believe she could become anything she wanted to be. We didn't offer a list of possibilities because that would have been too confining. From the time she was in first grade, Katie dreamed of becoming a veterinarian.

She held on to that dream for more than three years. I didn't take her seriously at first. Kids go through so many "careers" when they are growing up—fireman, nurse, teacher, dancer, doctor, etc. But Katie was serious. She had both the heart and the stomach for it. We happened along a poor snow-white cat once that had just been hit by a car and Katie didn't even flinch. She asked me to stop so we could make sure nothing could be done for it because, she explained, vets needed to be able to do that kind of thing.

In the fifth grade, Katie let go of the dream. She was struggling with school and thought it impossible. In a whisper she said to me, "Mom, I don't think I can be a vet. I'm not smart enough."

You're smart enough, sweetheart. Smart enough, compassionate enough, and a hard worker. Your brain processes language differently—that's all.

I have two children who wear tinted lenses, one some of the time and one all of the time. One had his problem identified early (second grade) and is doing well in school. The other was caught late, after several years of having her brain wired by the stress of room light and bright pages that caused her to experience a jumble of unstable words. She is doing much better now because she understands the importance of light in her environment. She compensates for it by turning the lights out, shading the page, or wearing tinted lenses.

I will always wonder whether early identification of Katie's problem might have wired her brain a little differently. If she hadn't experienced physical discomfort and visual distortions when she was very young, would she have some of the challenges she has today? I don't know. And science doesn't know for certain, either, because it has not fully investigated how aspects of light may cause some brains to react in a way that causes physical stress or perceptual distortions. In fact, most scientists don't even think light-based reading problems exist.

Remember James, the teen who was held back a grade and struggling in an alternative school? His mother tells me he is doing much better. The chronic headaches, stomachaches, and fatigue are gone, and after fourteen months in tinted lenses, he is returning to a regular high school. Way to go, James. Soon, few people will know James is sensitive to light. He plans to begin using a pair of custom-tinted contact lenses matching the hue of his glasses. Like Katie, though, James has residual issues with spelling and handwriting. But he can read for comprehension and meaning now at his grade level, and that skill alone will make a huge difference in his ability to be successful in school.

There is plenty of evidence to suggest that developing brains become wired according to the stimuli they receive. Infants born with cataracts, for example, undergo surgery immediately because, if vision is blocked in infants for too long, their brains do not complete the important connections necessary for visual perception to occur.

What might this mean for kids like Katie? Do young brains "wire" themselves to process dense text? If so, what is the long-term effect if this "wiring" includes physical stress and visual distortions?

They are chilling questions that some will dismiss. But, until science looks specifically at the issues, we won't know for sure how long-term exposure to visual stress and distortions may affect people like Katie and James.

Sensitivity to aspects of light isn't a cataclysmic health crisis. It is, instead, an invisible barrier to physical comfort and reading success. If ignored, it can *become* catastrophic for a child whose self-esteem and self-worth are shaped by school failure.

Color filtration used as overlays or worn as glasses or contact lenses is one way to address sensitivity to aspects of light. There are other ways that cost little to nothing. Avoiding or modifying problem light is one method. For decades, some individuals who instinctively knew they were sensitive to brightness, glare, or dark/bright contrast have dimmed the lights at home or preferred incandescent desk lamps at work. Unaware of Irlen syndrome, they didn't know *why* they preferred such light.

The following mix of strategies to use at home won't resolve issues for children struggling with reading as a result of light; but they can help. Katie and Jacob are good examples. These strategies work for Katie; they do not work for Jacob. The strategies are worth trying, however, to see if they can help.

1. **Encourage children to experiment with lighting.** If a child chooses a dim corner for reading, ask him why he chose that spot. If he says he likes it better or it is more comfortable, try an experiment. Move him to a variety of brighter locations (for example, under direct dining room light, under kitchen fluorescent light) and ask him how he feels about each. Listen for language that indicates comfort—not problems with vision or visual perception. The only thing Katie ever told us was that she was more comfortable or could read better in shadows rather than direct light.

2. **Observe the difference lighting makes in the length of time your child is willing to read.** If a child is more receptive to reading silently in one favorite spot in the house, there may be a reason. Don't discourage her from using this location. Regard it, instead, as an opportunity to observe her reading patterns under other types of light. Ask her to spend some time reading directly under incandescent light (the standard lightbulb) and under fluorescent light. Observe how much time

USING THE COLOR IN LIGHT

Suggestions offered here are derived from basic science and information provided by individuals sensitive to aspects of light.

✳ We think of sunlight as yellow. In fact, by the time it reaches us, it contains a great deal of blue. Some children who perform better with text filtered by blue also perform better with indirect or diffuse natural light as the light source. To improve the effect, experiment with turning off artificial light sources and partially closing window shades. Doing so deepens the blue and adds gray to room light.

✳ Fluorescent light varies in color depending upon the type of tube, age, phosphor, and firing mechanism. Therefore, it is unpredictable. Where multiple fluorescent tubes are used, high quality ballasts and the same model of tube should be used in every fixture. Individual tubes should not vary in color (you can tell by looking directly at the ends of illuminated tubes)— variation causes complications for light-sensitive individuals. To increase comfort, replace tubes and ballasts as soon as signs of weakened color or increased flicker appear.

✳ Incandescent light is warmer, leaning toward yellow and yellow-orange. Individuals whose visual systems benefit from these colors tend to prefer to read by incandescent light. Try experimenting with brightness as well as indirect vs. direct lighting until maximum comfort is achieved. If a child is willing to read longer in dimmer light, it is an indicator that such light is more comfortable to them.

💻 Computer and television screens flicker at a rate that is not supposed to be perceptible to the human visual system. Studies indicate, however, that some individuals are more sensitive to flicker. To reduce irritation, reduce brightness on computer screens. The next tip comes directly from Katie: try changing the background or page color of your computer screen. Her favorite color is a deep blue background with soft yellow print. In Microsoft Windows, go to the Control Panel, then to Display, then to Appearance. Here, choose the most comfortable Scheme and set the Item to Window. Then set the Color you prefer (click on "Other" for additional color choices). Once you do this, the background of your word-processing software will default to the colors chosen. Be sure to play with different hues and saturations. Even slight variation can make a difference. Caution: If you are sensitive to aspects of light, one or more background colors may stress your visual system. If you develop eyestrain, headache, or fatigue with a new background color, choose another.

NOTE: *Not all people sensitive to light benefit from these strategies. Some do. It all depends upon the sensitivity.*

she is willing to spend reading under each. If she is inclined to read longer in a favorite spot, observe the conditions in that location. What is the lighting like? Is it direct or indirect? Is it bright or dim? Lighting may be the very reason she chose this particular location.

3. **Observe the difference lighting makes in your child's homework patterns—for example, your child's ease in finding answers to chapter questions.** When Katie began to struggle, we moved her from doing homework in her bedroom, where she had instinctively figured out how to control the amount and type of light that reflected off her book pages, to the kitchen table. In our house, the kitchen table is in a dinette area and illuminated by six small 40-watt bulbs. Right over Katie's shoulders, however, is the kitchen, where four fluorescent tubes brightly light the room. When Katie began to struggle in school, we unwittingly moved her from lighting that made it *easier* for her to do her work (her bedroom) to the type of light that interferes with her ability to read efficiently (a mix of direct incandescent and bright fluorescent light). Because of the fluorescent tubes, light at our kitchen table is similar to the type of light used in Katie's classrooms. We moved our daughter in order to help her, not having a clue that some children are sensitive to aspects of light, including brightness, the color within light, and bright/dark contrast from a reflected image. If

we had known, we would have encouraged Katie to do her homework where she was the most comfortable.

Parents can observe this in their children by observing how they function under certain types of light. Once again, encourage a child to experiment with homework under different lighting conditions. Simply ask him where it is most comfortable for him to work. If he chooses a spot that is very dim, don't immediately move him into a brighter location. Instead, observe how fast and efficiently he works. Compare his progress under his preferred lighting conditions with how he works under other types of light. And *listen* to him if he tells you one light source is more comfortable than another.

4. **Don't experiment with color filtration; have children properly tested.** Playing with color can actually be detrimental to a child. Both Katie and Jacob react adversely to certain colors of tints. For Jacob it is pure red. For Katie it is anything other than blue-gray, and more specifically, a gray in the sea green or aqua range. Inappropriate color can cause physical symptoms, including strain, headaches, nausea, and irritability. It can mask the fact that a specific color will benefit a child. Children who demonstrate traits of sensitivity should be properly tested. If it is not possible, encourage them to modify the light in their environment. Additional ideas for helping light-sensitive children are provided in Chapter 15, "For Professionals."

5. **Encourage your child to use colored overlays correctly.** There are three basic issues to watch for where overlays are concerned: glare, proper color, and peer pressure.

Glare is a common problem with overlays. Overhead light can bounce directly off the surface and cause glare. Complicating this problem, though, is the likelihood that children with Irlen syndrome are more sensitive to glare than other people. This hypersensitivity occurs in varying degrees. This means that you may not be able to see glare that your child can perceive on an overlay. This makes it very important to ask a child regularly how the print looks through the overlay. If the child says "not very good," go the next step and ask why. "It's too bright" is an indication that the overlay is either the wrong color for the child or the child is perceiving glare. Help the child reposition the overlay to see whether a reduction in glare makes it more effective. If it does, remind the child to always position overlays to minimize glare. Overlays are not very effective if children must struggle with glare.

Proper color of an overlay for a child is determined by two factors: the needs of a child's unique visual system and brain, and the dominant color that is inherent within a light source. This means that changes in either can influence the effectiveness of assigned overlays. As Dr. Robinson has reported, there appears to be a biochemical basis for Irlen syndrome. Consequently, changes in biochemistry may be a reason some children require color changes from time to time. Additionally, every time a child changes classrooms, lighting conditions change, and this change can influence the effectiveness of overlays. It is important, therefore, to check regularly with a child to see whether overlay color continues to be appropriate. Sometimes, a modest change is needed. Other times a more dramatic change is required. Children who use multiple layers of overlays can be taught to adjust the layers so that they are most effective under specific lighting conditions. For example, if a child needs three layers of overlays for the regular classroom, lighting conditions in a reading room may be different and better addressed with only one or two layers.

Peer pressure can have a tremendous impact on a child's desire to use overlays, regardless of how much the overlays benefit the child. In October 2002 I became a certified Irlen screener. I did so for several reasons: to be a better parent advocate for children and families and to continue to learn more about light-based learning difficulties and color. I accept no fees for the screening I do. To date, I've screened several dozen children and have observed that they fall into two distinct categories: those who don't care what peers think when it comes to overlays and those who are socially "hyper-aware," meaning they are deeply affected by the perception of their peers. These children tend to be highly resistant to using overlays because they are fearful of being singled out by their peers. Such children can be encouraged to use overlays, but they should not be forced to do so. Other alternatives should be sought, e.g., modifying light directly above the child or allowing them to do their reading at home, where they can modify lighting conditions or use overlays. It is fairly easy to determine how a child will feel about using overlays by asking a few simple questions: "If one of your classmates says, 'What's that?' [referring to the overlay] what will you tell them?" And then, "If one of your classmates says, 'That's weird,' how will you feel?" I ask these questions of children being screened as a matter of routine—I learned from my own children how important they are. Jacob's answer: "I don't care. I need it." Katie's answer: "Well, I won't feel comfortable, and so I'll only use color when I absolutely need it." Answers like the latter give parents the opportunity to talk to their children about overlay use and peer pressure. It is an important discussion for every parent to have with a son or daughter.

Finally, consider overlays a piece of equipment your child uses to improve school performance. This means that overlays need to be examined occasionally for condition and quality. An overlay that is badly scratched or scuffed needs to be replaced. Parents need to stay on top of this; otherwise, it may go unnoticed. Overlays are inexpensive, costing about $3 per sheet.

6. **Children control how and when colored overlays or tinted lenses are used.** It is hard to be different. Your child may experience internal or external pressure not to use overlays or tinted lenses. Katie continues to struggle with both internal and external pressure. The internal pressure arises from not wanting to be different. The external pressure comes from skeptical children and adults who don't understand her need and question how she chooses to use her lenses.

Children need their parents' support and encouragement to use color. Ultimately, however, they control how and when it is used. Researcher G. L. Robinson and colleague P. J. Foreman noted the impact of social pressure in the use of color in a twenty-month study published in 1999 in the journal *Perceptual and Motor Skills*. In the study, they found that twelve out of eighty-eight participating children who did not consistently wear their tinted lenses chose not to, in part, because of peer pressure. Robinson and Foreman cited the work of three other researchers who found that children resisting the use of color were subjected to denigration, ridicule, bullying, and harassment.

Over time, peer pressure is not the only reason some children may choose not to use color filtration. Another significant reason: as reading skills improve, it becomes easier for some children to cope with shorter term classroom reading activities without assistance from color.

If children don't need colored overlays or tinted lenses, they should not be required to use them. Regularly I ask Katie and Jacob whether they still need their tints. Regularly I remind them that if they cease to benefit from color, they should stop using it. It has been my children's choice to use color for over three years. Jacob wears his tinted lenses all the time. Katie's use varies, depending upon her needs and her feelings about being different.

7. **Don't let struggles with school rob your family of joy.** Some parents may be better equipped to help their children than others. I'm not sure I was all that well equipped. Katie's struggle with school came at a time when I wasn't at the top of my game. Our children had lost two beloved grandparents, one after another. My own father was in declining health. I was struggling through health issues associated with a back injury, related sleep difficulty, and what was assumed to be the change of life.

Admittedly, I was a wreck. I might as well have been a 1970s AMC Gremlin with dents and dings and putty marks speeding too fast down the highway of life. My crankshaft was showing signs of stress and my engine block was at risk of dropping out. More important than any of it, though, was the beautiful little girl in my life who was hurting because she struggled to keep up with her classmates, and there wasn't a thing I could do to make it better.

In our house, Dad fixes the broken toys and Mom fixes and kisses the hurts and makes them better. I couldn't fix Katie's hurts. And my failure in that regard added a lot of stress to what already was a car in need of work. For a period of about two years, we were a rather joyless family.

Then understanding of how light was affecting Katie's ability to learn came into our lives. It came at just the right time. Even greater than the understanding of light and color, though, was our daughter's understanding that there wasn't anything wrong with who she was, how hard she tried, or her ability to focus.

Learning that she had light sensitivity was liberating for Katie. She finally knew her struggles weren't her fault. No one had told her it was—but that is what children will assume when they've been told there is nothing wrong with their visual systems, even though they sense physical stress in the form of chronic fatigue, headaches, or nausea or experience visual distortions. Who else could Katie blame but herself for her inability to succeed?

Even when the tint of Katie's lenses wasn't quite right, shading her eyes increased her energy and decreased the frequency of her headaches. She was happier and healthier. It made a difference. And receiving the correct tint made *all* the difference by allowing her to see how a stable page of text was supposed to look and feel.

Lest someone think that colored lenses are a placebo that did nothing more than remove a little pressure from Katie's life, think again. Stress did not lessen for our family. In fact, it grew. Six months after Katie received the right combination of tinted lenses, our children lost another beloved grandfather and a treasured family pet. A year later, their last remaining grandparent was diagnosed with cancer. A few months after that, I was sent off for major surgery. As all of this happened, *both* kids were benefiting from either controlling light in their environments or using tinted lenses.

Clearly, our family faced no less pressure. Yet by controlling light and using color, both kids experienced great improvement in silent reading and comprehension. Of this I am sure: being able to read and keep up in school with their peers made all the other stresses more manageable for both Katie and Jacob. What becomes of other children who are sensitive to aspects of light and face similar pressures? What happens when they do not have the opportunity to have their problems with visual stress and perception addressed? School failure? Mental illness? Experimentation with drugs?

When difficulties at school develop, families can benefit from taking stock of the stressors in their lives. Don't dwell on the stressors, just be aware of them and do what you can to protect your family's joy. Plan picnics, take mini-vacations, go to movies and laugh. Life is full of stress, so keep the family "car" in working order. Take it slow. Don't allow yourself to go too fast on the highway of life. Remember, your whole family is along with you for the ride.

All children are not sensitive to aspects of light. But for those who are, we have an obligation to figure out how to best meet their needs. These children and their respective families need to be identified, educated as to the issues associated with sensitivity, and provided options for addressing the problem. Modifying light in a child's environment for the most part costs little to nothing. Colored overlays are inexpensive. Tinted lenses are available, but they can be out of reach for low-income families. Options give *all* families the opportunity to address sensitivity to aspects of light in some way. Yet it requires teamwork—parents working with all the professionals involved in their children's lives.

FOR PROFESSIONALS

16

FOR PROFESSIONALS

For decades it has been assumed that reading in too little light harms children's eyes. Consequently, over the last hundred years, we have added ever increasing amounts of light to the school environment. Where did this thought that too little light is harmful come from and when was it scientifically tested? The idea may have evolved without adequate study during the middle part of the twentieth century, when productivity among factory workers was negatively impacted by poor lighting conditions. The solution back then was to add more light or brightness, not first to study the best type of light for the human visual system.

So when was a flood of fluorescent light scientifically determined to be the best type of lighting to promote learning? And when were children who struggle to read tested under a variety of lighting conditions to prove that more light is better or that type of light has nothing to do with the ability to read and learn?

I was not able to find answers to these questions. I did find, however, evidence to suggest that lighting has a different effect on the visual system than one might expect.

Sam Berman, Ph.D., is a physicist and former head of the lighting group at Lawrence Berkeley National Laboratory. LBNL is the nation's oldest government-funded scientific laboratory. For decades, Dr. Berman has been involved in the study of the light we use to illuminate our homes, schools, and places of work.

In the early 1990s, Dr. Berman and Dr. Don Jewett, a neurophysiologist and professor emeritus at the University of California Medical Center, completed an innovative study designed to measure how the human eye responds to certain types of light. The team's findings were significant and possibly underappreciated in terms of the potential impact on children in our schools.

Drs. Berman and Jewett found that more light is not necessarily better than less light for the function of the human visual system. Humans have at least two distinct receptive systems for light—the photopic system, involving the cones, and the scotopic system, involving the rods. The photopic system tends to be linked to brightness. The scotopic system is commonly associated with night vision. According to the duo's study, the scotopic system controls how much light is allowed to enter the eye and stimulate the human visual system, rather than our photopic systems. Their study found a correlation between the rods and the degree to which the pupil of the eye opens and closes, regulating the amount of light entering the eye. Furthermore, they found that lighting is better for the human visual system when it is scotopically enhanced— meaning, less light energy and more wavelengths in the blue-green range.

Dr. Berman and Dr. Jewett's study addressed only that part of the visual system that controls how much light is allowed to enter the eye. The study had nothing to do with the possibility that some visual systems may under- or overreact to specific wavelengths of light. The study does, however, support the idea that more light is not necessarily better for the average person. It also points out that scotopic aspects of vision, requiring less light energy, frequently are overlooked in contemporary indoor lighting practices. Their findings open the door to the possibility that science may operate under other faulty assumptions about light.

Other recent discoveries demonstrate there is much yet to be learned about how light affects the brains of mammals (including humans). In the February 8, 2002, issue, the journal *Science* announced that researchers at five different laboratories recently discovered melanopsin, a new protein in mammals that acts as a light-reactive pigment. It is the job of photopigments to collect wavelengths of light in living things and make use of the energy. Melanopsin already is being linked to how the human brain may use light to regulate the circadian clock, the master controller for 24-hour patterns of behavior and physiology. The newly discovered light-detection system also appears to be responsible for pupil constriction, which ultimately controls how much light is allowed to enter the visual system. Does melanopsin have a role in light-based reading difficulties? Time will tell.

Over the last forty years fluorescent light has evolved in its use in schools. During that period, too many health and learning problems have evolved for us to ignore lighting as a possible factor. How reading is taught in our schools may not be the only reason 10 million children in the United States are struggling with this particular skill. If lighting is a factor, new methods developed to teach reading will also be ineffective for some children.

How can each of us do our part to help children now? It likely will take another decade to sort out all the issues. Children can't wait. Their lives are shaped by what happens to them today, not by changes in lighting or vision screening practices a decade from now. Additionally, children like Jacob, who experience slight visual distortions in everything they see, cannot be helped by modifications in indoor lighting alone. For now, one of the few accommodations available to them is color in the form of overlays and tinted lenses.

IDEAS FOR EDUCATORS

Aside from parents, among the most important individuals in children's lives are the professionals with whom they spend up to seven hours a day—their teachers and other education professionals. Every school would benefit if one or more staff members were trained to identify and address the needs of children sensitive to aspects of light. This is a decision schools and individual educators must make. The goal of this book is to provide information for parents. It is not designed to be a training program or manual. Such programs are offered through other resources.

Educators can, however, try a number of low- or no-cost strategies to help children who may be sensitive to aspects of light. Some strategies—such as turning off a bank of classroom lights—can even save schools money. The following ideas come from our family's experience, as well as a mix of ideas offered by the Irlen Institute; Patricia J. Johnson, Ph.D., clinical neuropsychologist and founder of the North American Irlen Association; and Debbie Bowling, an Irlen practitioner and a certified teacher in the state of Texas.

Natural Light

Move children who exhibit traits of Irlen syndrome near windows where indirect sunlight filters through. If possible, the light should be directly behind children, and not to their sides. Directly behind is better because a bright, cloudy sky can be a source of problems. Some children who are sensitive to aspects of light, like Katie, benefit from a natural light source. Others, like Jacob, who experiences mild visual distortions even with natural light, do not.

Reduce Fluorescent Light

If possible, turn off one bank of fluorescent lights over the heads of children who appear to have light-based reading problems. Even better, move these children near a natural light source as earlier described *and* turn off a bank of overhead fluorescent lights. If you cannot turn off a full bank of lights, replace a working fluorescent tube with a nonworking fluorescent tube directly above a child. This will lessen the amount of direct overhead fluorescent light.

Supplement with Incandescent Light

Place an incandescent lamp with a low-wattage bulb near a child who exhibits traits of sensitivity. This is particularly helpful for individuals who benefit from color in the warm range. Yellow to yellow-orange are the colors prevalent in incandescent bulbs.

Minimize Instruction in Front of Windows or White Boards

Most people are aware that back lighting occurs when we stand in front of windows. Such lighting causes the visual system to darken shapes in the foreground. White boards, increasingly used in our schools over the last twenty years, can also be a source of problems for children sensitive to aspects of light. White boards reflect both light and glare. Instruction delivered by teachers standing in front of white boards can be distracting or uncomfortable for light-sensitive children.

Use of Overhead Projectors and White Boards

A bright white surface and black ink create a high-contrast image that may be difficult for some children to process. Consider using erasable markers in hues other than black (green or blue may be best). Also, consider muting the bright effect of overhead projectors with a colored transparency. Try a color most comfortable to the children who experience light-based reading difficulties in your classroom.

Computer Screens

Another no-cost intervention for children with light-based reading problems is to turn down the brightness on computer screens when they work with computers. Don't be surprised if brightness is cranked way down low. Katie prefers brightness in the 40 to 50 percent range. Encourage children to find a brightness that is comfortable for them and have them note the percentage. They need to be taught, too, to bring the brightness back to 100 percent before leaving the computer to avoid problems for the next student using the terminal.

Colored Overlays

The use of colored overlays is not as simple as it sounds. Because lighting varies, it can be a moving target. In order to be motivated to use them, children need to understand what they are for and their benefits. For some, the benefit of overlays is subtle. For example, how does one measure increased comfort? And what is comfort? Negative reaction to aspects of light does not have to involve headaches or strain. It can be as subtle as fatigue after no more than fifteen minutes of reading.

Also, visual distortions don't have to be dramatic. They, too, are often subtle. For example, a number of individuals aided by color have described conditions in which print is not a problem for the first five or ten minutes of reading. Progressively, however, it becomes more difficult for them to keep their focus on lines of text. Eventually, they begin to perceive distortions in the text—such as double images, words that appear washed out through the center, words that jiggle or otherwise move, or words that begin to appear as though they are rising and falling on the page. These are a few examples of how fatigue plays a role in both physical comfort and visual distortions.

If children don't understand that overlays are there to help them feel rested while they read, they may not understand why it is beneficial to use them. It is important to talk to children about the purpose of overlays. Other important factors, such as the following, will influence a child's use of overlays.

- **Color.** First and foremost, the color must be right for the individual child, and color needs sometimes change. Teachers need to explore this question with a resistant child. Simply ask if it feels comfortable or uncomfortable to use the overlay. If it is uncomfortable, a properly trained screener needs to reevaluate the choice of color.

- **Keep Them Clean.** Overlays need to be kept clean. Smudges will cause the same effect as smudges on a pair of glasses. Teach children how to use a gentle, color-safe cleaner to keep overlays clean and smudge-free. If children keep overlays in a manila envelope or folder, they stand a better chance of keeping them clean and scratch-free.

- **Condition of the Overlay.** Severely scratched or scuffed overlays also cause problems for children; consequently, the quality of the overlay needs to be monitored. Replace damaged overlays.

- **Glare.** A complicating factor in the use of overlays is glare. Children need to be taught how to look for problem glare and report it so that teacher and student can determine an appropriate solution.

- **Anxiety.** Children tend to be highly aware of being different. Anxiety will affect a child's use of overlays. Children who are not sensitive to aspects of light need to be taught not to tease or make comments about another child's use of overlays.

Tinted Lenses

Parents who invest in tinted lenses need the help of teachers to determine whether they are appropriate and helpful to a child. The same factors as those involved in overlays—color, cleanliness, condition, and anxiety—apply to tinted lenses.

The Irlen Institute reports that color adjustment in tinted lenses is needed within the first year 25 percent of the time. Parents need help to determine whether the tint color chosen is appropriate for a child's needs. If you do not observe notable improvement in learning over the span of a month, report it to a parent. Parents must decide what to do if it appears a tint check is needed.

Provide parents with constructive feedback as to a child's use of tinted lenses. If they end up in a desk most of the time, encourage the child to use them. Listen for reasons for resistance and help the child solve problems. If he or she still won't use the lenses, advise the parent. The goal is not to put undue pressure on a child to use tinted lenses. The goal is to work with the family to determine the source of resistance so that appropriate decisions can be made about the use of color.

Encourage Children and Respect Their Needs

This is perhaps the most important part of helping children who experience sensitivity to aspects of light. Jacob needs color all of the time. Katie needs it only under certain lighting conditions. Jacob does not need to be encouraged to use his tinted lenses, but he does need encouragement not to let teasing bother him. Katie needs to be encouraged to wear her lenses, because she wears them in some classes and not others. When she does need them, she feels awkward putting them on in front of her peers. She needs some control over when and where she uses her tints, yet she also needs encouragement to use them.

Colored overlays and tinted lenses are welcome in some schools and school systems and unwelcome in others. Some teachers have tried them and felt they were unsuccessful. Some administrators have found colored overlays and lenses to be difficult to support. In school systems where colored overlays have undergone formal studies, teachers were advised to pay close attention to how and when children used the overlays and to educate children in their proper use.

Debbie Bowling, a reading specialist who coordinated Irlen screening and the use of colored overlays for a school district in Texas, noted the following informal results in 2001 among students with reading problems using overlays on her school campus:

- 32 sixth graders averaged one year, three months growth in reading levels.

- 20 fifth graders averaged one year, three months growth in reading levels.

- 15 fourth graders averaged eight months growth in reading levels.

Bowling also noted that a number of children enrolled in special reading programs were able to move out of those programs and back into the regular classroom when aided by colored overlays.

Without active monitoring, children are less inclined to use overlays, say educators who have used the method over many years. When this happens overlays will, of course, appear not to be useful. Use of color in the classroom is still new and unusual. It makes sense, then, that children need support and encouragement from educators to feel comfortable with overlay use.

IDEAS FOR SCHOOL LEADERS

The power of leadership is all too frequently underestimated. The acceptance or rejection of new ideas often rests upon the values and goals of leaders. Consequently, school administrators and policy makers (that is to say, principals, special education directors, superintendents, members of school boards) have a vital role to play in the acceptance and use of color as an intervention for light-sensitive children.

Change doesn't happen by chance—someone has to make it happen. That someone can be a dedicated educator in your school system or it can be you, the educational leader. Either way, change comes about more smoothly when it involves careful planning that includes the following elements.

Articulation of Values

If school leaders don't value color as an aid for students, most classroom educators won't, either. Leaders need to communicate to parents and educators alike that change is needed—in this case, that children with light-based reading problems need to be identified and helped in order to make the process of reading more comfortable and productive.

Creation of a Strategic Plan

Most people benefit from a road map to get to a place they've never been before. The use of color is no different. A strategic plan can help individual schools or school systems establish realistic goals and objectives related to the introduction of colored overlays. In the state of Massachusetts, color is being embraced by some communities. Introduction of the program began with a $5,000 grant from the state legislature to fund the first year of preparation for one school-based study. Sending a team of teachers off for training is not expensive, $250 to $400 per teacher, nor is $3 to $9 per child for one to three overlays.

Time and Budget

Schools already are overwhelmed by demands on their time and financial resources. Staff training to identify Irlen syndrome and provide children with overlays does not have to be considered an infringement on system resources. If dozens of children in a school system become better students because of color, isn't it a worthwhile investment? Thousands of dollars saved in remedial instruction is merely an added benefit.

In 1989, William Hendrick, Ph.D., was working for the Jurupa Unified School District in California. In a single year, he observed twenty-five middle school students using color as an intervention improve their reading skills enough to move out of a remedial program and back into regular class-rooms. At the time, Hendrick recognized that the success of those twenty-five students alone translated to direct savings of $87,500 for one school year. Multiply that success times four—the minimum number of years remaining for the students before high school graduation—and the savings for that group of students alone is $350,000. The cost savings, however, does not compare to what students gain in terms of their ability to function and succeed in the normal school setting.

Staff Training

Budgeting needs to include staff training. First-year involvement may be as simple as sending a small team for comprehensive training and launching a pilot program in a single school. That is the way colored overlays were introduced in Duncanville, Texas, where two teachers pursued staff train-ing on their own. The staff members returned and launched a pilot pro-gram in one school. Today, Duncanville has a districtwide program.

Debbie Bowling and her colleague, Linda Sorensen, learned about the Irlen Method for screening children at a national reading conference, and upon their return, submitted a mini-grant request in their district to fund training to become Irlen screeners.

Sufficient Materials

To operate an effective program, teachers need to have a supply of materials available, including a supply of colored overlays in every color. Many schools also provide children with manila envelopes or folders to protect the overlays. Additionally, the Duncanville school system has developed tracking paperwork that helps teachers stay on top of children's needs related to overlays, as well as a teacher handbook.

Keeping the Vision Alive

Someone needs to make sure testing and intervention happen. Ultimately, this falls to school leaders. It is a circle that must remain unbroken in order for school-based screening and intervention to happen from year to year. When programs have ceased to be offered in schools, common reasons cited were:

1. Change in organizational leadership

2. Lack of administrative support

3. Lack of one individual at each school encouraging staff, answering questions, and monitoring program quality (education of teachers, parents, and students; effective use of overlays; and so forth)

Hendrick notes that: "In an era of ever-increasing pressure upon school administrators to find methods to enhance instruction and improve student test scores, any method that offers assistance to underperforming students should be carefully and fully considered." The pressure he refers to involves Individualized Education Program (IEP) goals, as well as state-mandated testing for high school graduation.

He supports colored overlays and tinted lenses because he himself has observed dramatic results for some students sensitive to aspects of light. Dramatic results can translate to dramatic cost savings. But more important, such results can shape the future for a youth on the journey to adulthood.

IDEAS FOR READING SPECIALISTS

Colored overlays and tinted lenses are not a cure-all for reading problems. Color filtration merely changes the relative power of wavelengths entering the eye (or the *color* of light). In some individuals, doing so makes the visual system more comfortable and less likely to activate visual stress and distortions.

Sensitivity to aspects of light appears to be a pervasive problem among individuals of all ages. The goal of testing for Irlen syndrome should be to identify individuals who have light-based reading problems and to provide education and options as to how those issues can be addressed. Irlen syndrome may be the only barrier to reading or it can coexist with other learning issues, including problems with language-related auditory perception related to dyslexia. In our family's experience, acknowledging and addressing Katie's visual distortions was the first step in a process to identify other learning problems. Once her ability to read improved, her confidence improved, too. We could then address issues such as attention and focus in class and word attack.

Standard perception tests used by psychologists and reading specialists will *not* catch Irlen syndrome. In fact, these tests may mask problems with reading-related visual perception because they do not typically involve the conditions that produce visual stress. Irlen syndrome is more apparent when dense blocks of text appear on a bright white page—the typical format for reading—and with exposure to such conditions over time (fifteen minutes of reading).

Reading specialists can help children with light-based reading problems by learning all they can about it. If possible, pursue training to become a screener. Then use screening as a tool to help sort through the different reasons children may struggle with reading and learning. Color is not designed to address all learning issues. Only those associated with light-based reading problems.

IDEAS FOR PHYSICIANS AND PSYCHOLOGISTS

The professionals with the potential to help families address reading and learning issues don't routinely talk to one another—meaning, what a family communicates to a vision professional or a physician may never be communicated to a school psychologist or classroom teacher. This is a

huge problem for children such as mine. As a family, we were communicating our concerns, but we shared a different set of concerns to a different
set of professionals who—apart from one another—dismissed the information as unimportant. It didn't occur to us that the problem might be
interrelated.

Physicians and psychologists can help a family sort through the issues
causing a child to struggle in school. In the case of Irlen syndrome, these
problems often have physical and psychological manifestations. When this
happens, a family will seek your help. If you know about these issues and
how they relate to learning problems, you may be able to help families
connect the dots. Consequently, the possibility of light-based reading difficulties needs to be considered and physicians and psychologists should
help families connect with appropriate intervention.

Here's how the controversy over color as an intervention for physical
discomfort and visual distortions began. Helen Irlen is a certified school
psychologist and licensed child and family therapist. Over thirty years ago,
she received her undergraduate degree from Cornell University and her
master's degree from the University of California at Long Beach (UCLB).

After working for ten years in public schools, Helen Irlen returned to
UCLB to become director of the Learning Disability Program and do
research with a group of adults with a history of learning problems. Her
research eventually led her to investigate visual perception associated with
reading and the various ways professionals in many areas have attempted
to address learning problems. Then and now, psychology has been the
branch of science assigned the task of addressing issues related to perception. She conducted her work entirely within her field of expertise—
psychology and education, not optometry or medicine.

Consequently, when she happened along color as an appropriate intervention for reading, she developed a school-based strategy for addressing
it—inexpensive colored overlays. She later found that some individuals
derive even greater benefit from custom-colored lenses.

In the interest of public protection, medical science requires conclusive testing before new interventions are accepted as safe and effective. But colored overlays and tinted lenses were not developed as a
medical intervention. Furthermore, by 1987 word of her work got
around to the media, who did what good newshounds do—they
reported the information to the general public. This occurred before
medically oriented testing could take place. A backlash of skepticism and

criticism for Irlen's work soon followed. Irlen was accused of being a charlatan who picked the pockets of parents eager to do anything to help their children.

What the skeptics didn't know, however, is that Helen Irlen herself is the mother of a child with severe developmental disabilities. It is a fact she has kept out of the public spotlight in the best interest of her son. She simply wanted to raise a healthy, happy, and self-sufficient child.

At twenty-seven, David Irlen is proving himself self-sufficient. He is a charming, goal-driven, and independent young man. My encounter with him was all too brief—over dinner one night with the Irlen family, during my first face-to-face meeting with Helen Irlen. I was privileged to sit with David and learn a little about him. He had recently earned his purple belt in karate and hopes to earn his black belt one day. He has a regular job he found on his own, and he speaks of it with passion and pride. Like his mother, David works in a center with young children.

Helen Irlen knows as well as any parent the hurts associated with having a child who struggles to find his place in the world. As a young mother, she struggled to find academic success for her own son and his complicated, multifaceted disabilities.

Sensitivity to aspects of light was not at the core of David's problems. But it *is* an invisible barrier to reading success for thousands of others. Helen Irlen has invested twenty years of her life in color filtration as an intervention because she has seen it work for light-sensitive children and adults. And she continues to see it work. Now that there are Irlen diagnosticians and screeners worldwide, Helen Irlen doesn't need to continue to see clients, but she does. She does it to aid in the development of a new area of science that is helping some children and families find perceptual relief and academic success.

In December 1999, G. L. Robinson and his colleagues published a paper in the *Australian Journal of Learning Disabilities* suggesting a biochemical basis for Irlen syndrome. If this connection is ever verified, a pill might one day solve the problem of inappropriate reaction to wavelengths of light, rendering overlays and tinted lenses obsolete. Helen Irlen not only knows about this research, the Irlen Institute supports it.

Without question, further research needs to be done to understand how modifying wavelengths of light calms the visual system and reaction in the brain. In the meantime, there are children who need help *now*. Physicians may find the Chart of Common Traits on pages 134–36 helpful.

The official position statement of the American Academy of Pediatrics on color as an intervention is a joint statement written in November 1998. It states:

Visual problems are rarely responsible for learning difficulties. No scientific evidence exists for the efficacy of eye exercises ("vision therapy") or the use of special tinted lenses in the reme-diation of these complex pediatric developmental and neurologic conditions.

From "Learning Disabilities, Dyslexia, and Vision: A Subject Review (RE9825)." To read the entire text, go to the American Academy of Pediatrics Web site at **www.aap.org** *and search on the term "Irlen."*

The opinion was crafted by members of the Committee on Children with Disabilities, American Academy of Pediatrics (AAP), American Acad-emy of Ophthalmology (AAO), and American Association for Pediatric Ophthalmology and Strabismus (AAPOS). Controlled studies by Evans, Wilkins, or Robinson were not included as references in the committee's citations. Material the panel did choose to cite, however, included two per-sonal opinions published in journals. One was an extensive editorial criti-cizing an article in *The New York Times*. The other was a two-paragraph letter to the editor appearing in the August 15, 1995, issue of the *Canadian Medical Association Journal* (*CMAJ*). Written by an M.D., the brief piece was critical of an earlier article appearing in the *CMAJ* reporting on litera-ture for and against color. The letter states: "reminds me of people who used to sell snake oil or who promise an herbal treatment for cancer with the proviso that only they can provide the treatment." Intriguingly, AAP/AAO/AAPOS reviewers chose to cite this two-paragraph opinion rather than the lengthier *CMAJ* article articulating the arguments for and against color filtration.

Colored lenses and overlays are not snake oil, nor are they a remedial strategy. They are simply a method of making the visual system more com-fortable and stable during the process of visual work. For both of my chil-dren, just knowing that they have a physiological barrier to the ability to read and perform work in school is a huge relief. If neither had tinted lenses today, they would *still* be better off. They know what interferes with their ability to perceive a page of text as stable and they know it has nothing to do with personal inadequacy or a psychological problem. Such knowledge is more important than colored overlays or tinted lenses themselves because it shapes self-perception and, ultimately, an individual's future.

Physicians are encouraged to look at the research on their own. References for and against color filtration appear in the back of this book. Published studies can be obtained through the National Libraries of Medicine or a hospital medical library.

IDEAS FOR VISION PROFESSIONALS

Some optometrists and hospitals in England, Ireland, Scotland, and Wales are screening for Meares-Irlen syndrome, as it is called by vision professionals there. Movement in this direction largely is based on the work of Arnold Wilkins, Ph.D., formerly of the British Medical Research Council and now with the University of Essex. Dr. Wilkins's work is for the most part ignored by ophthalmological associations in the United States, although they do cite a 1990 negative opinion of "scotopic sensitivity syndrome" by Harold Solan, an optometrist and researcher at the State University of New York, State College of Optometry. Curiously, the results of a study Solan published in 1998 suggesting that some children with reading difficulties *do* benefit from blue-tinted lenses are not cited by these organizations.

Ophthalmological associations in the United States consider scotopic sensitivity, an old term for sensitivity to aspects of light, a non-diagnosis. Optometry has a mixed opinion and, intriguingly, more optometrists appear to be recommending blue tinted lenses for some patients.

As of February 2002, the American Optometric Association (AOA) position on color acknowledges that one controlled trial demonstrated that "children with reading difficulties who were prescribed colored filters did experience reduced symptoms of asthenopia (strain, stress etc.); however, the filters may need to be individually and precisely prescribed." They also acknowledged that benefit from colored filters is not solely a placebo effect. Overall, however, the AOA cautions parents to "remain skeptical of the efficacy of any undocumented claims." *(From "The Use of Tinted Lenses for the Treatment of Dyslexia and Other Related Reading and Learning Disorders." The American Optometric Association's full opinion can be viewed at www.aoanet.org—from there, search on the term "Irlen.")*

In its list of references, the AOA does cite studies by Dr. Wilkins and Dr. Evans, but it does not cite any work by Dr. Robinson.

In a January 2001 article on the AOA's Web site, optometrist Leo Semes of the University of Alabama at Birmingham School of Optometry cautions that tinted lenses alone do not protect the eyes from bright sunlight. The Irlen Institute also cautions users of its lenses that they are not designed for sun protection; they do not block ultraviolet light.

For sun protection, every set of eyes benefits from sunglasses designed for UV protection. In his article, Dr. Semes also urges consumers to avoid blue lenses outdoors as they may enhance the sun's blue light, which may contribute to age-related problems with the eyes. This is a concern that needs further study.

Deciding what to say about Irlen syndrome to vision professionals was very difficult. After nearly a week of stewing, I finally asked thirteen-year-old Katie—by then a veteran of living with light sensitivity—what she thought I should say.

"I know what I would write, Mom," she said without hesitation. "I would tell the doctors they need to try it or they need to let someone they know who has trouble reading try it for a week. Then they'll know that color can work."

Great is the wisdom of a child.

Katie is right. Perhaps those who venture an opinion about color first owe it to children and adults like Katie to sit with them and observe firsthand the difference color makes. And, yes, color selection needs to be guided by a specially trained practitioner. It requires equal parts art and science. Using color incorrectly provides little benefit and may even be harmful, causing the very symptoms it is intended to circumvent.

IDEAS FOR RESEARCHERS

Research is vital in the role of safeguarding the public from sham medical treatments. When a hypothesis can be consistently replicated in scientific studies, then medicine begins to accept a therapy or treatment. Scientific studies cannot be replicated, however, if different variables are used from study to study. This is essentially what is happening with the study of color and its ability to address light-based reading difficulties. The most important factor needed to establish consistent study results is being ignored to one degree or another. The factor: lighting type. The following three studies with apparent negative results make the point.

Number 1

K. J. Ciuffreda et al., "Irlen lenses do not improve accommodative accuracy at near." *Optometry and Vision Science,* 74(5): 298–302 (1997).

Lighting Source: Soft illumination via incandescent (tungsten) lamp and reflected from a mirror. **Reading Test:** Snellen eye chart. **Summary statement** (re: effect of Irlen lenses): "The use of the Irlen correction did not have any positive effect on monocular steady-state accommodation at near."

Author Observation: This study uses the Snellen eye chart and soft incandescent illumination to test for effect of colored filters. Children with Irlen syndrome have passed such tests for years because lighting and use of an eye chart are conducive for testing visual acuity; they do not test for visual perception needed for reading. Testing related to reading and visual perception requires the same type of lighting conditions and reading materials used in locations where we ask our children to read.

Number 2

S. J. Menacker et al., "Do Tinted Lenses Improve the Reading Performance of Dyslexic Children? A Cohort Study." *Archives of Ophthalmology,* Vol. 111, Feb. 1993.

Light Source: Full Spectrum Fluorescent Light (Verilux Full Spectrum F40T12VLX) in a windowless room. **Reading Test:** Six passages, Macmillan series. **Summary statement** (effect of Irlen lenses): "One-way analysis of variance of reading performance showed neither improvement nor deterioration attributable to lens color or density when applied to error rates (formulas cited)."

Author Observation: Five pages into this study it states (paragraph four, page 218), "one could argue that perhaps there were individual performance improvers among the subjects." Study results also noted that in some cases, specific colors impeded some children's test results. Here are the three most significant individual performance improvers documented in Menacker et al., but never highlighted:

Child No.	% Improvement in Reading Speed	% Improvement in Error Rate	Optimum Color
4	35%	44%	Yellow
17	32%	72%	Yellow
18	115%	87%	Red

Note that in these three children the optimum color was *not* blue, the color some American vision professionals suggest is most effective. A suggestion as to why this study did not show benefit from blue: My daughter, Katie, performs well under full spectrum light, the lighting type used in this study. Full spectrum is well balanced in blue wavelengths. Katie performs well under blue-rich fluorescent light and poorly under red-rich fluorescent light. Katie might have performed well in this test with both the empty and "neutral" lenses. Her performance would have been impeded, however, by red-tinted lenses. Specific wavelengths and how they interact with the visual system *are* the problem.

Number 3

P. Blaskey et al., "The Effectiveness of Irlen Filters for Improving Reading Performance: A Pilot Study." *Journal of Learning Disabilities*, 23(10): 604–612 (1990).

Lighting Source: Unknown. **Reading Test:** Multiple. **Summary statement** (re: effect of Irlen lenses): "The subjects in the Irlen filter group did not show any significant gains in reading rate, word recognition in context, or comprehension."

Author Observation: Five pages after the summary statement is the following (paragraph 2, page 609): "Our data suggest that Irlen filters may have a positive effect for some individuals who have essentially normal decoding skills but are unable to gather information effectively or sustain effort for adequate periods of time because of discomfort associated with reading." Sustained reading is, and always has been, a central issue with Irlen syndrome. As the visual system fatigues or comes under stress, reading ability deteriorates. Furthermore, applying color does not mean children will become instant readers. Once a proper color is found, children will have an easier time learning to read. Lighting type is not specifically mentioned in this study; therefore, how light may have affected the results of the test is unknown.

For studies to replicate results related to the effects of color, they must, at the very least, include the following:

1. Tints need to be specifically prescribed and not involve generic color.

2. Individual improvement needs to be examined, in addition to group results.

3. Lighting needs to be carefully controlled. Under ideal conditions, studies need to identify the type of light most problematic for each test subject and use that type of light for testing.

4. Fatigue plays a major role in problems associated with light-based reading problems. Studies need to involve sustained reading, not brief reading exercises, since problems typically emerge after five to fifteen minutes of reading. This is important for one other reason: sustained reading is what children are asked to do in schools and at home.

Further research needs to be done. But testing procedures need to be standardized so that they properly measure the sources of the problem (light and sustained reading) and the potential for improvement (oral and silent reading *after* reading instruction—color only removes a barrier to reading; it does not teach children to read). Our children have taught us that all light is not the same. Type of lighting and its effect upon test subjects deserve to be considerations in every study.

OUR CHILDREN'S FUTURES

17

OUR CHILDREN'S FUTURES

"One thing I have learned in a long life," Einstein once wrote, is "that all our science, measured against reality, is primitive and childlike—and yet it is the most precious thing we have." If Einstein, with his tremendous genius, felt this way, what does it say of anyone who would readily discount the experience of thousands of children and adults who exhibit light-based reading difficulties? Moreover, why isn't it common practice to ask children struggling with reading how they feel physically or what they experience during the process of reading? Neither the Snellen eye chart nor perception tests commonly used in schools replicate the reading experience. Why not?

Another great scientist was fascinated with light, but few people outside of physics are aware of his fascination. Just four years after inventing the telephone, Alexander Graham Bell envisioned and created another device that would have as much, if not greater, implication for humankind. He called the device the "photophone" and he called it "the greatest invention I have ever made; greater than the telephone."

Developed in 1880, Bell used it to transport voice messages on wavelengths of light. It did not involve the transmission of sound by electrical wires; only a device that projected sound toward a mirror and a special receiver. But the photophone became a dusty idea on a shelf when Bell could not overcome interference by cloud cover. It would be decades before the photophone's science would contribute to light-based fiber optics.

Light is an amazing thing. Perhaps the question we should be asking is, with its incredible power and potential, why *wouldn't* it interfere with reading ability in some children? We already know that human bodies vary in how they react to other external influences, such as smells and common allergens. Why wouldn't the human visual system vary in how it receives and reacts to waves and particles of light?

The theory of color as an intervention is simply this: visible light comes to us in the form of wavelengths that humans experience as color. Some people have visual systems that are more sensitive to properties of light. In these people, such wavelengths may cause an over- or underreaction that triggers problems throughout the visual system. These problems ultimately translate to some kind of perceived visual stress—fatigue, physical discomfort, or visual distortions. In the most serious form, they cause seizures and a world filled with fractured images. Finally, these anomalous reactions become more apparent with ever-increasing amounts of visual stress. This theory is based upon the works of a number of researchers.

In our family's experience, there are at least two very distinct manifestations of sensitivity to aspects of light—minor visual distortions in everything perceived by the visual system (Jacob's problem) and fatigue, physical discomfort, and visual distortions associated with reading dense text (Katie's problem). Other manifestations include agitation and inattention that appear similar to ADHD, physical stress that may appear as chronic fatigue or depression, nausea, fractured images, seizures, and more.

THE NEED TO WORK TOGETHER

In addition to his contributions to science in the way of inventions, Alexander Graham Bell contributed something else that is often overlooked. He believed science is best served when it is *collaborative* and not conducted in isolation.

The question of light-based reading difficulties—and other possible health problems linked to light—needs a collaborative scientific approach. It needs experts from a host of disciplines working together to address the puzzle. Children and adults from all walks of life need the question settled.

In the meantime, parents need to know that sensitivity to aspects of light is a potential barrier to reading. For many children, it is a barrier easily addressed either by modifying sources of light or through the use of carefully chosen color.

In the process of learning about color filtration, I asked practitioners independent of schools how often they have the opportunity to test children from minority groups for sensitivity. They say it is seldom. Most kids being fitted with tinted lenses are white and from middle- to upper-income families. Expense and word of mouth relegates intervention to this group. This is unfortunate because sensitivity to aspects of light does not discriminate. Any child may be affected. Communities that may need color the most to help break the cycle of poverty and violence are least likely to have it in the tool kit of options to help children.

Serious problem behaviors that tend to cluster in the same individual and reinforce one another, as the Carnegie Council on Adolescent Development puts it, can begin young in life. They can begin when a child is pressured to perform in school and that child cannot live up to expectations.

The importance of early school success has a foreboding connection to a study of learning characteristics conducted in the late 1990s among Colorado prison inmates by Judith Whichard, Richard Feller, and Ruthanne Kastner. They randomly sampled inmates from six different incarceration sites and published their results in the September 2000 issue of *The Journal of Correctional Education*. Their finding: out of 155 inmates tested, 72—or 46 percent—had moderate to severe sensitivity to aspects of light. The percentage in the general population is estimated to be closer to 12 percent.

The average cost of keeping one individual in a United States prison for one year, according to the National Center for Policy Analysis, is $25,000. The cost to build a new medium-security prison facility can be over $100,000 per bed. The average cost of an overlay is $3. Screening for overlays, if it is not available free through schools, costs $80. The average cost of tinted lenses: $500.

The best studies demonstrating the existence of sensitivity to aspects of light and the benefits of color may be research done in schools. One of the most recent and comprehensive studies is the Pioneer Valley Project in Massachusetts. Funded in part by the Massachusetts State Legislature and Massachusetts Department of Education, the study included thirty fourth graders—fifteen special education students and fifteen non–special ed. Two weeks after the students began using carefully selected colored overlays, average test scores for accuracy increased by one year, one month for the special education group and one year, four months for the non–special education group. After using colored overlays for three months or more, accuracy increased by an average of two years for the special education group and three years, three months for the non–special education group. The average improvement in comprehension for both groups was two years, three months.

Individuals associated with the study note that excellent results were achieved in part because of the cooperation of teachers. Did they change their methods of instruction? No. Changes made included encouraging children on a daily basis to use their Irlen overlays, making sure students used their overlays correctly, and revisiting the appropriateness of colors to the specific needs of children throughout the study.

A proponent of funding for the Pioneer Valley Project was Senator Stanley Rosenberg, assistant majority leader of the Massachusetts State Senate. In a brief telephone exchange, I asked Senator Rosenberg about his support of that funding. Rather than mention the dollars that could be saved when even a few children move out of special education and into regular classrooms, he spoke first about the emotional suffering that could be avoided. He was keenly aware that the ability to read, remain focused, and feel successful in school shapes children's futures in a variety of ways. There are potential cost savings to states—but, more important, as Senator Rosenberg pointed out, there is an opportunity to help shape the lives of children.

In 1999, a California energy consulting firm completed an unrelated study that indirectly supports the Pioneer Valley results. Fluorescent light is the type of light most commonly associated with fatigue, physical discomfort, and visual distortions. The Heschong Mahone Group evaluated the effects of natural sunlight in elementary schools in three western United States communities. In Fort Collins, Colorado, it found 7 percent across-the-board improvement in both math and reading scores in locations where natural light was plentiful. In Seattle, Washington, the firm found an average improvement of 9 percent in math and 13 percent in reading in schools with an ample natural light source. In the Capistrano Unified School District in Orange County, California, it found that students on average performed 20 percent better in math and 26 percent better in reading when aided by natural light.

HOW DO WE HELP THOSE WHO NEED IT MOST?

For most children, one or more overlays or a simple light color of tinted lens is all that is needed to accommodate for sensitivity to aspects of light. Whether children are better served by overlays or tinted lenses depends upon individual need. Katie and Jacob's problem with light is more severe than most. They need tinted lenses. Our family could afford them. Many cannot.

This reality prompts an important question that must one day be addressed. How do severely impacted children whose parents work at low-wage jobs get the tinted lenses they need? Good question. Currently, there is no universal answer. The best suggestion is for parents to direct this question to:

- Your local school. Specifically the departments responsible for staying on top of federal and state laws regarding accommodations for children with learning needs.

- The government agencies responsible for providing children with an appropriate education. This includes state or provincial offices of education (see page 212 for Web resources).

There is no need to put every child in tinted lenses and there isn't enough money to change the way we light our schools. Such strategies wouldn't work anyway—children sensitive to aspects of light vary in their lighting needs. But there *is* enough money for research as to which lighting causes some children the greatest problems (types of light, types of fluorescent tubes, age of ballasts, age of the tubes themselves, etc.). Governments and private foundations spend billions of dollars annually to investigate issues related to human disease and development, including reading difficulties.

If billions of dollars are spent to study other issues, doesn't it make sense to study how different types of light affect children who struggle with reading problems and inattention?

Lighting standards throughout the world are in the process of changing. Some businesses are moving toward Triphosphor T-8 lamps in order to improve lighting conditions and save money. They are also moving to high-frequency ballasts that fire at a faster rate, reducing flicker and requiring less electricity. Also, in the Pacific Northwest in the fall of 2001, homeowners were sent free compact spiral fluorescent tubes to use in place of incandescent bulbs. It was part of a promotion to encourage the switch from incandescent light—which wastes much of the energy needed to create light—in favor of the new, more efficient spiral fluorescent tubes.

Before we make such changes, should we know more about how lighting type affects *all* human visual systems—including those abnormal systems that may react adversely to specific properties of light? Changes in fluorescent lighting may not cause problems for the average human visual system. But if it has the potential to cause fatigue, discomfort, attention issues, or visual distortions in *millions* of children struggling to read and learn in schools worldwide, isn't it worth knowing first what the range of impact may be?

If sensitivity does indeed vary from person to person, as Helen Irlen first suggested in the early 1980s, then it will be impossible to create an indoor lighting source perfect for every person. Teaching individuals who are light sensitive how to modify the light in their environments or when and how to use colored overlays and tinted lenses is a far more practical solution. Years from now, the ultimate solution may come from a pill that functions like an antihistamine to prevent under- or overreaction in the visual system in the first place. Currently, however, there is no such pill.

Research is the backbone of change in scientific circles. Parents need to be aware of this. Much of the research conducted throughout the world is funded by governments, which means it is funded through our tax dollars. Parents have a right to be heard as to how they want their tax dollars spent. The best way to be heard is to contact your elected representatives. In the United States, that is members of Congress. In Canada, it is members of Parliament. For the benefit of children struggling in school, write to your representatives and ask them to push for studies examining the impact of all types of light and lighting conditions on the human learning process. Ask them to make sure individuals with light-based reading difficulties, or Irlen syndrome, are included.

A Sample Letter

[Insert Date]

Congressman/Senator/Member, House of Parliament [Insert Name]
[Choose a congressman/senator/member representing *you*]
[Insert Address]
[Insert Postal Code]

Dear Congressman [Senator or Member, Insert Last Name],

Millions of children are struggling to read in our schools. Focus to date has been almost exclusively on how reading is taught. A significant body of evidence exists to suggest that reading instruction is not the only issue. (See references below.)

The evidence indicates that human visual systems and brains *vary* from person to person in how they react to light. For as many as 12% of children, this may result in physical discomfort, visual distortions and/or inattention when systems become stressed or fatigued during the process of reading (immediately or within 5 to 15 minutes).

[If you have a personal example, insert here.]

This is not a problem of vision. It is a problem of how the visual system and brain react to and interpret light. Ironically, standard vision screening removes conditions that might identify the problem—bright light and/or dense and crowded blocks of text, common components of reading. Inexpensive solutions to this problem exist, but families are not getting the information they need.

This is an urgent issue in need of your help. Please do what you can to push for funding for further research as well as initiatives that will provide families easy access to appropriate testing and intervention.

Sincerely,

[Insert Your Name]
[Insert Your Address]
[Insert Your Phone Number]

References:
The Light Barrier, 2002, by Rhonda Stone, St. Martin's Press
Dyslexia: A Psychosocial Perspective, 2001, edited by Morag Hunter-Carsch, M.Ed., Whurr Publishers (see Chapter 3)
Dyslexia and Vision, 2001, by Bruce J. W. Evans, Ph.D., Whurr Publishers, London, U.K. (see Meares-Irlen Syndrome)
Visual Stress, 1995, by Arnold J. Wilkins, Ph.D., Oxford University Press, Oxford, U.K., and *Reading Through Colour*, 2003, John Wiley & Sons
Reading by the Colors, 1991, Helen Irlen, Avery Publishing Group

E-mail or postal addresses for United States Congressmen: www.congress.org—At the official congressional Web site, go to the section marked "U.S. Congress" and click on "Elected Officials." Look for a map, click on your state, and find a list of your senators and representatives.

E-mail or postal addresses for Canada's Parliament: www.parl.gc.ca—There, go to the section marked "Senators and Members." A number of listings are available, including a listing for members by province and territory.

Before sitting down to write, be clear about what you want to say. Feel free to reference this book as well as the research mentioned throughout. If you have a personal story to tell, share it. Remember to keep it brief. Close the letter by asking your representative to push for research dollars to study how different types of light affect children struggling in our schools. Ask for a national initiative that will help families gain access to appropriate screening and intervention.

When you have finished writing your letter, send a copy to this address:

(in the U.S.)
    Director, NICHD
    National Institute of Child Health & Human Development
    Bldg. 31, Room 2A32, MSC 2425
    31 Center Drive
    Bethesda, MD 20892-2425

(in Canada)
    Minister of Health
    Division of Childhood and Adolescence
    Health Canada
    Jeanne Mance Building
    Postal Locator 1909C2
    Ottawa, Ontario K1A 1B4

If our government leaders are not asked to look into this, it likely will not happen. There are no major sources of funding such as those provided by the pharmaceutical giants, nor are there any major professional associations pushing for the study of light, its effects on the human brain, and the ability of color to correct light-related problems. There is only a grass-roots group of screeners, diagnosticians, a few optometrists (mostly in the United Kingdom and Europe), and a few teachers throughout the world doing what they can to identify children and help them.

"CONCERN FOR MAN"

As a family, perhaps we ought to have quietly used color to help our children overcome their problems, then moved on with our lives. We chose a different path, one that likely will draw much criticism. I am not a scientist. I am just a mom. Yet beyond the impact of light-based reading difficulties on other children, our family is aware that at any given moment Katie and Jacob may be ordered to remove their glasses by an uninformed adult, causing them embarrassment and putting them at risk of fatigue, physical discomfort, and/or visual distortions. My children face two ongoing challenges: their physical sensitivity *and* narrow, uninformed opinion.

"Concern for man and his fate," Einstein said, "must always form the chief interest of all technical endeavors. . . . Never forget this in the midst of your diagrams and equations."

I am an average mom with two beautiful children. For me, a slice of heaven on Earth is the smell of my daughter's freshly baking focaccia or the sound of her long fingers stroking *Für Elise* on the piano. I can't help but smile at my son's passion for the sport of the month or his on-key vocal rendition of "Tomorrow." Parents live for moments like these. In our family's experience, a child who struggles with reading and homework has less time for baking, piano practice, sports, singing, and the general enjoyment of life.

For some children, properties within light are an invisible barrier to reading and personal success. For some children, color overcomes the barrier.

REFERENCES
REFERENCES
REFERENCES

To minimize duplication, references are listed only once, in the chapter where they first relate to the discussion of light-based reading problems. Please note, however, that all of the references influence information presented throughout this book.

Chapter 6. A Threat to School Success

Willard B. Bleything, "Juvenile Delinquency: The Role of Optometry in Remediation." *Journal of Behavioral Optometry*, 9(4):99, 1998.

Willard B. Bleything, "The Health Profile of the Juvenile Delinquent." *Journal of Optometric Vision Development*, Vol. 28, Winter 1997.

Getting the Facts About Adolescent Substance Abuse, a fact sheet available online through The National Clearinghouse for Alcohol and Drug Information.

Great Transitions: Preparing Adolescents for a New Century, The Carnegie Corporation of New York, Carnegie Council on Adolescent Development, October 1995.

"Learning Related Vision Problems—Education and Evaluation," a resolution passed by the Maryland PTA, 1998, and the National PTA, 1999. Lead author: Nora Putt, Maryland PTA.

The National Center on Addiction and Substance Abuse at Columbia University (CASA), Web site at **www.casacolumbia.org**.

U.S. Department of Health and Human Services, Substance Abuse and Mental Health Services Administration, Web site at **www.drugabuse statistics.samhsa.gov**.

Chapter 7. Life-Changing Discoveries

Sandra Blakeslee, "Study Ties Dyslexia to Brain Flaw Affecting Vision and Other Senses." *The New York Times*, September 15, 1991.

George M. Bohigian, Chairman, "Dyslexia—Council on Scientific Affairs." *Journal of the American Medical Association* 261: 2236–2239 (1989).

Merrill Bowan, O.D., "'Learning Disabilities, Dyslexia, and Vision: A Subject Review': A rebuttal, literature review and commentary," *Optometry*, the Journal of the American Optometry Association, 2002; 73: 553–75.

J. B. Demb, G. M. Boynton, and D. J. Heeger, "Functional Magnetic Resonance Imaging of Early Visual Pathways in Dyslexia." *The Journal of Neuroscience*, 18 (17): 6939–6951.

M. C. Diamond, A. B. Scheibel, and L. M. Elson, *The Human Brain Coloring Book*. (Color Concepts, 1985).

Kristian Donner, "Progress and Paradigm Shifts in Vision Research." *Perception* 28 (1999).

Bruce J. W. Evans, *Dyslexia and Vision* (Whurr Publishers, 2001).

B. J. W. Evans et al., "Optometric Characteristics of Children with Reading Difficulties Who Report a Benefit from Coloured Filters." *John Dalton's Colour Vision Legacy*, Chapter 10.7, 1997.

Albert M. Galaburda, "Ordinary and Extraordinary Brain Development: Anatomical Variation in Developmental Dyslexia." *Annals of Dyslexia* 39 (1989).

L. E. Hughes and A. J. Wilkins, "Typography in Children's Reading Schemes May Be Suboptimal: Evidence from Measures of Reading Rate." *Journal of Research in Reading* 23 (3) (2000).

G. W. Hynd et al., "Brain Morphology in Developmental Dyslexia and Attention Deficit Disorder/Hyperactivity." *Archives of Neurology* 47 (1990).

Helen Irlen, *Reading by the Colors—Overcoming Dyslexia and Other Reading Disabilities Through the Irlen Method* (Avery, 1991).

Helen Irlen, "Scotopic Sensitivity/Irlen Syndrome—Hypothesis and Explanation of the Syndrome." *Journal of Behavioral Optometry* 5(3) (1994).

Jeffrey Lewine, "Clinical Applications of Magnetoencephalography," a presentation to the Japanese Clinical Neurophysiology Society, October 2001.

M. S. Livingstone et al., "Physiological and Anatomical Evidence for a Magnocellular Defect in Developmental Dyslexia." *Proceedings of the National Academy of Sciences* 88:7943–7947 (1991).

Olive Meares, "Figure/Background, Brightness/Contrast and Reading Disabilities." *Visible Language* 14: 13–29 (1980).

S. J. Menacker et al., "Do Tinted Lenses Improve the Reading Performance of Dyslexic Children? A Cohort Study." *Archives of Ophthalmology* 111 (1993).

John J. Ratey, *A User's Guide to the Brain: Perception, Attention, and the Four Theaters of the Brain* (Pantheon, 2001).

W. H. Ridder III et al., "Not All Dyslexics Are Created Equal." *Optometry and Vision Science* 74 (2) (1997).

G. L. Robinson and P. J. Foreman, "Scotopic Sensitivity/Irlen Syndrome and the Use of Coloured Filters: A Long-Term Placebo Controlled and Masked Study of Reading Achievement and Perception of Ability." *Perceptual and Motor Skills* 89: 83–113 (1999).

A. J. Simmers, L. S. Gray, and A. J. Wilkins, "The Influence of Tinted Lenses upon Ocular Accommodation." *Vision Research* 41: 1229–1238 (2001).

H. A. Solan et al., "Eye Movement Efficiency in Normal and Reading Disabled Elementary School Children: Effects of Varying Luminance and Wavelength." *Journal of the American Optometric Association* 69(7) (1998).

"Reading by the Colors," produced by Joseph Wershba, *60 Minutes*, May 8, 1988.

P. Whiting, G. L. Robinson, and C. F. Parrot, "Irlen Coloured Lenses for Reading: A Six-Year Follow-Up." *Australian Journal of Remedial Education*, 26(3): 13–19 (1994).

Arnold J. Wilkins and Elizabeth Lewis, "Coloured Overlays, Text, and Texture." *Perception* 28: 641–650 (1999).

A. Wilkins et al., "Double-Masked Placebo-Controlled Trial of Precision Spectral Filters in Children Who Use Coloured Overlays." *Ophthalmic and Physiological Optics* 14: 365–370 (1994).

A. Wilkins et al., "Preliminary Observations Concerning Treatment of Visual Discomfort and Associated Perceptual Distortion." *Ophthalmic and Physiological Optics* 12 (1992).

A. Wilkins, "Technical Note—Overlays for Classroom and Optometric Use." *Ophthalmic and Physiological Optics* 14 (1994).

A. Wilkins, *Visual Stress* (Oxford University Press, 1995).

M. C. Williams et al., "Effect of Wavelength on Performance of Attention-Disordered and Normal Children on the Wisconsin Card Test." *Neuropsychology* 8 (2): 187–193 (1994).

B. G. Zifkin and D. Kasteleijn-Nolst Trenite, "Reflex Epilepsy and Reflex Seizures of the Visual System: A Clinical Review." *Epileptic Disorders* 2(3) (2000).

Chapter 8. "Kids Like Us"

Anne A. J. Anderman, "Physicians, Fads, and Pharmaceuticals: A History of Aspirin." Published online in the *McGill Journal of Medicine*, an international forum for the advancement of medical science by students, 1996.

Sarita Belmont, Elsie Dorain, and Georgianna Saba, *A Study to Test the Effectiveness of Reading with Irlen Colored Overlays for Students with Scotopic Sensitivity/Irlen Syndrome*. A Pioneer Valley Pilot Project, Pioneer Valley, Massachusetts, 2000.

Hattie Bernstein, "Light Sensitivity Brought Darkness." *The Sunday Telegraph*, January 5, 1997.

Heather Black, "Emily's Violet Colored Glasses." *Woman's World*, October 19, 1999.

E. Chronicle and A. J. Wilkins, "Colour and Visual Discomfort in Migraineurs." *Lancet* 338: 890 (1991).

Guilford Middle School Scotopic Sensitivity Report Findings for Academic Year 1998–99, July 6, 1999.

Matt Hansen, "Discovering the Wonderful World of Words—Teen Embraces Reading Following Recent Diagnosis of Scotopic Syndrome." *Jackson Hole Guide*, April 28, 1999.

"Aspirin" from *Invention Facts and Myths*, www.IdeaFinder.com.

Irlen International Newsletter, February–July 2001.

Irlen International Newsletter, August 2000–January 2001.

Phyllis Kreuttner and Irene Strum, *An Intervention for Students with Low Reading Achievement: A Report for the New York City Schools*, 1990.

"Migraine Update," available online at the National Institute of Neurological Disorders and Stroke Web site at www.ninds.nih.gov/health_and_medical/pubs/migraineupdate.htm, July 1, 2001.

Lawrence Osborne, "Midnight's Children." *The New York Times Magazine*, September 16, 2001.

G. L. Robinson, P. J. Foreman, and K. Dear, "The Familial Incidence of Symptoms of Scotopic Sensitivity/Irlen Syndrome." *Perceptual and Motor Skills* 83: 1043–1055 (1996).

Thomas D. Rossing and Christopher J. Chiaverina, *Light Science—Physics and the Visual Arts* (Springer-Verlag 1999).

Linda Shaw, "Hey, Kids, Want to Get Better Grades?" *The Seattle Times*, reprinted in the *Yakima Herald-Republic*, October 17, 1999.

Larry B. Silvers, "Controversial Therapies." *Journal of Child Neurology*, Vol. 10, Supplement 1, January 1995.

A. J. Wilkins, "Visual Sensitivity and Hyperexcitability in Epilepsy and Migraine." Andermann and Lugaresi, eds., *Migraine and Epilepsy* (Butterworth, 1987), 339–365.

"About XP," an article on the official Web site of the Xeroderma Pigmentosum Society, Inc., online at www.xps.org.

Chapter 9. How Do We See?

Joel Achenbach, "The Power of Light." *National Geographic*, October 2001.

Jim Breithaupt, *Einstein—A Beginner's Guide*. Hodder & Stoughton, 2000.

M. C. Diamond, A. B. Scheibel, and L. M. Elson, *The Human Brain Coloring Book*. Color Concepts, 1985.

K. R. Dobkins, "Moving Colors in the Lime Light," *Neuron* 25:15–18, January 2000.

Lighting in Residential and Commercial Buildings (1993 and 1995 Data), an online resource of the Energy Information Administration, United States Department of Energy, 1998 (www.eia.doe.gov).

B. J. Evans et al., "Effect of Pattern Glare and Colored Overlays on a Simulated-Reading Task in Dyslexics and Normal Readers." *Optometry and Vision Science* 71(10):619–628 (1994).

"Medicine," *Seeing Our World in a Different Light* by Linda Hermans-Killam, October 2001, an online resource of the Infrared Processing and Analysis Center, California Institute of Technology.

"What Are the Best Light Bulbs to Use in These Fixtures?" *Welcome to Lighting Principles*, Lighting Research Center, 2001, Rensselaer Polytechnic Institute (www.lrc.rpi.edu).

John Ott, *Health and Light: The Effects of Natural and Artificial Light on Man and Other Living Things*, Ariel Press, 1990.

John Ott, *Light, Radiation and You—How to Stay Healthy*. Devin-Adair Pub., 1985.

"The Father of Full Spectrum Light," an article at **www.ottbiolight.com**.

David Park, *The Fire Within the Eye: A Historical Essay on the Nature and Meaning of Light*. Princeton University Press, 1997.

"Visual Cortex" and "Lateral Geniculate Nucleus," Introductory Biological Psychology Tutorials by Sandra Nagel Randall, and Lyle K. Grant, Athabasca University, Athabasca, Alberta, Canada.

Thomas D. Rossing and Christopher J. Chiaverina, *Light Science: Physics and the Visual Arts*. Springer-Verlag, 1999.

"I Hate Fluorescent Light" by Eric Strandberg, *Home Lighting News*, Northwest Lighting, 2000, Lighting Design Lab (www.lightingdesignlab.com).

The Secret Life of the Brain, a co-production of Thirteen/WNET New York and David Grubin Productions, 2001.

"The Eye and the Retina," "Basic Visual Pathways," and "Central Visual Pathways," The Washington University School of Medicine Neuroscience Tutorial, 1997, an online resource (thalamus.wustl.edu/course/eyeret.html).

Arnold Wilkins, *Reading Through Colour*, John Wiley & Sons, 2003.

Arnold Wilkins, *Visual Stress*. Oxford University Press, 1995.

S. Zeki, "Color Coding in the Cerebral Cortex: The Reaction of Cells in Monkey Visual Cortex to Wavelengths and Colours, *Neuroscience* 9: 741–776,

Chapter 10. Bridging the Gap

John Bruer, *The Myth of the First Three Years: A New Understanding of Early Brain Development and Lifelong Learning*. Free Press, 1999.

A. J. Wilkins et al., "Colored Overlays and Their Benefit for Reading." *Journal of Research in Reading* 24(1):41–64 (2001).

R. S. Worrall, "Detecting Health Fraud in the Field of Learning Disabilities." *Journal of Learning Disabilities* 23(4):207–212 (1990).

Chapter 11. Signs, Symptoms, and Color Filtration

National Institutes of Health, National Institute of Child Health and Human Development, April 13, 2000, news release: "National Reading Panel Reports Combination of Teaching Phonics, Word Sounds, Giving Feedback on Oral Reading Most Effective Way to Teach Reading."

National Institutes of Health, National Institute of Child Health and Human Development, March 2, 1998, news release: "NICHD-Funded Researchers Map Physical Basis of Dyslexia" (based upon the research of S. E. Shaywitz et al., Yale University).

Chapter 12. Not Dyslexia and Not ADD/ADHD

Daniel G. Amen, "Looking into Inattention and Impulsivity: The Prefrontal Cortex," in *Change Your Brain, Change Your Life*. Three Rivers Press, 1998.

"Rallying the Armies of Compassion," Foreword by President George W. Bush, April 24, 2001, available online at www.whitehouse.gov/news/reports/faithbased.html.

The Future of Children: Special Education for Students with Disabilities. Center for the Future of Children, The David and Lucile Packard Foundation, Spring 1996.

"Frequently Asked Questions (FAQ)," CHADD Web site (Children and Adults with Attention-Deficit/Hyperactivity Disorder), available online at www.chadd.org/faq.htm.

Karen Donnelly, *Coping with Dyslexia*. The Rosen Publishing Group, 2000.

"Research into Dyslexia," the Dyslexia Parents Resource, available online at www.dyslexia-parent.com/research.html.

Bruce J. W. Evans, *Dyslexia and Vision*. Whurr Publishers, 2001.

C. G. Gordon, "Visual Anomalies in Dyslexia: A Review of the Literature." *British Orthoptic Journal* 54:34–39 (1997).

Dyslexia—A Psychosocial Perspective. Morag Hunter-Carsch, ed. Whurr Publishers, 2001.

Daphne M. Hurford, *To Read or Not to Read: Answers to All Your Questions About Dyslexia*. Scribner, 1998.

G. Reid Lyon, "Report on Learning Disabilities Research," adapted from testimony given before the Committee on Education and the Workforce, U.S. House of Representatives, July 10, 1997, and published online at www.ldonline.org/ld_indepth/reading/nih_report.html.

G. Reid Lyon, "Solid Research, Solid Teaching." U.S. Department of Education Community Update, April 2001.

Anne Marshall Huston, *Understanding Dyslexia: A Practical Approach for Parents and Teachers*. Madison Books, 1992.

Sam Goldstein, and Nancy Mather, "Attention and Impulse Control— What to Do When Your Child Can't Concentrate or Lacks Enough Self-Control to Learn," in *Overcoming Underachieving—an Action Guide to Helping Your Child Succeed in School.* Wiley, 1998.

"The ABC's of ADD," National Attention Deficit Disorder Association (ADDA) Web site, available online at www.add.org/content/abc1.htm.

National Institute for Child Health and Human Development, Request for Applications: HD-03-012, Research in Adolescent Literacy, Dec. 19, 2002.

S. Ogden, S. Hindman, and S. Turner, "Multisensory Programs in the Public Schools: A Brighter Future for LD Children." *Annals of Dyslexia* 39, 247–267 (1989).

Lucy Jo Palladino, "What is ADD?" in *Dreamers, Discoverers and Dynamos* (formerly titled *The Edison Trait*). Ballantine Publishing Group, 1997.

Sylvia O. Richardson, and Gordon F. Sherman, *Doctors Ask Questions About Dyslexia: A Review of Medical Research.* The International Dyslexia Association, 1994.

Harold A. Solan and Leonard J. Press, "Optometry and Learning Disabilities." *Journal of Optometric Vision Development* 20 (March 1989).

Carol S. Spafford et al., "Contrast Sensitivity Between Proficient and Disabled Readers Using Colored Lenses." *Journal of Learning Disabilities.* 28(4) (1995).

Melissa J. Thomasson, "Hints on Coping with Attention Deficit Disorder," published online on the Dyslexia Awareness and Resource Center, www.dyslexia-center.com/add02.html.

Frank R. Vellutino, "Dyslexia." *Scientific American* 256(3) (1987).

Chapter 13. Solving the Mystery of Irlen Syndrome

B. Blackman, "Phonological Awareness," *Handbook of Reading Research Vol. III*, 2000, Lawrence Earlbaum Associates, Inc.

G. Coles, *Misreading Reading—The Bad Science That Hurts Children.* Heinemann, 2000.

A. E. Farstrup and S. J. Samuels, *What Research Has to Say About Reading Instruction*, International Reading Association, 2002.

R. Flippo, editor, *Reading Researchers in Search of Common Ground*, International Reading Association, 2002.

K. Goodman, *What's Whole in Whole Language?* Heinemann, 1986.

U. Goswami, "Phonological and Lexical Processes," *Handbook of Reading Research Vol. III*, Lawrence Earlbaum Associates, Inc., 2000.

R. L. Hotz, "Brain scans can detect dyslexia, showing root of reading problem," *Los Angeles Times*, Aug. 3, 2002.

J. LeDoux, *Synaptic Self—How Our Brains Become Who We Are.* Penguin Books, 2002.

M. McKinney, "Reading Help May Alter Brain Activity in Dyslexia," Reuters, April 30, 2002.

National Reading Panel, "Teaching Children to Read/Summary Report," *Report of the National Reading Panel*, April 2002. Summary report can be viewed at: www.nichd.nih.gov/publications/nrp/smallbook.htm.

J. M. Schwartz and S. Begley, *The Mind and The Brain: Neuroplasticity and the Power of Mental Force.* ReganBooks, an imprint of HarperCollins, 2002.

B. A. Shaywitz, K. R. Pugh, A. R. Jenner, J. M. Fletcher, J. C. Gore, S. E. Shaywitz, "The Neurobiology of Reading and Reading Disability (Dyslexia)," *Handbook of Reading Research Vol. III*, Lawrence Earlbaum Associates, Inc., 2000.

F. Smith, *Understanding Reading—A Psycholinguistic Analysis of Reading and Learning to Read*, 2nd Edition. Holt, Rinehart and Winston, 1978.

R. Stainthorp and D. Hughes, *Learning from Children Who Read at an Early Age.* Routledge, 1999.

Tadlock, D. R., "A Practical Application of Psycholinguistics and Piaget's Theory to Reading Instruction," *Reading Psychology* 7(3) 183–195 (1986).

E. Temple, G. K. Deutsch, R. A. Poldrack, S. L. Miller, P. Tallal, M. M. Merzenich, J. D. E. Gabrieli, "Neural deficits in children with dyslexia ameliorated by behavioral remediation: Evidence from functional MRI," *Proceedings of the National Academy of Science Early Edition*, 100(5): 2860–2865 (2003).

L Trei, "Remediation training improves reading ability of dyslexic children," *Stanford Report*, Feb. 25, 2003.

Chapter 14. The Right Way to Get Help

Kenneth Anderson, "The Reading Wars: Understanding the Debate Over How Best to Teach Children to Read." *Los Angeles Times*, June 18, 2000.

Gerald Coles, "No End to the Reading Wars." *Education Week*, December 2, 1998.

L. Croyle, "Rate of Reading, Visual Processing, Colour and Contrast." *Australian Journal of Learning Disabilities* 3(3) (1998).

B. J. Evans et al., "Optometric Correlates of Meares-Irlen Syndrome: A Matched Group Study." *Ophthalmic and Physiological Optics* 15(5): 481–487, (1995).

B. J. Evans et al., "A Preliminary Investigation into the Aetiology of Meares-Irlen Syndrome." *Ophthalmic and Physiological Optics* 16(4):286–296 (1996).

B. J. Evans et al., "A Review of the Management of 323 Consecutive Patients Seen in a Specific Learning Disabilities Clinic." *Ophthalmic and Physiological Optics* 19(6): 454–466 (1999).

"Learning Disabilities Association-Sponsored Symposium on Chemical Hormone Imposters and Child Development," Jerry Heindel, *Children's Health Meeting Report, Environmental Health Perspectives* 108(8) (2000). A resource of the National Institutes of Health.

Helen Irlen, "Scotopic Sensitivity/Irlen Syndrome—Hypothesis and Explanation of the Syndrome." *Journal of Behavioral Optometry* 5(3) (1994).

R. Johnson et al., "The Vision Screening of Academically and Behaviorally At-Risk Pupils." *Journal of Behavioral Optometry* 7 (1996).

Kathleen Kennedy Manzo, "More States Moving to Make Phonics the Law." *Education Week*, April 29, 1998.

Kathleen Kennedy Manzo, "Whole-Language Model Survives Despite Swing Back to Basics." *Education Week*, March 17, 1999.

G. L. Robinson and R. N. Conway, "Irlen Filters and Reading Strategies: Effect of Coloured Filters on Reading Achievement, Specific Reading Strategies, and Perception of Ability." *Perceptual and Motor Skills* 79 (1 Pt 2): 467–483 (1994).

G. L. Robinson and P. J. Foreman, "Scotopic Sensitivity/Irlen Syndrome and the Use of Coloured Filters: A Long-Term Placebo Controlled and Masked Study of Reading Achievement and Perception of Ability." *Perceptual and Motor Skills* 89: 83–113 (1999).

"UCSD Shiley Ophthalmologists Discover Relationship Between Eye Condition and Attention Deficit Hyperactivity Disorder," an article referencing a study by R. H. Ventura, D. B. Granet, and A. Miller-Scholte on the University of California-San Diego Web site, April 12, 2000.

Chapter 16. For Professionals

"The Use of Tinted Lenses for the Treatment of Dyslexia and Other Related Reading and Learning Disorders." The American Optometric Association.

Marcia Barinaga, "Circadian Clock: How the Brain's Clock Gets Daily Enlightenment." *Science* 295 (5557): 955–957, February 8, 2002.

"The Coming Revolution in Lighting Practice," by Sam Berman, published online in *Energy User News* (www.energyusernews.com), November 8, 2000.

Sam Berman, "Energy Efficiency Consequences of Scotopic Sensitivity." *The Journal of the Illuminating Engineering Society* (Winter 1992).

"Joint Policy Statement Affirms OD's Role in Care for Students with Dyslexia," an article appearing on the College of Optometrists in Vision Development Vision Conditions Web site at www.covd.org.

"Learning Disabilities, Dyslexia, and Vision: A Subject Review (RE9825)," a joint statement of the Committee on Children with Disabilities, American Academy of Pediatrics, American Academy of Ophthalmology, and American Association for Pediatric Ophthalmology and Strabismus.

B. Coyle, "Use of Filters to Treat Visual-Perception Problem Creates Adherents and Sceptics." *Canadian Medical Association Journal* 152(5): 749–750 (1995).

G. L. Robinson et al., "Understanding the Causal Mechanisms of Visual Processing Problems—A Possible Biochemical Basis for Irlen Syndrome?" *Australian Journal of Learning Disabilities* 4(4) (1999).

K. G. Romanchuk, "Skepticism About Irlen Filters to Treat Learning Disabilities." *Canadian Medical Association Journal* 153:397 (1995).

Alfredo A. Sadun, "Dyslexia at *The New York Times*: (Mis)Understanding of Parallel Visual Processing." *Archives of Ophthalmology* 110 (1992).

R. Tyrrell et al. "Coloured Overlays, Visual Discomfort, Visual Search and Classroom Reading." *Journal of Research in Reading* 18(1): 10–23 (1995).

Chapter 17. Our Children's Futures

Alexander Graham Bell Family Papers at the Library of Congress, American Memory/Library of Congress. Available online at memory.loc.gov/ammem/bellhtml/bellhome.html.

Jim Breithaupt, *Einstein—A Beginner's Guide*. Hodder & Stoughton, 2000.

Ira Flatow, *They All Laughed . . . From Light Bulbs to Lasers: The Fascinating Stories Behind the Great Inventions That Have Changed Our Lives.* HarperPerennial, 1993.

"Development of Zebrafish Mutagensis and Screening Tools," the National Institutes of Health Program Announcement. Release date: March 19, 2001. Expiration: March 1, 2004, unless reissued.

"Bell's Photophone." *Today in History*, June 3, 2001, American Memory/Library of Congress.

J. A. Whichard, R. W. Feller, and R. Kastner, "The Incidence of Scotopic Sensitivity Syndrome in Colorado Inmates." *Journal of Correctional Education* 51(3) (2000).

INTERNET RESOURCES
INTERNET RESOURCES

INTERNET RESOURCES

For mailing addresses and telephone numbers, go to the Web sites listed below. If you do not have access to a computer, contact your local public library for assistance.

Irlen Syndrome

www.Irlen.com
The Irlen Institute
Explanation of color to address Irlen syndrome, as it relates to physical discomfort, visual distortions, migraine headache, and autism, as well as a comprehensive list of Irlen practitioners in thirty countries.

www.ceriumvistech.co.uk
Cerium Technologies
Explanation of color to address Meares-Irlen syndrome, testing procedures used by vision professionals, and a list of screeners in eighteen countries.

www.essex.ac.uk/psychology/overlays
Arnold Wilkins
Explanation of color to address Meares-Irlen syndrome, brief reference to other related conditions, and a list of more than 150 published articles by Dr. Wilkins.

Dyslexia

www.dyslexia-parent.com
Web site of the Dyslexia Parents Resource

www.interdys.org
Web site of the International Dyslexia Association

www.ldac-taac.ca
Web site of the Learning Disabilities Association of Canada

ADD/ADHD

www.add.org
Web site of the National Attention Deficit Disorder Association

www.chadd.org
Website of Children and Adults with Attention-Deficit/Hyperactivity Disorder (CHADD)

www.nimh.nih.gov
Web site of the National Institute of Mental Health (U.S.)
To locate the latest information on ADD/ADHD, go to the Web site, click on Publications and look for the ADD/ADHD question-and-answer file. You can also perform a search for ADHD on the NIMH Web site.

www.hc-sc.gc.ca/english/search.html
Search engine of Health Canada Online
In the search field, type ADHD and enter. A variety of recent articles will appear.

Regional Resources/Disability Rights

These sources can help you locate regional resources to explore your rights for comprehensive academic screening.

www.pacer.org
Parent Advocacy Coalition for Education Resource (PACER Center—U.S.)
The list can be difficult to find. Once at the PACER Web site, go to National Information and scan down until you come to an interactive map; click on your state for listings.

www.disabilityresources.org
DRM Disability Resource Monthly Guide to Disabilities on the Internet (U.S.)

www.ldac-taac.ca.
The Learning Disabilities Association of Canada
The Learning Disabilities Association of Canada offers a Web site and list of resources available throughout Canada. Go to Directory and look for resources by province.

Government

www.congress.org
The official Web site of the United States Congress.

www.parl.gc.ca
The official Web site of Canada's Parliament.